Caging the Rainbow

Caging the Rainbow

Places, Politics, and Aborigines in a North Australian Town

Francesca Merlan

University of Hawai'i Press • Honolulu

03 02 01 00 99 98 5 4 3 2 1

Library of Congress Cataloging-in-Publication Data

Merlan, Francesca.
Caging the rainbow : places, politics, and aborigines in a North Australian town / Francesca Merlan.
p. cm.
Includes bibliographical references and index.
ISBN 0-8248-2001-0 (cloth : alk. paper).—ISBN 0-8248-2045-2 (pbk. : alk. paper)
1. Australian aborigines—History. 2. Australian aborigines—Social conditions. 3. Australian aborigines—Government relations. 4. Human territoriality—Australia—Katherine (N.T.) 5. Spatial behavior—Australia—Katherine (N.T.) 6. Geographical perception—Australia—Katherine (N.T.) 7. Katherine (N.T.)—History. 8. Katherine (N.T.)—Social conditions. 9. Katherine (N.T.)—Race relations. I. Title.
GN667.N6M47 1998
994.29'0049915—dc21 97-48596
CIP

Designed by Kathleen Szawiola

CONTENTS

LIST OF ILLUSTRATIONS

PREFACE

THIS BOOK is an ethnographic exploration of change and continuity in the lives and social orientations of Aborigines around the town of Katherine in the Northern Territory of Australia (map 1).

Though the book's focus on *town* life is somewhat unusual among Australian Aboriginal ethnographies (but see Cowlishaw 1988, Dagmar 1978, Sansom 1980), this is crucial to my approach. I first spent almost three continuous years around Katherine (1976–1979) and have spent time in the area every year since then. From my early focus upon the differential socio-spatial orientations toward hinterlands and their manifestations in daily life characteristic of the camps and people of the Katherine Aboriginal scene (chapter 1), I came to realize that the town had a centrality in their lives that I could properly explore only by writing an avowedly intercultural ethnography. That is, it could not presuppose the autonomy or independence of the social field as solely indigenous, or Aboriginal, but needed to explore interrelationships constituted as ones between Aborigines and others over time and at different levels. The attempt to understand continuity and change in this light leads me to examine socio-spatiality from a number of perspectives on the Katherine scene and to relate that scene throughout the book to wider contexts.

Chapter 2 is an account of the relationships of an Aboriginal woman to the town whose connection with it not only spanned her entire life and the great change in the town since World War II, but whose familial background is centered on the town. That is shown to be crucial to her understanding of the evanescence of a former "place" in Aboriginal terms, in what is now the main street of Katherine town and also relevant to understanding changes in the socio-territorial identity of the town in Aboriginal terms (chapter 4). Chapter 3 explores the relations of Aboriginal people to hinterlands and shows elements of dissolution and of continuity in those relationships.

Government Aboriginal affairs policy in Australia has clearly shifted since the early 1970s, from a more coercive and directive project of "assimilation" to one of "self-determination." National concern with the character of the indigenous "self" has been at the basis of reconstitutive measures, including land rights in the Northern Territory. Chapter 5 places the Katherine scene, and the emergence of the land rights era, in the context of the changing formation of the Australian nation-state and the terms central to it: "people" and "land." Analyzing the implications and effects of wider (national and international) movements in public thinking and policy and relating them to the Katherine scene, I suggest that many aspects of the recent relationship between Aborigines and the Australian nation-state can be best understood as mimetic, or imitative (Taussig 1993), rather than coercive in character. In the imitative relationship, questions of representation are important. Aborigines, like other Fourth World or indigenous peoples, are highly susceptible to others' representations of who and what they are, and this susceptibility plays a large role in shaping their conditions of life. Issues of the deployment and authority of specifically *anthropological* representations on the Katherine scene and the wider indigenous scene are developed throughout the book.

Chapter 6 examines the contestation over definition of spaces within the town in interactions between Aborigines and others. It provides a counterpoint to chapter 2 in showing some of the unhomelike aspects of the town from Aboriginal perspectives. It also contrasts with chapter 5 in pointing to continuous, as well as new, elements of repression and contestation in the relations between Aborigines and others within the town, some of these elements—as white townspeople would observe—actually having become more intense since the liberalization of Aboriginal affairs policy.

Chapter 7 renews the focus of chapter 2 on places as differentiating in Aboriginal terms by exploring the recent appearance of a place near the town and relating this to wider issues of indigenous cultural creativity, the burdens and constraints imposed upon it, and the accusations of "invention" that have figured largely in recent "sacred sites" disputes and heritage issues in Australia.

In the conclusion (chapter 8), I argue that the mimetic character of the intercultural relationship between Aborigines and the nation-state needs to be seen as part of a social technology of imitation, continuous with other forms of Western invention in its tending toward reproducing the world as knowable, boundable, and manageable.

It is difficult to properly acknowledge all the people who have shaped this work, because it has really been in the making since I first came to Katherine in 1976. Many of the people who contributed to it beyond measure have passed away in the years since then: Alice and Peter Mitchell from the Gorge camp, Gordon Bulumbara from Barunga, Maggie Datba from Mudginberry, Willy Byers from Kalano, Nida Waramburr and Ruby Allison from the western side, and recently, Peter Jatbula, originally from Gimbat but very much from town, too, and Elsie Raymond, originally from Delamere and Willeroo, but also a person of Katherine town. Katherine reminds me of them.

Among many others I would particularly like to acknowledge for having taught me about the town and its environs at close quarters and from more distant vantage points are Julie Williams, Sandy Barraway, Nipper Brown, Bill Harney, Phyllis Winyjorrotj, Ivy Brumby, Patsy Brown, Daisy Bordurlk, Noel McDonald, Mae Rosas, Jessie Roberts, Betty Lardy, Jimmy Conway, Lulu Jilimbirrnga, May Page, Mae Rosas, Maggie Datba, Amy Dirngayg, Sarah Heppelwhite, Ruby Ngalwara, Lily Kruger, Nellie McCoy, Graham Campbell, Nida Lowe, Tom Kelly, George Kelly, Gary Cartwright, Fred Costello, Mick Maloney, Marnie Evans, Eddie Ah Toy, Tex Moar, Jimmy Forscutt, Wally Christie, Norman Jensen, Mae Govan, Michael Somalios, Bill Windolf, Pearl Ogden, Judy King, Mike Canavan, Ted Lowe, David Ross, Larry Ah Lin, and Lana Quall.

Henry Scott was extremely generous with his time, discussing with me aspects of Katherine's history in detail. For their information and help concerning Katherine town's history of roads and works, I thank Dan Darben (chief district engineer 1965–1974) and Trevor Troy (Transport and Works, Katherine). For the detailed information they were willing to supply about the history of the Commonwealth Scientific and Industrial Research Organization (CSIRO) "hot springs" camp, I am grateful to Ted Morris and Lindsay Phillips. Tom Kerwin and Noel Buntine gave me some interesting insights into the recent pastoral history of the Katherine area, and Mike Nicholas, John Havnen, Robert E. Lee, John Ah Kit, and Mick Peirce, perspectives on Aboriginal organizations in town. I am grateful to David Dalrymple and Ruth Morley, both formerly associated with Katherine Aboriginal Legal Aid Service, for information on its functions in Katherine and the surrounding area and for discussion of "dry area" and other alcohol-related issues. Robyn Morris, Kerryn Taylor, Ken and Julie Barnes, and Jane Dowling were generous in discussing with me aspects of institutional separatism between whites and blacks in Katherine, only some of which I have been able to incorporate here.

I got much friendly assistance from staff at the Commonwealth Archives, Darwin, the Northern Territory Archives Service (where I would especially like to acknowledge Jenni Wright), and at the Katherine Historical Society. My thanks also to John Roberts and Peter Johnson of the cartography section in the Department of Geography, Sydney University.

Among academic colleagues, I thank Lowell Lewis for reading and commenting on some chapters, Les Hiatt for his critical reading of a draft of this manuscript, and Jeremy Beckett both for comments on a draft and for the long-term inspiration his own work has been to my efforts to revise "Aboriginal studies" in appropriately intercultural terms. I particularly thank Fred Myers for comments on a pre–final draft of this project, which have helped me cast it in its final shape. I also salute Steve Feld who, at a late stage, encouraged me to drop some of the dry language and keep the stories.

Finally, I want to thank Alan Rumsey—my husband, colleague, and hardest-working critic—who read through a number of drafts, offering numerous suggestions and comments. And James and Jesse. It was hard for them to see why I wanted to write this—too much work, not enough fun—but they were patient and came to take a personal interest in the book—or, at least, in Mommy's finishing it.

One

Places and People of Katherine Town

MANY WRITERS have observed that, in the ways in which Aborigines position themselves around settler locations—missions, pastoral stations (ranches), and towns—they have tended to reproduce, within a small space, differentiated orientations to "country," the lands to which they regard themselves as having primary ties. This chapter gives an account of the diversity of spatial orientation among Aboriginal people to the town of Katherine. It also begins to explore how this diversity relates to their differentiated and changing ties to hinterlands outside the town.

No doubt, such spatially relative orientation reflects continuity in practice from precolonial times. Thus, Bell (1983:8), writing of the Central Desert settlement of Warrabri north of Alice Springs, noted of the distribution of locally recognized social groupings that "Warlpiri and Warumungu oriented their camps to their traditional land west of the settlement, while Alyawarra and Kaytej oriented their camps to the east. Contact between east- and west-siders was minimal and occurred in the service core of the settlement where the whites lived and worked" (see also Myers 1986:34–36 concerning

Western Desert peoples' spatial orientations in a settlement context and Kolig 1981:12–22 and Memmott 1991:44 for comparisons with situations in remote northwestern and southeastern Australia, respectively). Often, such spatial arrangement even continues to be strongly manifested in "fringe camps" around complex urban centers (see, e.g., Sansom 1980 writing of "fringe dwellers" around Darwin, the Northern Territory's chief city). The extent to which urban encampments are appropriately understood as spatially relative to each other and differentially oriented toward hinterlands depends upon the extent to which the Aboriginal people concerned sustain salient concepts of socio-territorial identity and differentiation under the particular sociohistorical conditions and reorientations they have experienced. Such concepts are quite strongly maintained among many Aboriginal people living in Katherine, in varying ways on which this book seeks to provide perspectives.

Recognizing that spatial orientation is a constitutive dimension of social identity and difference is an important element of understanding towns like Katherine "in Aboriginal terms." In varying but significant measure, many Aboriginal people of Katherine see their lives in terms of "where," in relation both to other Aborigines and to non-Aborigines.[1] Among many Aborigines, it is generally important where one is from in the sense of having socially recognized connection to country, where one has been in the course of one's life, and where others are to whom one is closely linked. To varying degrees, these socio-spatial orientations are mirrored—partly realized in forms of social practice and also altered over time—in the way that Aborigines position themselves in relation to the town (moving in and around it), in the ways they relate to other people, and in the spaces they typically occupy.

To many Katherine Aborigines, whites and other outsiders are obviously originally from somewhere else, not from the range of country that they know. Yet outsiders have been around Katherine for a long time, and some have had strong and far-reaching influence upon Aborigines' lives, as employers and workers established in local places.

Aboriginal social and spatial orientations to town and hinterland, and the relations between these, have not remained static. However, Aboriginal people envision the temporal dimension of these relations variably. Sometimes they do not recognize, or have in mind as a possibility, that changes in social identification of people and territory have come about for which good "objective" evidence can nevertheless be presented. (Building on some material in this chapter, chapter 4 deals explicitly with the question of variable recognition of change and the emergence of new forms of historical consciousness in the town setting.)

Towns and other places of settler development had significant effect upon Aboriginal populations in earlier times and still do, in changing ways. Such centers were always in places with access to water and other requirements for settler life and livelihood. Such siting inevitably disrupted Aboriginal people, often forcing them into situations of competition with settlers and introduced animals.

In the Katherine region, exploration for the establishment of the Overland Telegraph from the 1870s and initial pastoral settlement from 1879 at Springvale just downstream of the present town (see map 1) doubtless caused the decimation of Aboriginal numbers and, very likely, the swift, near extermination of Aboriginal people of the immediate area near the town, as this grew. Over time, however, Aboriginal people from further afield were also displaced and relocated toward centers of settler activity (see Stanner 1958), and dependencies of various kinds grew between Aborigines and settlers. New patterns of interaction among Aborigines also developed in these contexts, and social identifications and territorial attachments doubtless underwent revisions. (Chapter 4 outlines some of the evidence for change in Aboriginal socio-territorial identification of the Katherine town area. It is also shown that the relation to these processes of change has not been the same for all Aborigines, and that varying perspectives on the town area exist among them.)

Much anthropological writing about Aborigines has arguably been "traditionalist," reproducing idealized representations of those now commonly called "indigenous peoples" as they allegedly are, but in terms of what is understood as their past. To the extent that writings depict the present as (idealized) past, they must fall short of adequately describing and theorizing the nature and extent of change experienced by Aboriginal people and the character of contemporary sociocultural formations in which Aboriginal people participate. David Riches (1990:72), an anthropologist and Eskimologist, has argued that such problems of representation are common to a large body of anthropological writings about the Eskimo, much of which remains preoccupied with "an Eskimo tradition seen in isolation and/or as an inertial force influencing Eskimo activity vis-à-vis the non-Eskimo world." This characterization may be widely applicable to writings about indigenous or "Fourth World" peoples encapsulated in modern nation-states (Manuel and Posluns 1974, Graburn 1981). Perhaps Marilyn Strathern's (1992a) diagnosis of "postplural nostalgia" is apposite, a contemporary condition within such states in which we fear the apparent diminution of human cultural heterogeneity. Traditionalist accounts of indigenous peoples support a vision of the world in which at least some portions of it, some peoples of it, remain customary, unchanged, and therefore different from "us," inherent and unreflective in their relation to their "culture."

My attempt to supersede an undoubtedly strong legacy of traditionalism in the anthropological literature concerned with Aborigines[2] involves seeking to dissolve constricting dichotomies between persistence and change, between "traditionality" and (presumably) non- or posttraditionality. I assume neither to be more fundamental than the other, and begin where I assume dimensions of both persistence and change to have some relevance as subjective dimensions shaping social practice in the lives of Aboriginal people as I got to know them. I assume in my writing about the Katherine scene the notion of an intercultural setting, in which distinctions between that which is historically persistent and that which is not, although regularly cast in terms of difference between "Aboriginal" and "non-Aboriginal" by social actors themselves, are always open to forms of reconceptualization and practical revision by them, as well as being analytically problematic.

In keeping with this, the reader will find that I do not begin with traditional anthropological categories of description and analysis of Aboriginal social organization (e.g., "tribe," "clan," "kinship," and so on), though I critically discuss certain of these in following chapters. My method of exposition of the diversity of Aboriginal orientation to the town is to give an account of my own growing acquaintance over time with Aboriginal people, "mobs,"[3] and camps. At the end of the chapter I reflect on the significance of whom I came to know and draw some conclusions concerning the differentiated relations of Aboriginal people to the town.

In conformity with my attempt to privilege neither persistence nor change, it is important that revisions of spatial orientation among Aboriginal people be understandable as sociohistorical process. The revision of socio-territorial identities and orientations among Aboriginal people can only be analyzed in the light of their long-term, changing experience with settlers and others who continue, in some ways, to be outsiders to them. It is useful for the reader to have in mind some of the main periods and tendencies in settler "management" of Aborigines to understand how these have informed relations of power, difference, and inequality between "Aborigines" and others.

Until the last several decades, there were strong administrative attempts in the far north to keep people then called "natives" away from regional towns like Katherine but also to concentrate them and make them sedentary. Even into the 1960s, administrators attempted, with some success, to keep them in certain kinds of rural environments, including missions, government settlements, and on pastoral properties where their labor was useful. In towns, it was felt, they would be subject to the demoralizing influences of alcohol (opium was also common in an earlier period), prostitution, idleness, and disorder (Attwood 1989, Cummings 1990, Austin 1993 give useful indications of contemporary "scientific" concepts and moral precepts that guided the "protection" and separation of Aborigines from settlers in different parts of Australia). Nevertheless, working against such concepts and practices of separation was the ever-present attractiveness of inexpensive native labor. As workers, natives might live in and around places of settlement, with all the forms of "contact" this might imply.

Around Katherine, Aborigines congregated in considerable numbers on peanut and vegetable farms from the 1920s, having previously gathered around the developing rail-line and along the river near the growing town. From 1918, prohibited areas ordinances were gazetted around Katherine (as around other Territory towns); these stipulated that Aborigines were to be within town areas during the day only if engaged upon the legitimate business of an employer and were not to be there between sunset and sunrise. Despite such prohibitions, native encampments existed in the vicinity of towns like Katherine, allowing the campers access both to town and to outlying areas and their food resources, important to survival. It generally proved difficult to control native movements and presence to the extent the ordinances appear to suggest.

Following the Japanese air attack upon Darwin and Katherine in February 1942 (which killed one native in Katherine), natives were collected and interned in one of the Army camps or compounds around Katherine. Internment brought people unknown to one another into close contact for the first time and exposed them to what they generally experienced as a comparatively liberal military regime of work and rationing (Hall 1989). These compounds were broken up after the war and most of their occupants from distant places returned to their areas of origin; but large numbers of natives were moved to government settlements, and these (like Bamyili, more recently renamed Barunga, 80 kilometers east of Katherine, to which I refer in several places in this book; see map 1), became permanent.

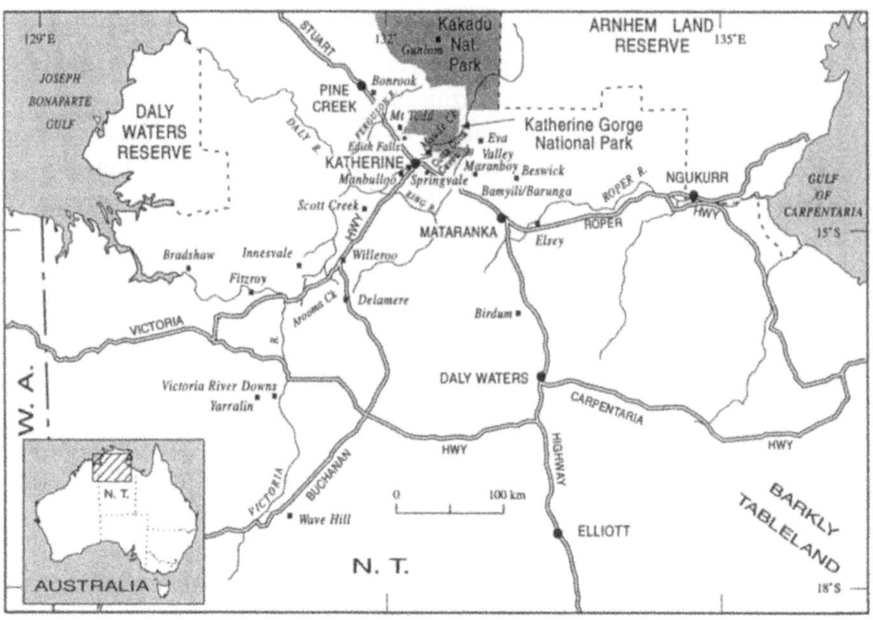

Map 1. Katherine Region Locations

After the war and the departure of most of the military, efforts at close control were resumed and even heightened by the modernization and professionalization of the Native Affairs Branch.[4] Natives were to be in Katherine town and the surrounding rural area as properly managed labor. Only able-bodied adults were, in theory, to be allowed around the town, housed, fed, and paid a small wage by their employers. Children and the unemployable were to be kept out of town, on settlements or pastoral properties. A 1952 census by a Native Affairs Branch officer of Aborigines situated in and around the town revealed only 105 people, mainly adult men and women, distributed over about thirty town and peri-urban locations (Commonwealth Archives, F1 52/648).

This situation changed dramatically in the 1960s. Efforts to modernize the pastoral industry and to improve overall working conditions included union-led efforts to establish a pastoral award, or minimum wage. (Useful accounts of early and changing conditions of Aborigines on northern pastoral stations include Stevens 1974, Berndt and Berndt 1987, Rose 1992.) The modernizing policy shift at broadened governmental levels was part of the general tide of change in the postwar period, and was chiefly accomplished by Paul Hasluck, Australian minister for territories from 1951 to 1963. This shift began with revision of the older style of protectionism and the introduction of a universalist welfare model that nevertheless assured the special management of Aborigines as "wards." In these terms all but six (full-blooded) Aborigines in the Northern Territory were gazetted in the Register of Wards, completed in 1955–1956. (See Cummings 1990, chapter 6 for fuller discussion.) The 1953 act was repealed by the Social Welfare Act introduced into the Northern Territory Legislative Assembly in 1964. The concept of "wardship" was removed from the 1964 bill, along with provisions that had allowed their removal and detainment.[5]

A national federal referendum of 1967 established the willingness of approximately 90 percent of the Australian electorate (but not including white or other residents of the Northern Territory who could not exercise the franchise; see Bennett 1989:53–54 for details and analysis) to change two sections of the Australian constitution widely considered discriminatory toward Aborigines: section 127, which had excluded them from federal census, and section 51 (xxvi), which had restricted the powers of the Commonwealth in making laws in relation to "aboriginal people in any State." With the elimination of these restrictions, the scene was set for a much greater role for the Commonwealth in Aboriginal affairs policy and administration.

In 1965 the federal Conciliation and Arbitration Commission, in a move that would greatly affect the Northern Territory, agreed upon a minimum pastoral wage, but thirty months' "adjustment period" was allowed to pastoralists. The latter argued that their relations with Aborigines were not economically rational: based partly upon traditional attachments of Aborigines to particular locations, pastoralists had had to assume paternalist duties of care that, they warned, would become unbearable if a minimum wage were set. If forced to pay a minimum wage, they would, for example, have to turn off from their properties the large numbers of unemployable Aborigines they maintained.

The pastoral award broke many of the links that had been established between pastoral properties and the encampments of Aborigines who had lived and worked on them, often under deplorable conditions, and created a dramatic influx of Aborigines into regional towns like Katherine. By 1970, officers of the Welfare Branch, the successor agency to Native Affairs, counted approximately three hundred Aborigines camping in and around Katherine, the majority at four principal locations. These correspond closely with today's main Aboriginal "town camps" (see Map 2), with a further eighty persons distributed over thirteen additional locations.

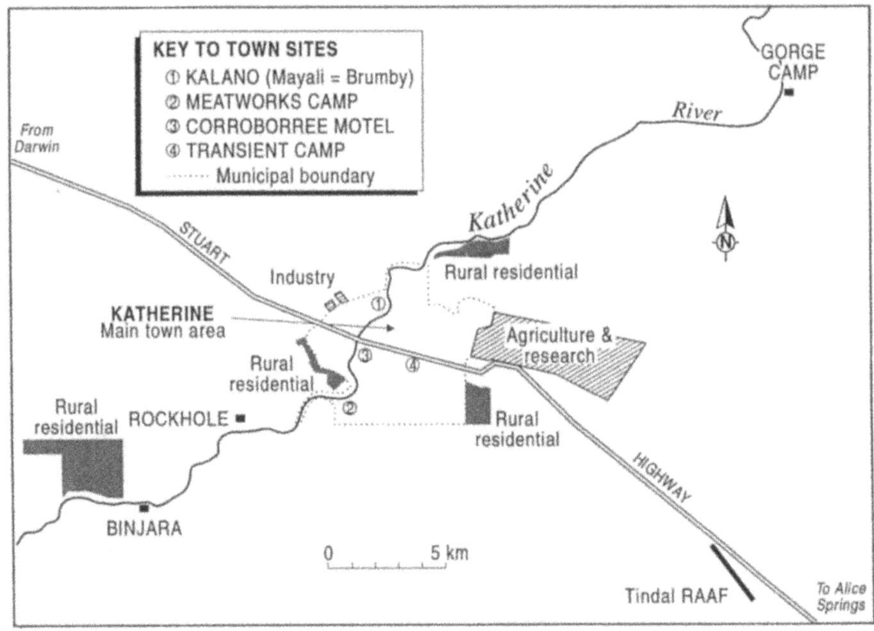

Map 2. Katherine Aboriginal Town Camps

Though many white townspeople and administrators were incensed by the influx, and both hoped and deluded themselves that it was temporary, in retrospect it is clear that the earlier situation of close management of Aborigines' presence around towns had changed for good. From 1967, the District Welfare Office decided that some existing tent communities would have to be legitimated and steps taken to provide some services to, and to regulate, these "fringe camps" (see Lea 1987:58–68 for details). The eventual softening from "fringe" to "town" camps (House of Representatives 1981) minimized the spatial remove that characterized most of them, at the same time suggesting the possibility of their more genuine inclusion within town spaces.

In 1974, a town-area Aboriginal organization called Kalano Association was established under the auspices of the regional branch of the Department of Aboriginal Affairs (DAA), the establishment of which was part of a wider shift from principal management by state- and territory-level agencies.[6] In 1970, again under the auspices of the DAA, the first six houses intended for Aboriginal occupancy were completed on what was then the eastern fringe of Katherine town. (Inasmuch as many of its residents, as I recount further on in this chapter, identified themselves with country west and south of town, this location in Katherine was thus not within the portion of town where many had previously camped informally. Though spatial separation from non-Aborigines has always been an element in the siting of Aboriginal residential locations around the town (and has been to some extent preferred both by Aborigines and by others), the subsequent years have seen continual struggles and efforts concerned with the acceptance and service provisioning of Aboriginal camps (see, e.g., Loveday and Lea 1985, Loveday 1987) and with the location and acceptance of Aboriginal residents, especially those considered "traditionally oriented," in other forms of housing (especially subsidized Housing Commission locations) more widely distributed throughout the developing town's residential areas.

And so, to a view of Katherine as I came to know the town around this time.

People from South and West

I first arrived in Katherine in the wet season of 1976. It was early February, and the build-up to the wet, the hottest period in this part of northern Australia, had broken. The weather had begun to be bearable because the rains came almost daily. From New Orleans where I had been teaching at Tulane University, I had applied for and received a research grant from the Australian Institute of Aboriginal Studies in Canberra. Officers of the institute had suggested to me several places in Australia where I might do research, provided that I choose an area where there was still much to learn and record about local languages and the people who spoke them. Of several areas suggested by the institute, I chose Katherine, on the basis of little specific knowledge and few preconceptions about the form of life that Aboriginal people might be living. I later understood that the relative availability of research funding was part of the attention newly focused on Aboriginal affairs and particularly fostered by the Whitlam-led Labor government, 1972–1975.

In a few weeks in Canberra, I had gained some familiarity with the general Australianist literature on language and social organization, but it gave me little sense of what the Aboriginal people I would meet might be like.

I drove down the "track," the Stuart Highway, from Darwin, quaking as I went over the railway trestle at Adelaide River that still, at that time, served as thoroughfare in the wet season whenever the main road was impassible. The dirt along the way was very orange in places, and the trees struck me (who had just come from the lushness of Louisiana) as bare and spiky, and the vegetation, especially the short, ferny-looking cycad palms, as something from the great age of dinosaurs.

The long vehicular bridge that spans the Katherine River at what is called the High Level had been completed only shortly before I came to Katherine. Before that, traffic had entered town via the Low Level crossing well downstream, over a concrete causeway that had been one of the improvements made during the military occupation of Katherine during the Second World War.

As I came close to Katherine, I saw what was obviously an Aboriginal camp on the north side of the river, separated from the main town, just before the vehicular bridge (location 1, map 2). It was close to the road, so that I could see distant figures of people moving about and clothes hung to dry on sections of barbed-wire fence. The camp's main shelters were small cinder-block cubicles, but there was also a clutter of tent tarpaulins, children's bikes and toys, a couple of old vehicles, tins, bed frames, upturned flour drums. The ground was muddy, and there was standing water in places.

I soon learned that this camp, like the bridge, was sometimes known as the High Level after its position on the river in relation to the town. It was also known to some white residents as Silver City, in mocking reference to its strewn and unkempt appearance. Over decades, many Aboriginal camps had existed along this riverbank (earlier also known as Northbank), with the river an important marker and physical realization of spatial separation between the town and the Aboriginal campers.

Katherine's principal business and office area (the town then had a population of less than five thousand) extends along the main street, a segment of the Territory's major north-south road, the Stuart Highway. On my first arrival, the town seemed quiet, and I learned it was rained in from several directions.

Later I came to see this quiet in relation to an annual round, mainly in terms of the drastic seasonal contrast characteristic of Australia's monsoonal north between the wet and the dry. For much of the year—roughly from May to September—no rain falls. From May to about August, the sky is bright blue and cloudless, the days are clear, and the nights cool. But from September to November, the buildup to the wet is marked by increasingly humid heat from which there is no relief. The hottest temperatures (up to 38 or 40 degrees Celsius) occur during October, November, and December, during the buildup, and the relative humidity is also highest then, about 80 percent. The sun is intense, the air close, and one's body is constantly covered in a light film of sweat, producing its own minimal cooling effect. For people, like many Aborigines, who go barefoot, sand and bare, exposed ground are burning hot, necessitating movement from one tree or shade patch to another if one walks around. By October or November, the first rain brings welcome relief as the buildup turns into the wet. Eventually, rains and freshening northwesterly winds come daily, and most of the annual rains fall from January to March. Rivers rise with the runoff and sometimes become raging torrents of floodwater carrying branches and trees along and leaving vegetation high up in trees as high-water marks visible the year round. Grasses flourish and grow tall along the rivers. In Katherine, white and black alike flock to the High Level bridge to see the level of the river after heavy rains, marked in meters on the concrete pylons of the old railway trestle that spans the river just downstream. I had arrived in Katherine in mid-wet. Travel can be restricted if rains cover the roads at creek crossings and occasionally even at the built-up river crossings over the Stuart Highway.

I had no contacts in Katherine. As I made a purchase at a local shop, someone who looked like the proprietor asked me what I was doing in town, and I told him. He knew the names of a couple of local languages and assured me that they were nearly the same. I came to know that answers like these might be wildly inaccurate, as his was. Uncertain where to go, I walked up and down the main street. As I loitered, a savage fight quite unexpectedly (and also unusually, for it is not an everyday occurrence) erupted between two white men dressed in stockmen's clothes in front of a store on the main street. One finally got the other on the ground and started kicking him in the face. A few passersby gathered, and eventually the combatants were separated. Somewhat shaken and with the echoes of the blows still thudding in my head, I continued walking slowly along the main street, now more uncomfortable as a person with no evident purpose.

Aboriginal people came and went; they were in the majority on the main street for some of the time, concentrated in certain places along it. Some sat on the sidewalk in front of what was then the main street's largest shop, Katherine Stores ("Since 1926"). A couple of very striking old Aboriginal men were there, one with a huge mop of white hair, the other white-haired and slight, walking on crutches. Some of the women, who wore colorful but shapeless dresses, were sitting talking to each other, and

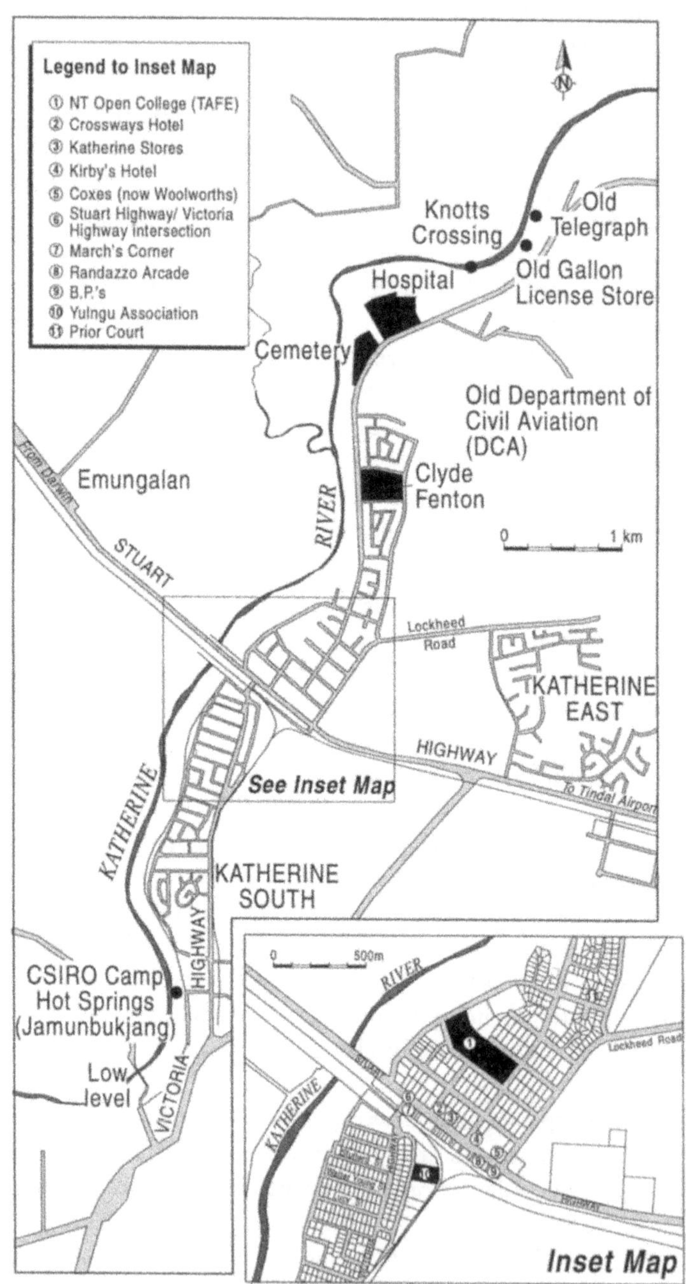

Map 3. Katherine Town Locations

children were running about on the sidewalk, eating ice creams. Children and adults were barefoot. The groups of Aborigines I came near were speaking Kriol English,[7] which was only partly comprehensible to me at that early stage, but still clearly distinguishable from an Aboriginal language.

Some Aboriginal people were at the southern end of the main street, near a large building called Randazzo Arcade. I saw a sign pointing upstairs to the Department of Aboriginal Affairs. I went up, and an elderly secretary took my name, then led me in from the waiting room to meet two officers. They looked very spruce in light shirt and shorts, knee-length white socks, and walking shoes, a kind of attire then unfamiliar to me but that I later came to recognize as fairly standard tropical gear among northern Australian public servants and other office workers. Some Aborigines who have worked in public service roles have adopted this style of dress.

The officers heard what I had come to do, and one offered to introduce me to a "responsible" Aboriginal couple. He shortly drove me to a small cluster of half a dozen houses on the eastern edge of town in an oval street called Prior Court—the first set of houses, referred to above, completed for Aboriginal occupancy in 1970 (location 11, map 3). He pulled up to a gray brick house with a tree and a sagging wire bedstead in the yard. There were children everywhere, and a lithe woman who seemed to be of early middle age perched on the bedstead. Sitting below her on the ground, legs straight out in front of her and back effortlessly erect, was an older woman with several fingers and toes missing, a leper. The atmosphere was tense. People seemed to be alarmed at this unexpected visit and (I imagined) especially at me, a stranger. The yard was littered with bones, papers, tins, and items of old clothing. The official introduced me to Elsie, the woman on the bedstead, and she extended her hand briefly, looking slightly sideways. He explained to her that I was trying to learn something about the local languages and people and commended me to her and to her husband, Kaiser, who appeared from inside the house. Shortly, the official drove away.

I tried to explain that I wanted help finding out about local languages and where people were from. I did not understand their Kriol well and had to listen carefully. I also told them something about myself: that I had come from overseas, that I was here without family, and that I had seen and wanted to meet some Aboriginal people on the main street but it had been hard to start to talk to them, since I didn't know anyone. By this time I had been there a while, struggling with myself not to leave quickly, despite the sense of tension I felt. These remarks about myself seemed to elicit sympathy. Although Kaiser remained cautious, Elsie said she would call me "granddaughter," and she told me that the appropriate social category term for me would be *nangala.* She quickly corrected herself, saying, really "properly," *yinggangala* in Wardaman, her language; *nangala* was the Mudbura word for it, from Kaiser's language. She would teach me "proper" Wardaman.

Elsie and Kaiser explained to me who all the people around the place were, including their own sons and many people who they said were close relatives of theirs, sitting on the lawn in front of the next house a short distance away. I assimilated only a little of this. It was some weeks before I understood the family relations they had summarized for me. Elsie had a high-pitched voice and rapid, indistinct style of speech, partly due to the loss of some of her teeth. Her movements were supple and her manner quicksilver. I immediately found her winning, but it was only after a few weeks, when we had begun to travel together and she to show me the country she knew around Katherine, that I became enchanted by her deftness as she made our trips the occasion to do what she obviously found completely absorbing: looking for bush foods. I would watch her admiringly as she would walk unhesitatingly out along the bigger branches of fallen trees partly submerged in Katherine River to toss her fishing line just where she had learned a turtle or fish was. Or I would be delegated, and armed with a waddy (stick), to stand at one hole of a goanna (large lizard) network she had found while she, bending effortlessly from the waist, would begin digging at another with improvised digging stick in one hand, the other hand serving as scoop to clear the loosened dirt away.

Elsie and I began doing a lot of language work, but in short stretches, for rarely would an hour or two go by without our being visited, or going to make calls around town ourselves. She told me that she and many of her relatives were Wardaman, but they were closely linked to other countrymen of the Victoria River region, including those she called Nungali, Ngaliwurru, Jaminjung, and Mudburra, Kaiser's people (map 4). The Wardaman came from southwest of Katherine, from Willeroo and Delamere Stations (see map 1). Kaiser, on the other hand, was from Wave Hill, a place which had become known to Australians as the site of a strike of 1966 by Aboriginal stockmen, who walked off demanding better wages and living conditions, and then rights to their own land, in what has conventionally come to be seen as a first step in the subsequent land-rights movement (see Doolan 1977, Hardy 1968, Rose 1992).

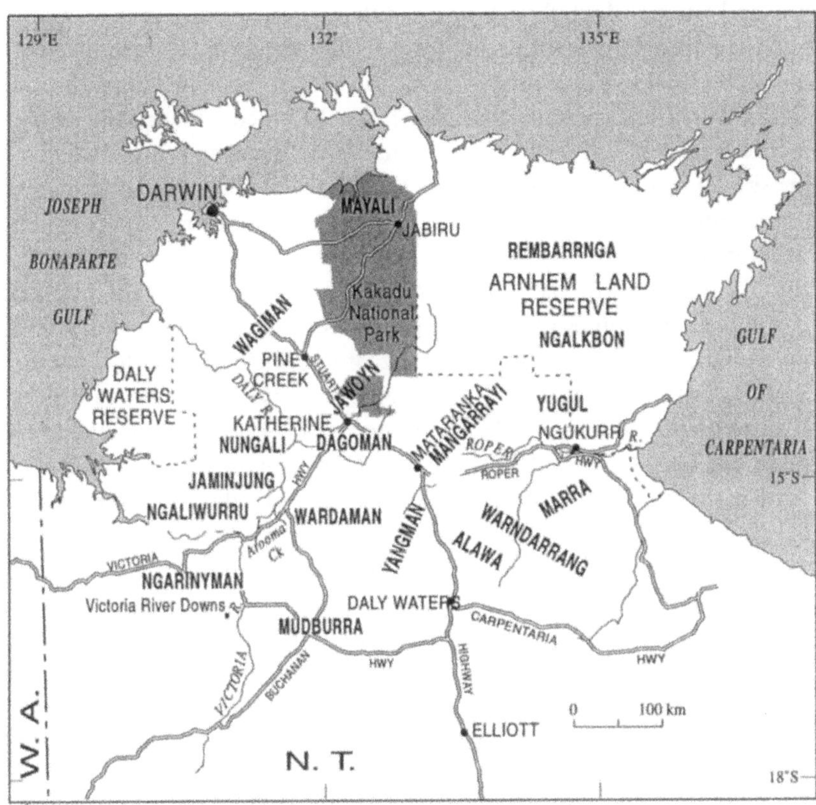

Map 4. Distribution of Socio-territorial Groupings

Elsie herself had grown up on Willeroo and Delamere but together with Kaiser had been in and around town for some years. She had done housework, and he had been yardman at the hospital for some time, until he had been pensioned off with chest problems. She knew Katherine well, but especially the southwestern sector of town in all its particularities of place-names, Dreaming associations, and personal ties. She was always pointing out to me places and features of town that related to the Wardaman experience of movement back and forth between the town and the stations to the southwest where they and other Victoria River Aborigines had worked: from Manbulloo, with its head station not far outside Katherine town past the meatworks, to Willeroo, Innesvale, Delamere, Victoria River Downs, and Coolibah and Bradshaw to the west. She showed me the place where the "loading" (supplies) used to be brought from the railway and left for Manbulloo. We visited the old army camp sites on Manbulloo and along the Victoria Highway within the town area that dated to the Second World War military occupation of Katherine, including the old World War II army camp where her father had died, whence she, at her mother's request, had returned to Delamere. We drove and then walked to the sites of camps where she and Kaiser and the children had lived, in the southwestern part of town, on the racecourse or near the river, in the years when it was still possible for Aboriginal family groups to tuck themselves away in independent campsites in close proximity to town. She pointed out the sites of houses of Europeans for whom she had worked and told me the Aboriginal names and dreaming associations of places all along the Victoria Highway, first close to town and then, as we traveled more widely, as far south as Willeroo and Delamere. Always, she wanted to get away from town and go fishing and foraging; when any animal or bush food was sighted, she was unstoppable. My Land Rover seemed to be parked along the road as much as it traveled, while we (sometimes as many as twenty of us, especially on the longer and more exciting expeditions) chased goannas; hurled missiles to knock blanket lizards out of trees; stalked bush turkeys; raced for bush plums, wild apples, and oranges; stopped to dig yams and plat potatoes.

As far south of the town as Wugimadgun, or Scott Creek, Elsie told me, was not Wardaman country, but belonged to people called Dagoman, of whom very few remained.

One day we set off (stopping frequently to pick up *yidawurru* [wild melons] along the road, with Elsie and the children as usual spotting them well before I did) to Willeroo, where a few Wardaman and other Aborigines who worked seasonally were periodically living in the Aboriginal camp.

Southwest from Katherine the country is fairly flat savannah, with occasional hilly relief. But as one approaches what Elsie and others call "Willeroo country," the terrain becomes more remarkable. One can see long distances to sweeping table-topped hills that rise from country sloping toward the Victoria River Valley. Near Willeroo Station is an almost perfect cone-shaped hill, called Warnmarring. The Wardaman vision of the country, as conveyed to me by Elsie and others, is that a King Brown snake traveled to Warnmarring and then on to Muymuy, Willeroo Station homestead, from a long hill to the west called Mawuyaya (Poison Place). At this place, Aborigines who belonged to it or were familiar with it could collect venom on a spoon, so it was said, to poison an enemy.

Everyone agreed that the Willeroo Station area belonged (in Aboriginal terms) to a man named Claude Manbulloo, his sister, their father's sister Nida, and others of Claude's relatives on his father's side. By this time, all of his father's many brothers and sisters, except for his aunt Nida, had passed away. (Nida herself died in 1992.) Claude was seen as the effective senior person and landholder of this family, as his aunt, even then, was regarded as "old people." At Willeroo I met Nida, who was living in one of the hot, fly-infested tin sheds that the station provided. She was a gentle old woman, with work-enlarged hands, softened now from disoccupation, and large eyes that always seemed vague; her eyesight may have been impaired. But she was in command of her mental faculties and kindly sat and talked to me about the country in which we were sitting. She obviously preferred speaking to Elsie and to me in Wardaman, and I listened intently and tried to understand as much as I could. Claude had not come with us, as he was away working on the Daly River. He had a reputation as a thoroughly experienced stockman and a powerful, reliable worker out in the bush, but as a "grog-eater" when in town—something he has now entirely put aside.

Behind the Willeroo homestead rises a scarp called Bijbarnang, from which *girribug*, the long-tailed "pheasant coucal," threw clapsticks. Some of these were still to be seen on the flat below in the bed of Aroona Creek when I first visited Willeroo and into the 1980s, in the form of three-to-four-foot-high, shaped and smoothed, elongate stones. They have since disappeared.

Nida told me (and other old people often referred to this story too) about a white station worker named Roy Bartlam, who, Aboriginal people say, annoyed by nighttime didgeridoo (wooden drone pipes) playing, had shot up the Aboriginal camp.[8] According to Nida and another old woman, Daisy Gimiyn, the Aborigines had all run up the escarpment to Bijbarnang after Bartlam came down to the camp at night and in the morning had speared Bartlam's horse out from under him as he came after them.

Nida pointed out a spring on the hillside near Bijbarnang called Wiyorlwonyang, which has an almost lidlike cover. Further south along the scarp, a native bee place was a sorcery site for male Aborigines of Willeroo: the bees would be enjoined to attack and to pockmark images of unfaithful women made on a smooth rock surface.

At Muymuy itself, Nida, Elsie, and others showed me, between the homestead and the Aboriginal camp, a ghost gum, the form taken by the traveling King Brown snake. As we walked around the Aboriginal camp, people pointed out trees under which they themselves had given birth to certain of their children or where other women's children had been born. They said that Aboriginal people were buried farther along the creek, which separated white and black living spaces in the homestead area. They recalled the burials there of some specific individuals, but there were also said to be earlier burials of people no longer individually remembered. All around were named places replete with memories and significances: births, names, fights, white-inflicted punishments, elopements, flight, revenge, Aboriginal spearing of an early white traveler. Willeroo country was still vital in the way that all these episodes and memories were thoroughly integrated into a landscape crisscrossed by King Brown, Taipan, Pheasant Coucal, and other *buwarraja* ("Dreamings," or creator beings); significances were inscribed in places in both personal and Dreaming terms. The Dreaming has a vertical dimension in the higher table-topped hills to the south, around a place called Galamberremang. These uplifted hills were said to have risen above *ngabayardu* (the flood), and thus allowed some people to be saved long, long ago.

Much farther to the south, in what is now Gregory National Park, an eerie-looking pyramid-shaped hill called Barnanggaya, or alternatively Barnanggarni, had also provided refuge for some people above the floodwaters. Linked as high places of refuge in these flood stories, Galamberremang and Barnanggaya tower over the country and communicate with each other at long distance. As well, Barnanggaya is a *warrija* (crocodile) Dreaming site at which *barnangga* (owlet nightjar) and another bird, *warrura*, argued over the distribution of a crocodile catch. It is the country of Elsie's "second" father, Ngamunugarri (called Tarpot in English), who was formerly an active participant in our visits to country and had done stock work throughout the area when younger but is now definitively "old people" and much more sedentary.

Running south from Muymuy, Claude's country, was Elsie's own special country; it extended to Winybarr (a spectacular, deep-sided water hole on Innesvale Station, adjacent to and formerly part of Willeroo), Wugleni (Johnstone Waterhole), Yiwarlarlay (a place now known for its gigantic rock painting of the Lightning Brothers, Jabirringgi and Yagjagbula), and Yerriyn (Old Delamere Station). The earliest white settlement in Elsie's country had been at Monborrom, Old Willeroo, in the Moray Range. Newspaper reports I later found tell that Aborigines attacked and speared the station's manager, Scott, in October 1892 and carried off a large amount of food and other supplies. This attack gained them only temporary respite from the advance of pastoral occupation. Punitive expeditions were mounted from the Katherine area for the Scott killing. Contemporary newspaper accounts indicate what public opinion expected these expeditions to accomplish: "I think the pursuing parties will be bound to have recourse to firearms in making arrests and unless a swift and terrible example is made of them no one will be safe in travelling about as before. The immense booty and the easy way in which it was secured will render them more impudent and treacherous than ever" (*Northern Territory Times and Gazette*, November 14, 1892). There is, however, no newspaper record of what was done, a silence that contrasts sharply with detailed newspaper accounts of the murder scene and the partial discovery by search parties from Katherine of the pilfered supplies. This period may be the historical background to episodes related to Elsie by her father. He told her about places near Johnstone Waterhole where many Aborigines were shot while the remaining few came in to Willeroo. As we traveled around and talked about Willeroo country, I was struck by the way that venomous snakes moving through it converged on Muymuy, the present Willeroo homestead. Did those dangerous presences somehow represent a merging of the dreaming stories with the colonial Willeroo past?

At Willeroo, the Aboriginal camp itself was ablaze in the sun: small, square, galvanized iron structures on concrete slabs, in a cleared area, with no shade trees, no running water, and no electricity. About twenty people were in residence there on our first visit in the wet season of 1976. They had received from the station portions of a "killer," or beast (beef), and had laid these on leafy boughs on table surfaces in the middle of camp. The flies rose from the meat in dense clouds everytime anyone came near. The heat in the camp was intense, the humidity stifling. It seemed to me nearly incredible that babies and children could have survived their infancy here; and indeed, many did not.

Despite an unfriendly reception from the homestead, I had thoughts of moving to Willeroo for a while (though I later learned that the manager had contacted his Sydney office for advice on how to turn me down). Not long after that, my interest in moving there disappeared anyway, for at about the time of the annual Katherine Show, in July, the management took the Aboriginal station workers into town with their swags (bedrolls), promising (I was told by camp residents) to pick them up in a couple of weeks after the show was over. Instead, it seems from their account, the manager never collected them, but brought all their things and dumped them at the High Level camp. The urbanization of Aborigines who had lived and worked on pastoral stations had occurred in variant forms on many properties since the late 1960s with the implementation of the pastoral award wage and was made nearly complete at Willeroo by that episode.

Even as this move into Katherine was occurring, some of the Wardaman people I knew (including Elsie's family) were beginning to try to gain rights to some land on Willeroo, by excision. There was some strength of feeling among Wardaman families about moving back onto country. How they might face the many practical problems that would have arisen was left for consideration when the time came. I helped in writing petitions and submissions to government agencies; some they wrote themselves, younger people serving as the scribes, older people affixing signature or cross. They tried to get first one location, then another, but their requests came to nothing at that time.[9]

In the meantime, many of the people who had come in from Willeroo, and others in town, still felt an immediate need for a living area of their own. The living site closest to town, with which Wardaman and other Victoria River people had long familiarity, was Manbulloo Station. This was close enough to town to enable people to reach its services; but interest in residence there was limited to families who originated from what Katherinites call the western side and who had a family history of work on western pastoral properties, usually including Willeroo, Delamere, and Manbulloo.

There had been an Aboriginal camp on Manbulloo until 1974, when the last few people had been removed by the manager of Vesteys, the British company that held the property. Manbulloo was operating at low levels by then as a cattle property, and the Aborigines on the station were now seen as a problem rather than a labor pool. No longer welcome there by 1977, Wardaman people moved to a number of places in town, especially to the High Level, as well as to a new site, called Bunjarri,[10] on Manbulloo.

As I mentioned above, some western-side Aboriginal people of Katherine regard Manbulloo Station as in Dagoman country, and not Wardaman. But a few older Wardaman people are the most knowledgeable about places and place-names on Manbulloo. The station area holds memories for all those who lived there, worked there, and performed ceremony in the vicinity of the station homestead, regardless of "tribal" affiliation. A burial ground of those Aborigines who died there has been demarcated as a sacred site. A pattern on the ground that looks like a footprint is regarded as Dreaming by Aborigines who lived on Manbulloo.

It quickly became clear to me that those Aboriginal people who have familiarity with both Manbulloo country and Willeroo country have less full and specific sense of the meaningfulness of sites in the former. In the main, the area southwest of Katherine, including much of Manbulloo, is now a landscape of named places, mainly creeks and sites along the Katherine and King Rivers, with specific Dreaming associations but little elaboration of stories or connections among sites. There is little remaining sense of larger-than-life creator figures, like the King Brown at Willeroo. At Manbulloo, significance for Aborigines is now focused mainly on the station homestead area, around which people lived and worked, with nearby ceremonial grounds and burial places. A few places, as interpreted by older Aboriginal people, still hold clues to the spectacular meanings formerly associated with them (briefly alluded to in chapter 4); but most of these have now become obsolete through lack of commonality. The sense of places as linked and forming Dreaming tracks that connect and intersect as a larger regional system has faded. (In chapter 4 I consider how the evanescence of Dagoman identity is linked to the fact of the town's growth and existence as a regional center in which vivid socio-territorial identity has proven difficult to sustain in older Aboriginal terms.)

People from North and East

As I came to know many of the Wardaman people around town, I also became aware of people called Jawoyn, some of whom lived at the Gorge camp north of the township at the mouth of Katherine Gorge National Park (location 5, map 2), an increasingly important tourist destination. White townspeople seemed to think only a few Jawoyn remained; they were considered a "dying tribe" (see Maff n.d.: 6). Elsie and her mob knew the Gorge people, but they were not close familiars, and their paths crossed mainly in town.

I decided to visit the Gorge camp, but for some time the road was flooded. By the time it became passable, I knew a few of those old people slightly including an old lady, Alice Mitchell, whom I had met in Elsie's company. Both Alice and I called Elsie "granny." Alice had always been friendly to me, and it was with her that I first went out to the Gorge camp.

The camp, it turned out, had only rudimentary facilities: a water tank, which was occasionally filled by a truck from Kalano; shacks of galvanized iron and wood scraps and tent flys; and a few latrines. There were a few iron bedsprings outside, hooks and high places from which things could be hung, and fireplaces with some cooking pots. Special possessions and clothes were largely stored in old, battered suitcases and duffle bags. A few half-finished didgeridoos were propped against trees.

The day I first went out to the Gorge must have been a pension day, or close to it, though I did not record this in my diary. We had been in Alice's camp only a short while when it became apparent that some of her camp mates, mostly old people including her husband and several of his elderly male companions, had earlier returned from town with grog and were in the middle of a fight. We heard angry shouts, and a few old men and women came into view. One of the men had a scrap piece of galvanized iron in hand and scaled it across the clearing toward where we were sitting, though not, it seemed, specifically targeting us. Alice started shouting as loudly as the rest and told them to stop swearing in front of her white lady little sister. A few glanced at me without much interest; some, glassy-eyed, continued the fight all around the camp for some time. Contents of some of the suitcases were scattered; any of the numerous skinny and hairless dogs that got in their path were unceremoniously kicked out of the way and ran off cowering and yelping piteously. Alice suggested that we leave again, but I shook my head, determined not to be driven away now that I had finally gotten there. When Alice saw that I was not to be moved, she and I just sat and talked quietly until the commotion died down. Before I left some hours later, she had introduced me to some women and her old husband and several other men of similar age who sat off by themselves, nursing a few cans of beer. She introduced me to them loudly, but they were impassive, just nodding a quiet greeting: they seemed to want to be left in peace.

Alice shortly took to treating me the way she treated her other female camp mates, explaining that since I was her "little sister," I had to work for her. (The social category Elsie and Kaiser had given me translated into comparable Gorge camp terms and made it plausible for Alice to classify me as her sister.) I could begin by going with her to pick up some firewood in my Land Rover.

That was the start of a friendship that lasted ten years, until Alice's death. Gradually, I began to know all the camp occupants, including the old men who had seemed so remote at first. Among them were Norman Rankin ("Eyeglass," Alice called him, or *dum-muya*, Jawoyn "eye-sick," as he was known around the camp) and Peter Mitchell, Alice's dour, slim and handsome old husband (whom Alice always called, in Jawoyn, "our," that is, her and my, husband, to his perennial discomfiture), who seemed to feel that silence suited him; he became loquacious only occasionally, when drunk. He was also known to other campers and to some Aboriginal and white people in town as Peter Carpenter, a name commemorating the occupation he had followed in the postwar years at Beswick, a pastoral property to the east of Katherine, developed as an Aboriginal training center after the Second World War. There was Tommy Birrgalaju, an old Mayali man who was camp-bound, having lost a leg, and his wife, Alice (called Barrakjowotj [scorpion hand] in reference to her having been bitten by a scorpion). I learned she belonged to the same Jawoyn clan group, Wurrkbarbar, as Sandy Barraway, a man I later came to know well, first at Barunga and then in Katherine. It emerged that I would call Alice Barrakjowotj *jongwok* (auntie), since Sandy, on a few days' acquaintance, pronounced me *madak* (daughter)—a term that also fitted with Elsie's classification of me from the Wardaman side.

There was also Alice Barrakjowotj's son, Roy Anderson. There were old Harry and Alice Gardaygarday, Mayali people originally from the north, who had worked on Eva Valley Station in the 1960s and had been among those who had sometimes walked from Eva Valley through to Katherine town via the Katherine Gorge. There was Sandy Fredericks and his large family, also Mayali; when younger, Sandy had walked with his father from Katherine back to a distant place, Jowow'mi, not far from the Arnhem coast, for ceremony. One of Alice Mitchell's constant camp companions was Nancy Galaworga, originally from the Roper River area. Alice would order her about mercilessly, tapping her walking stick on the ground to promote "hurry up." There was Charlie Williams, usually known by his Aboriginal name, Na-Daymaniya, and his co-countryman Jerry Dempsey or King. Both were Rembarrnga, of a socio-territorial identity of the Arnhem plateau different from Jawoyn and Mayali, but with whom people of the latter two felt familiar. Jerry's father, Lightning, had become a police tracker in Katherine for the policeman, old Bob Woods, decades before, and Jerry had stayed on. These and other Gorge campers, most of whom were elderly, after a while came to tolerate and even expect me.

As I have noted, some of the steady Gorge camp residents were Jawoyn, an identity they conceived in terms of its association with a territory and a language. They all said that the Gorge and the river down to and including the township were Jawoyn country, part of a much larger stretch of country they identified in this way, and that their language was Jawoyn (see chapters 4 and 5). Mayali people like Tommy Birrgalaju and Sandy Fredericks had originated from farther north.[11] Most campers spoke Jawoyn and Mayali, and all understood both. They had in common their years of experience along this portion of the Katherine River north of the township, based in shared residence on pastoral properties and farms along the river and also on the peanut farms that had been established in the 1920s and 1930s in attempts to create farming employment for Europeans.

Among the European employers that all these old people had known in that earlier era were Nigel Bruce and Bert Nixon, and a brief sketch of both, and of the work that Aborigines did, is important to understanding the relation between that past and their present at the time I got to know them and some of the sociohistorical particularity of their experience as northeasterners.

Nigel Bruce came to Katherine in the 1920s from New South Wales, where he had been a bank employee. He took up land in Katherine and got into farming. Henry Scott, a long-term Katherine resident (see chapter 2) remembered him as "one of the first blokes who set up a cotton ginnery here," and he came to own large portions of land along the Katherine River. His lifestyle on the Katherine was "very spare, yes, like er, all he had was an old iron bed, no mattress or anything, only a few peanut bags I think were on that . . . old fowls, you know, you'd wake up in the morning and there'd be fowl dung all over him, so he lived a pretty, yeah, oh, a very crude old life."

Jawoyn and Mayali worked on Nigel Bruce's peanut farm for rations. Some labor was required over about half the year, from December to June, depending on the state of technology and farm machinery at particular periods.[12] From June to about October some farmers who tried vegetable crops made some use of Aboriginal labor. Given this round, little Aboriginal labor was required from about October or November to about March. Most Aborigines, like Alice and her mob, were let go for at least some of that period. They would get some rations, tobacco and other supplies and live for periods of time along the river, up against the escarpment that rises to the north of Katherine, or go on top of the escarpment to hunt porcupine and kangaroo and also, sometimes, to smoke the opium ash that they could purchase at Mrs. Knott's store near the old Katherine crossing or at Chinese establishments in Katherine.

Nigel Bruce was around Katherine so long that he became a fixture to Aboriginal people, a way of measuring a span of lived time. There are still many who can say they grew up "langa old Nigel Bruce, langa Bruce farm." One family is surnamed "Bruce" after him. But Nigel Bruce came to grief. Some Katherine old-timers claim that he was set up, that a new policeman in town bought a bottle of plonk (cheap wine), planted it on Bruce's farm, and told an Aborigine where it was. When he went to get it, the story runs, Nigel was arrested for supplying alcohol and got six months for it. Certain of Bruce's long-term acquaintances refuse to believe that he ever supplied alcohol to blackfellas on his property. Whatever the truth of that episode, Aborigines (like Peter Mitchell, and Alice, and their camp mates) told me it was common practice for bosses to give them small amounts of alcohol, including metho (methylated spirits), from time to time, but that there was a common conspiracy of silence: neither Aborigines nor whites were supposed to tell.

Nixon lived on the Katherine River at a time when Aborigines who came to work on the peanut farms were still mobile over considerable distances, footwalking, as they say. At least from time to time, there were camps of Aboriginal people on the major rivers to the north, and some Aborigines of northern origin have told me about movements back to their country of origin for the performance of ceremony. It is clear, however, that the density of the Katherine River encampments and the relatively fixed nature of the pastoral and rural employment that drew people to them also resulted in the performance of ceremony on the river, in close proximity to the town. People from as far away as locations on the Roper River have told me stories of walking to the Katherine River to attend ceremony; the stories I have heard probably date to the 1930s. Oral interviews with Bert Nixon in 1982 show that he knew of this activity and its location. In that later context he saw this knowledge as confirming his authority to protest and contest land rights and sacred sites legislation and its implementation.

There were camps over such long periods on Nixon's property that the partly continuous, partly changing sets of people who lived there formed personal attachments and ties to places on his property. Sarah Andrews, a Jawoyn woman, described to me the deposition of her father's bones at a place called Wiyawa, a creek that seasonally is reduced to a set of small, blue water holes. To this place, a few kilometers away from the Nixon home, Aborigines retreated to fish, hunt, and gain access to the escarpment during periods when they moved away from the homestead.

Nixon held a set of views about Aborigines that seem to be common, if not typical, among men of his life experience. He struggled to establish himself in primary industry. From the Depression era well into the 1960s, he had as his workers Aborigines who were relatively unsophisticated in the practices of wage labor. They were generally content to work for keep and pocket money, or perhaps a small wage. In many cases, at least, such people felt they had a personal, rather than simply economically instrumental, relationship with the boss, often asymmetrical in that there was dependence on the Aboriginal side and control on the white side. No doubt, Nixon's identity as Na-Gartbam (a Mayali-speaking clan to which he was attributed an affiliation) was not a straightforward acceptance of him as a peer but a partial masking of many aspects of unequal power between him and his workers, including the conditions that allowed him to "marry" an Aboriginal woman—live with her in the long term, with some Aboriginal acceptance of this as a marriage. There are many instances of Aboriginal workers staying with the same boss for a long time or of there being a binding relationship between some family member and the white employer—sometimes, but not always, a sexual one. By the time of my research in Katherine, Nixon, like many other whites who lived through the transition from the earlier labor conditions—which they considered as natural, not requiring comment—to later welfarism, saw Aborigines as having been "spoiled."

This, then, was a central person whom the Gorge campers had known as employer and holder of land on which they had lived, worked, and sometimes hunted and foraged, and who, from that position of command, had known them in some ways intimately, in others ways very little. Although the Gorge campers might greet Nixon when they saw him in town or ask after him, by the 1970s in most ways their lives and his had diverged. Put more sharply, they were no longer of any use. I did not know of Bert Nixon's ever having visited the Gorge camp over the years I have visited there, despite the fact that up until the time he died, old men who had been among his most constant workers were living there.

As the rural subsistence life such as they had known on the river properties became less possible from about the mid-1960s, Aboriginal people who had lived in that way for years formed camps on the river, at the Two Mile, in the rocks near the old Department of Civil Aviation (DCA, map 3) and along rock formations slightly farther from the river where the Japanese had bombed in 1942, and elsewhere; they also camped near the mouth of Katherine Gorge, employed by a small-scale tourist operator, Ray Groves, from about 1968 to cut didgeridoos in the high country above the gorge and to decorate them. Welfare benefits became available to some in the form of old-age pensions and, in the cases of some with children, child endowment monies.

Aside from relatively recent developments relating to Katherine's having become a major tourist destination,[13] the Gorge campers no longer had many intense relationships with whites. When I got to know them in the latter 1970s they seemed to want to consolidate their apartness: to fish and forage along their beloved Katherine River and to live in their Jodetluk camp close to the now paved Gorge road. The nearest telephone was at Maude Creek Station, a pastoral property a few kilometers down the road. They might expect occasional lifts from rangers and others coming past from Katherine Gorge. Some of them would spend periods of time in town, mostly at certain camps at Mayali-Brumby on the High Level. Most of the regular Gorge camp residents were old people, who considered younger people, even their younger relatives, to be too much trouble and nuisance. A few younger people with close ties to older campers, however, did live there at times. In the general complaint about younger people, the elderly were partly thinking that they wanted to bring their grog back to camp, drink it quietly, and have their privacy, without the fights and "humbug" they felt they often got from younger people, especially during drinking sessions. It became clear to me that these old people shared a familiarity with each other and with this part of the Katherine River that had its roots in the earlier Aboriginal way of life around Katherine town, which in its particular combination of seasonal, rural employment, blended with subsistence activities, had already come to an end. Most wanted better amenities in camp—better houses, water, and so on—but did not want to be fully drawn into the processes and politics of development of Aboriginal organizations and facilities in town.

By the time I got to know them, a pattern of life lived largely apart from whites and regular relations of employment had become established. The Gorge people spent time in their camp cooking, washing, sitting around, and visiting with each other. They continued to move around their domain near the Gorge on foot, and then with my Land Rover often available to them, also downriver toward the township.

We walked around the hills near their camp, which they called Jodetluk (a Jawoyn name meaning place of the *jodet* ["left-hand kangaroo," a wallaby that "waves" its left paw as it hops], by which name this camp became known. They showed me a King Brown Dreaming stone in the dry hills away from the river, which had to be looked after because, if kicked over, it would release a plague of snakes. We drove in to favorite fishing spots along the Katherine River downstream from the Gorge, often to Marlunba, the Maude Creek junction with the Katherine River. They spoke of many places farther away from the river where they used to walk around; I knew them only as names and relative locations along the river, not as living spaces. I was surprised and grateful one day when I showed up and Peter, Alice's old husband, motioned to me and led me on a long, almost wordless walk around the hilly hunting area Alice called Jimartbaman, only speaking to name a few places that opened to our view and looking for signs of wallabies as we walked. With that, people in camp began to say I was really learning something about the Katherine River: a gift to me from Peter, Alice's and my old husband, gone now (since 1988) to join Alice in the Katherine Cemetery near the hospital.

The Gorge campers also continued to walk to places along the Katherine River to fish—one of their favorite places was Wun.gurri, which they knew as a boy and girl Blue-tongue Dreaming—usually making outings of a single day's duration. Sometimes I would go along. They would collect the few things necessary to them—billycans, tea and sugar, bread, tobacco, fishing lines and hooks—and walk across the road, then slowly thread their way along to the river, where they could sit quietly for a day's fishing, always attentive to what they were learning from line and water about the presence of fish and turtles, often talking little, each person intent on his or her doings for hours at a time. Sometimes people would call up and down the bank for the loan of a knife, or tobacco, or bait. These calls would be answered in a leisurely fashion in due course. Alice was often an exception to the general practice of not questioning others about their catch, as she tended to have a much more incisive and even invasive style, something everyone else recognized about her and generally tolerated. Whenever I was along, she would hector me a little to do the camp work of building a fire, hauling water, and so on; the others tended to be less bossy toward me and to share the work. I was always very obviously Alice's "little sister": it was she who had brought me to their camp. And it was sometimes (though not always) through her that those less willing to risk direct requests, with the possibility of refusal they entailed, would ask me for things, rides, money, help.

Toward afternoon, after a day of fishing people would gradually come together, one making a fire, starting to boil the billy, and putting fish in the ashes to roast. The loose, general sense of being together along the river but in a condition of individual absorption in one's fishing gradually reshaped itself into a togetherness around the fire, with increased exchange of talk, often about the immediacies of food, fire, and tea. After a simple meal of fish, bread, and tea, fish set aside for those back in camp would be wrapped in paperbark or any available store wrappings and tucked into the billycan, along with cups and other equipment. People would start slowly back toward camp.

Or sometimes, in the first period I got to know them, the Gorge people would form a little party to climb *waykan* (on top), up to the heights overlooking the gorge to search for trees to cut as didgeridoos, as they had done for years. On these expeditions, over time, I began to feel that I was learning something of my companions' mode of absorption. The departure from camp was generally unhurried. The steepest part of the climb was usually made without talking. The loudest noises became the swishing of grass from our passage and the occasional rattle of rocks as they rolled from under our feet down the slope. Time seemed to slow as we worked our way up to the top. I soon realized that this, for me at least, was the experience of having uninterrupted opportunity to minutely observe the country through which we were walking as someone, at least for a time, entirely subject to it. I would watch my companions' reactions to it and their continuing recognition of it and signs of their earlier passages through it as they moved toward previous campsites, cut trees, and known rock pools on top. The slowing-down sensation was the absence of other immediacies against which to measure the passage of time, except for our movement through the country.

Over months, the experience became an increasingly subtle one for me, as I learned more about some of the things they were watching for and learned something of the layers of the past to which those markers belonged and of the people with whom they were associated. As the objects of their attention became better known to me, there was a curious paradox in that though time seemed slowed, such days of walking always seemed to me to pass very quickly, and the time between rising and lowering sun seemed very short. I found this changed experience of duration restful, and I believe that the Gorge campers generally found such outings refreshing and completely absorbing. On other days, back in camp, the campers would finish and paint the "bamboo" (as they call the didgeridoo in English), with the men doing most of the main designs but Alice and other women applying much of the Arnhem-style crosshatched in-fill. The work was done carefully and without haste, by a few people sitting under a tree, with little pots of color carefully mixed on the ground, the bamboos, the brushes, a little fire, timely talk—a small world of familiar and absorbing activity.

The patterns back at camp, however, were variable. Some days would pass in which some people seemed satisfied just to be where they were. But other days—pension day, and frequently, any days when there was some ready cash—they would have a sense of urgency about getting into town. Then, the thrall and the unhurried but steady character of our walks through country, and of the painting, was obliterated. Occasionally when I arrived from Katherine, nothing would do but I must turn around and straightaway take people back to town for shopping. The focus was on grog, but not all money was spent on it. The old people would generally spend first on some food and tobacco. But they often seemed to skimp on that to have money for grog. After I had observed the patterns of their life, I became hard-nosed about not "carting grog." I would take people to shop and would carry any amount of groceries, carefully sorted into personal piles as they saw fit in the back of my Land Rover. But I would not cart grog. I saw no other way of dealing with this without becoming subject to all sorts of further, related demands: to drink some on the way back, to go back for more when the bought supply was exhausted, and so on. (On the fortnightly pension day, the white Kalano bus would show up and take people to town for shopping; grog was forbidden on it, too. Some campers, to circumvent these prohibitions, would come back via taxi, despite the cost—about $A18 one way at that time. Pension day was always followed by several days of heavy drinking, sometimes fighting, then the thinner times until the next pension.) So I was generally willing to pick up people, even if they were drunk, if they were not demanding to cart grog back; sometimes people already drunk would not renounce such demands, and I would leave them behind. Far from blaming me, those of my passengers who were not then drunk or drinking usually encouraged my actions.

As I became better known in the camp, requests to me for money, too, were common; I sometimes acceded to them, sometimes did not. How I responded depended not simply on my means at the time, but also on a continuous updating of my sense of relationship with particular individuals and with the camp at large.

As I got to know the Gorge people better, I would occasionally ask some of them for money or to buy food and drink for me as well as for themselves as we were driving around. Sometimes, after I had been around for awhile, people (especially Alice's mob) would do this without my asking or would offer me some of their own food and tea in camp. That meant a great deal to me, because it seemed to me that it implied some acceptance of my presence. I wrote in my diary in the first period I was there that these seemed to me to be the least accessible and accepting Aboriginal people of any I had met around Katherine. They seemed resigned to their history of interaction with whites, but under their present conditions of life, chose to keep such interaction to a minimum. This choice was obviously also that of the whites they had known. A few people, such as the Gorge head ranger mentioned above, enjoyed a measure of their recognition as someone familiar to them over the long term and as someone who occasionally stopped for them on the road and brought them meat. In some ways explored in later chapters, Aboriginal concepts of place are permeable; so, to at least a considerable extent, are relations with persons. Gradually, the Gorge campers began to let me share their company on terms that became increasingly comfortable for all of us. I didn't always learn a great deal of objective information, or even necessarily ask questions (although I generally continued my learning of the languages they spoke, Jawoyn and Mayali, and thus might ask some questions about word reference, meaning, or use. Most of the old people came to tolerate and even encourage this and sometimes made me small, on-the-spot gifts of understanding as we talked). Our walks around the country were important in the mutual process of familiarization. After a while I felt that they had overcome some of their earlier reserve and had allowed me to participate in ways of being with them that seemed to me very rich. But this experience did not seem transferable or even easily explicable to other people: it had only come through my spending time with them, largely on their terms. Certainly, to most townspeople who remarked it, the Gorge people's manner of life seemed degraded, the occasional public drunkenness of many the most obvious aspect of their behavior, and their existence apparently without future.

The Gorge people themselves had a view of the relation between past and present characterized by a sense of the disappearance of their elders and contemporaries from the scene. Often Alice, who had a spectacular command of the web of kin relations and life histories linking Jawoyn people and some long-term co-resident Mayali and of the membership of Jawoyn *mowurrwurr* (clans) (chapter 3), used to recount these connections to me. Her knowledge of all these interpenetrating systems of identification and identity construction went back well before World War II. She herself used to weave stories of life on the river around Katherine, repeopling places with the names of those who had spent time there (often including herself), reconstituting time-specific "mobs" and events in memory. Through our frequent conversations, most intensively after 1980 when I began formally gathering data for the eventual Katherine Area Land Claim (chapters 3, 5), I entered, at least partly, into the thought-world of Alice and some other older people and became able to recognize the names of people long dead, to place them temporally and spatially in the Katherine landscape, and to think of networks of other people still living in terms of their relations to these forebears. Alice, like Elsie, had a truly profound and broad view of a region and its people. But when I would ask Alice whether particular people had left descendants or whether certain clans were extant, she would often say *bu-ny-joyoyinay* (they've died).[14] This was a perspective of the older Gorge camp people generally—not that they have no relatives in an absolute sense, but that *relevant* close others, with whom they had shared a life and a way of life, were becoming scarce. Together, we had seen a number of the older Gorge campers die; and those remaining saw to the necessary rites, including seclusion of the remaining spouse (if there was one) and the eventual smoking (purification) of the people and the camp after the requisite period.

In 1978 the Department of Aboriginal Affairs established Yulngu, an Aboriginal resource association, in Katherine, and this organization undertook to provide better housing for the Gorge people. It also became the catalyst for a certain vitalization of Aborigines' involvement in "cultural" activities and events, such as arts and crafts manufacture, the formation of dance troups, the establishment of a regional language center dedicated to the maintenance and preservation of local Aboriginal languages, and so on—matters not taken up in detail in this book.

Up until then, Kalano Association had provided tent flys to Gorge campers (which they paid off in small fortnightly installments) and had filled water tanks, carted firewood, and made rubbish collections—minimal provisions for a group of largely elderly people. Indeed, Raymond Fordimail, then a Jawoyn man in his late twenties rising to prominence, who was community adviser at Barunga but whose full aunt Topsy Mandawma was a long-term Katherine River resident and latterly, Gorge camper, said at the time that the old people were living like "wild dogs." His main reference seems to have been to inadequate water and toilet facilities. And they themselves said they wanted houses and a bore.

Those facilities began to be established. When the Katherine Gorge

Land Claim was heard from 1983, even though the precise area of the Gorge (by then, Jodetluk) camp was not under claim, the Gorge campers said they wanted to stay where they were, and they wanted to gain long-term title to the camp area. In fact, the area of the Gorge camp could not be claimed because it was not vacant Crown land, the only type of land that may be claimed under the Land Rights (Northern Territory) Act. The camp was on the property of Maude Creek Station, the homestead of which was a few kilometers downstream, off the other side of the road. But because the old people were so attached to the camp, which also was starting to have improved facilities, a trade-off was arranged whereby the old people gained a special purpose lease to Jodetluk area, in return for which the Jawoyn claimant group as a whole agreed to drop the claim to a portion of Crown land adjacent to the Maude Creek property. During the land claim, the whole set of parties participating were taken to Jodetluk to show the campers' strength of attachment to the area. In the course of the visit, the old people showed everyone (among other sites) the *jurrang* ('King Brown' [snake]) Dreaming stone, which they said should not be kicked over. This display was met with skepticism by some locals who chose to come along on site visits throughout the claim; they expressed the belief (their evidence was never made clear) that this was only recent invention (see chapter 7).

By 1987, the Gorge camp had town electricity, a water bore and electric pump, pit toilets, reticulated power mains, and some houses and laundry facilities, the designs for which they had been consulted about. There were twenty-five to thirty steady Gorge camp residents, as there had been eight to ten years previously, although there were different individuals: more younger members of certain families were staying there, and some old people had gone.

By 1987, Alice too had died. I got a phone call from her in July or so 1986, at my Sydney home where she had stayed with us a couple of years before, her first and only trip to Australia's south. She told me that she was ill; neither she nor I knew how ill. I wanted to go to see her but was in a difficult phase of pregnancy and did not go immediately. Sick as she was, when I told Alice of my condition, she was enraptured: she herself had never had any children, and we had often spoken of this (though she had acted in loco parentis to a couple of related children in particular). In some ways, she regretted her own childlessness deeply, and here was I, her little sister, producing a child for us, to which she would have some kind of continuing relationship! She rallied enough on the phone to start bossing me:

I must come as soon as possible and bring the little *balang* or *beliyn* along. But she died within a few weeks, of liver cancer. When I did finally get back to Katherine, some months later with my new child, I went to the Gorge camp and asked Maggie Ryan, our old mutual friend, to take me to Alice's grave in the Katherine Cemetery. Maggie did so, and as we approached the now slightly worn mound, I burst into uncontrollable tears. I had not even vaguely intended to wail as I had sometimes seen Gorge campers do, in the Aboriginal mode, when their camp mates died; but I did anyway. Maggie did the best she could, maybe slightly surprised despite all our time together—for she had, after all, spent her life in the Katherine River school of hard knocks—that a whitefella would do that. "I love you," she tried to console me. We sat awhile on the ground, and then I took her back home. Maggie is gone now too.

There is now increasing rural development on either side of the Gorge road, within the area over which the Katherine River people hunted and foraged and where they worked on the peanut farms and for pastoralists like Bert Nixon. The area just north of the township, especially around the old telegraph station, is more intensively populated now by white families; and there seems every chance that real estate on the Katherine Gorge road will appreciate in value, given the economic significance of the Katherine Gorge National Park, now called Nitmiluk National Park and owned by the Jawoyn people as a result of the Katherine Area Land Claim.

The core, elderly population of the Gorge camp continued to decline and now, in the mid-1990s, the camp is sometimes deserted. Occasionally, a few people from Barunga or Mayali-Brumby go to stay there for short periods. Maybe the emptying out of the camp will turn out to be temporary, following some recent deaths, but the existence of the houses (better accommodation than some Aboriginal people in Katherine have yet) has not been enough to draw or keep a permanent population there. The people who lived on the river for decades, who hunted and foraged over it in their accommodation with whitefella pastoral and agricultural enterprise, were the ones who wanted to live on the river, and they stayed there as long as they could, in most cases until they died.

People in Between: Changing with the Town

Some of the people who later will be shown to be central to the understanding of socio-spatial shift in and around Katherine town live or lived at another Katherine camp called the Rockhole. It is at a pleasant location, about twelve kilometers south and west of the town on the Katherine River (map 2), and reached by the Florina road which, like the Gorge road area, is being more intensively settled, largely by white families. The Rockhole camp, as the name suggests, has been developed on a pool or water hole of the river. The camp as such began to be developed from the early 1970s, but the area was used by Aboriginal people, under different conditions, from a much earlier time. On the other side of the Florina road, away from the main river, is an area known to have been used by Aborigines as a major ceremony ground well before World War II, a period at which the fathers of those who were senior individuals during the 1970s and 1980s were in their prime.

The development of pastoral and other rural properties on and near the river disrupted earlier Aboriginal use of the area. The first pastoral property in the district was Springvale, for a time the jumping-off point for pastoralists traveling farther west, into the Victoria River area and toward the river valleys of the Kimberleys, where pastoral exploration and development were under way. From Springvale, manager Alfred Giles directed exploration for good outlying pasture lands, as far as eventual Delamere and Willeroo Stations (Giles 1928). An outstation of Springvale was established at Delamere in 1880; and by the early 1890s there was a station homestead in the Moray Range, at Monborrom, or Old Willeroo, where Scott had been speared in 1892. There was a period of brutal frontier violence, to which certain stories that Elsie knew seem to relate. But by the time ethnologist Baldwin Spencer visited Willeroo in 1912, hosted by owner Tom Pearce (a well-known Katherine personality, earlier the owner and manager of the Sportsman's Arms pub in Katherine), the main period of frontier violence, with its doubtless considerable toll of Aboriginal lives, was over. Spencer found an Aboriginal camp that appeared settled in to the pastoral work routine.

Springvale was abandoned as unviable in 1886, and the Giles family moved to Bonrook Station, where they managed to make a living selling beef to consumers in the nearby mining town of Pine Creek. For a long period Delamere and Willeroo, together with Manbulloo Station, which had been established on the river near the growing town of Katherine, were owned by a single British company, Vestey's, with the result that Aboriginal workers were shifted around over the larger company area as work required. Some workers were also brought to these properties from further afield, many from the Victoria River Downs and Wave Hill Stations (see map 1). By the Second World War, people who considered themselves Wardaman, from farther south around Willeroo and Delamere, predominated at Manbulloo. However, they continued to recognize the area as Dagoman. The small remaining number of people recognized as Dagoman were their co-residents and consociates at Manbulloo and around Katherine town.

The settler population of Katherine town swelled during the years that the railway line extension from Pine Creek, and eventually the Katherine River bridge, were being built. Among these railway workers were a number of Russians, some of whom later settled around Katherine, taking up rural blocks and developing peanut farms. On the river south and west of the town, several locations are thought of by Aborigines in terms of their associations with Russians. Nearest to the town was Jimmy Zimin's, not far from the Low Level. Downstream opposite Manbulloo Station homestead is Long John's, where a farm was developed by a Russian fully known as Long John Ivanetz. Even further along is Galloping Jack's; Jack, or Germogen Sergeev, as he was actually named, used to entertain the locals with his feats of horsemanship in the main street of town. There were other Russian farmers on the river, but those mentioned stayed and reshaped Aboriginal identifications of place along the river. They are also commemorated by Europeans: Zimin worked for the Commonwealth Scientific and Industrial Research Organization (CSIRO), experimenting with variable depth of peanut plantings. It was on some of the land he had formerly worked that a meatworks was established in 1963. Long John, together with Bert Nixon, worked supplying the army with vegetables during the war. Galloping Jack, when he had a good peanut crop, would donate a pound of his income to each pensioner in town. In those terms, they are remembered not so much in relation to the country that they worked, but for the contributions they made to the development of the agricultural potential of the local economy. They are also remembered by white townspeople for their hard work, their love of strong liquor (which they sometimes shared with local Aborigines), and (for some) their exotic flair. In the early days, some of the Russians lived rough, and during those times some had female Aboriginal companions—and as Aborigines remember, did not scruple to share them with their Aboriginal husbands.

Aboriginal numbers at Manbulloo were large in the period before the Second World War, sometimes ranging upward of two hundred. Town whites saw these people as "bushy" and unsophisticated. From time to time, Elsie Raymond and members of her extended family were among their number. They worked on the stations and had relatively little access to town. From at least the Depression period, the river farmers also relied on obtaining Aboriginal labor via Pine Creek well to the north. After the workers were paid off and returned by train to Pine Creek, they obtained rations from the local Chinese-run store, Ah Toy's, and then returned to their places of origin until it was time for the work season to begin again.

In this way, a number of Mayali families, originating from north and east of Pine Creek, returned year after year. Some Mayali, and other Aborigines of Arnhem origin, also made their way to the Katherine farms via Maranboy, a major tin mine developed to the east of Katherine from 1913 (see map 1). Maranboy attracted very large numbers of Mayali, Ngalkbon, Rembarrnga, and Jawoyn people. Joint occupation of the mining camp area laid the basis, in the forms of intermarriage and other interaction, for the later co-residence of these people of Arnhem origin at army compounds and later, after the Second World War was over, at the settlement of Bamyili (now Barunga) and nearby Beswick Station.

A postwar employment opportunity developed for Aboriginal people that was to result in the first major, recognized or licit camp within close reach of the town. Before the war there had been an Aboriginal compound on the Katherine River in the vicinity of Maude Creek junction, managed with the assistance of a man whom local Aborigines remember as Mr. Long of the Aborigines Inland Mission. During the war, an Aboriginal compound was established at the Donkey camp, a large pool in the Katherine River a bit farther downstream. At the end of the war, some Aborigines were still living at this army camp; some were also living on the river in the southwestern area of town, in an area that had been an army hospital. CSIRO took over an army experimental farm and opened an agricultural research station in Katherine (see map 3), its main purpose to improve crop varieties suited to this part of the tropical north. Aboriginal labor was used for clearing, planting, driving, various forms of crop testing, and experimentation; and, of course, where there was a white staff, there was also considerable demand for domestic labor, housekeeping, and child minding.

At first, Aboriginal workers were picked up from their river camps and taken to work at CSIRO, then returned at night to their camps, but management decided it might be advantageous to all concerned to develop a residential Aboriginal camp at CSIRO for these workers. Walter Arndt became officer in charge in 1947. Over his years at Katherine CSIRO, he was to take great interest in the Katherine area's Aboriginal heritage (see chapter 4). Working with him Arndt had L. J. ("Flip") Phillips, who came to the Katherine station as technician crop agronomist, became an experiment officer, and eventually took over as officer in charge after Arndt left in 1959. Phillips and Ted Morris, who was lab technician for some years from 1966, still live in Katherine, and both have kindly given me insights into life at the CSIRO camp; other views and information have come from Aboriginal people who lived there.

Both Morris and Phillips spoke of the Aboriginal camp as friendly, intimate, and exceptionally clean. Each mentioned that no special pressure had to be placed on the residents of the Aboriginal camp to keep the place up: they always kept it tidy, kept their own fowl, and tended gardens. To both men, the present Katherine camps contrast strongly with the tidiness of the CSIRO camp. Families lived in temporary housing with verandahs out front and created their own cooking areas outside the houses. There were pit toilets. The houses were about three hundred yards away from the bosses' houses. Workers' families were provided with rations, and for a time, there was a workers' mess. CSIRO white staff exercised considerable control over pay and rations: recipients were not allowed to withdraw all money at once, for example, but were required to leave some over into the following week. Ted Morris commented that men rather than women appeared to control the money and that, when they were away from camp working where there was an available source of bush foods or fish (as when they were sometimes taken to work for short periods at the Daly River CSIRO), they would save their rations to bring back to their families.

Sometimes, I was told, family members came to stay at CSIRO (for example, when they needed hospital care), so the camp served some of the functions of a transient camp. Phillips remarked that Aborigines saw CSIRO as a "top job"; it offered Aboriginal people the combination of communal camp life, secure employment, and a benevolent management who, at least when they thought it necessary, got involved in camp disputes, sometimes offering to help settle matters (as Phillips said) "with a waddy" (stick). Ted Morris estimated that during periods in the mid-1960s, there were up to two hundred people staying at the CSIRO camp. Phillips observed that in the early years, the campers would take off downriver along the river toward the Low Level, sometimes carrying spears, for weekends of foraging, fishing, and hunting. A basketball court was created for the children, who also occupied themselves playing football and swimming at the river. For adults, cards were a regular in-camp pastime.

Soupy Marapunyah, an Aboriginal man, was regarded as principal camp spokesman. At least, he most clearly mediated between the blacks' camp and CSIRO personnel. Soupy was northern Jawoyn; he originated from the Pine Creek area, and the country he identified as his own lies within Gimbat Station, far to the northeast of Katherine. Morris said of him that he "stood out, he was a magnificent specimen, and took pride in his work." Phillips, too, was unstinting in his praise, describing Soupy as a "top man." The most obvious representative of the Aboriginal camp, then, was a foreigner to Katherine, someone recognized by Aborigines as nonlocal, but no longer an outsider, for he had married a local woman with long-term family connections to Katherine (though she had previously been promised to a Wardaman man).

Arndt took an interest in Soupy, one that grew particularly through Arndt's inquiry into the significance of a dangerous and sacred locality that Soupy told him about in his "country" to the north (Arndt 1962, 1966).

Some of the CSIRO white personnel, politically and socially liberal, were concerned with the question of Aboriginal acceptance and advancement within the town context. Phillips and his wife took Soupy's wife, Amy, and Ivy, the wife of another CSIRO worker, Henry Brumby, to a town ball in Katherine. Phillips noted that "half the town moved the other way. It was the local people born and bred who really objected" and also that Amy and Ivy were "paralyzed."

CSIRO staff also wished to see promising Aboriginal children allowed to attend school. Many local white parents opposed the idea, and so they sought alternatives. On Thursday nights adults were allowed to attend classes to learn road signs so they could get driving licences. Some children were given lessons by the CSIRO bookkeeper and his wife. Later, when some children did begin to attend school, the bookkeeper would check their clothes to make sure they were acceptable, because inadequate personal hygiene was commonly given by some white parents as a reason Aboriginal children should not be allowed to go to school with their own children.

Phillips, like other long-term Katherine residents, also commented on the fact that there was de facto segregation in the town cinema: all the Aborigines, some followed by their dogs and pigs, would sit down front, on the ground, and all the whites behind, on chairs. Once, Soupy wore to the cinema a three-piece suit that Phillips had given him in 1949 to get married in; but it may have been considered "flash," Phillips thought, because that was the last time he wore it.

Another key camp resident, one who belonged to a family more closely linked to the town area, was Eric Morgan. Eric was especially befriended by Flip Phillips, and older members of his family had been with Arndt in the early years of the camp. Eric had some schooling and could read and write. Along with Henry Brumby, he was regarded as an excellent truck and machinery driver. In Ted Morris' words, Eric "looked like an ordinary town blackfella" (that is, unlike Soupy, who looked more striking and robust, a "bush blackfella"). He showed Ted Morris places in the limestone country around the town that his mother's first husband had regarded as his own country. (Her later husband, Eric's own father, was Jawoyn.) Despite Eric's familiarity with the town area, he did not assume the status of camp leader.

A third significant figure in the camp was a man named Steven Watson. He was a Southern Arnhem Lander, who when young had received some education from missionaries at Goulburn Island off the northern coast of Arnhem Land. More fully an outsider than Soupy, Watson had come to Katherine during the Second World War period. I met Steven shortly after I came to Katherine; when I met him, I recognized him as one of the people I had seen on the main street on my first day there, swinging along near Cox's store on his crutches (for one of his legs was deformed) with a crowd of people from the Rockhole camp.

Steven, a Christian, deplored the use of tobacco and alcohol. He married a local woman (there were old rumors told me about how he had "pinched" her from her former husband) and settled in Katherine, becoming a steady resident at the CSIRO camp.

White CSIRO personnel encouraged at least one young Aboriginal boy to attend Gatton Agricultural College in Queensland, where Arndt had studied. Intimidated at the idea of going so far from home, he did not do it; but the proposal is another indication of the personal interest that CSIRO administrators took in some of their workers and their families.

Thus, the CSIRO camp brought together Aboriginal people from both western and northeastern sides, providing resources in a way not typical of any other town location at the time. It was a locale stabilized by managing whites' well-intentioned interest in it and probably also stabilized from within by becoming home to a core of Aboriginal people who saw themselves as linked to the locale and like it becoming transformed through wartime and postwar town expansion. At least some of them still saw the town as developing in relation to the limestone expanse, to the rock forms now incorporated into the CSIRO Four Mile farm and the thermal pool in the river at the CSIRO camp.

Both Ted Morris and Flip Phillips spoke of the dramatic effect of alcohol use upon the coherence of the CSIRO camp. Shortly after the passage of the Social Welfare Ordinance of 1964, which legalized Aborigines' consumption of alcohol, Morris said the CSIRO men "started not turning up for work"; even the stalwarts like Soupy were affected. At that time, alcohol use was still uncommon among Aboriginal women. He added that the men "used to go to the pub, get plonk and take it back to camp. Flip's house was the first they came to." Thereafter, both men felt, problems of camp management became severe; levels of violence within the camp increased, and Ted Morris feels that over time, there has been a marked escalation in levels of violence toward women. Phillips said, "Most blokes who worked for me had died five years after the grog came in."

In April 1973, Soupy Marapunyah's eldest son, Jimmy, was killed in a car accident; alcohol was involved. Everybody who knew Soupy emphasized that this son was his pride and joy and that he grieved terribly for him. Several days after Jimmy's death, Soupy died; some who were close to him say he poisoned himself in his anguish. Ted Morris observed, "When Soupy died, it [the camp] disintegrated. Before, when you went down there, you saw Soupy." He reported Soupy as having said about the clean and tidy appearance of the camp, " 'We been have'im standard to keep up.' " Steven Watson may have aspired to leadership, and especially, to moral authority related to his giving of the Christian message, but in Morris' view, Soupy was "really it." After Soupy's death, some camp members left and went to Bamyili settlement (see map 1).

For some time before this, a white man named Peter Lewis, who worked with underprivileged (including Aboriginal) children in town, had taken camp residents out for weekends on one of the CSIRO trucks. It had become especially important to women and children to go out, away from town, after the grog had begun to preoccupy and consume their men. He often used to take them to the area of the present Rockhole camp, on the Katherine River. Ted Morris maintains that the Aboriginal workers at CSIRO were never made redundant; with the grog, they became unfit, not turning up regularly enough to work to collect wages.

After several significant men in the CSIRO camp, including Soupy and Henry Brumby, had died in the early 1970s, Steven Watson and other camp residents spent some time living at the High Level (around location 1, map 1). But he soon led some of them to the Rockhole, which was to be a nondrinking camp. Those who chose not to go to the Rockhole nevertheless had to move away from CSIRO, where long-term residential arrangements had now come to an end. From the mid-1960s onward, other Aborigines from pastoral properties also came into town, dislocated from pastoral stations in numbers as a result of the decision to implement award wages. The combined camps of the Aborigines living on the riverbank in the southern section of Katherine town extended from opposite the CSIRO camp right up to Walter Young Street (see map 3), in an area sometimes known as the High Level bottom camp. The day was fast approaching when housing and other provisions for these people around the town would have to be given serious consideration, despite the evident reluctance of many townspeople. Steven Watson was a charter member of Kalano Association which, when formed in 1974, had among its principal aims the acquisition of residential property, planning of housing, and provision of alcohol rehabilitation.

In the late 1960s, one Aboriginal CSIRO family had been considered responsible enough to be let an ordinary, European-style house in Stutterd Street, in the southern sector of Katherine town just off the road that winds near the river (map 3). But they experienced problems: as the grog problem grew, other people would stop in at their house and make it difficult for them to maintain it. The facilities were overused, and eventually the toilet became blocked. Not knowing what to do about such problems, family members poured fuel down the toilet and lit it on fire, exploding it. The family shortly returned to their previous style of camping, first at the High Level, and eventually at Rockhole.

There was another, smaller camp known as "Northmeat" or the "Meatworks Camp" near the abattoirs (location 2, map 2). Most of the small number of households were centered on older white men and their Aboriginal de facto wives or companions. Many of these women were Mayali and had been around Katherine town for a long time, some of them from the early days of work on the peanut farms. Small numbers of people continued to camp in this location into the 1980s, when they were compelled to move away for lack of tenure of the land.

In my early days in Katherine, there were still small temporary camps in a number of locations, for example, around the dump and other places in the southwestern part of town. There was as yet no formally designated transient camp, as there now is (location 4, map 2). (Both Transient camp and the acquisition of a former motel as an Aboriginal hostel [see location 3, map 2] came about after the setting up of the Katherine-based Aboriginal resource association, Yulngu, under the auspices of the Department of Aboriginal Affairs from 1978.) This, however, is now known as the Warlpiri camp, its residents oriented toward their country and the large settlement of Lajamanu 350 kilometers southwest of Katherine. When there began to be a significant influx of people from Lajamanu into Katherine in the mid-1980s, many Katherine Aborigines were apprehensive. The new presence changed the mix of Aboriginal people in town. Warlpiri are stereotyped by other Aborigines as fierce and more confrontational in style than themselves. Nevertheless, there has been a steady social incorporation of Warlpiri into the Katherine area Aboriginal scene: grogging and intercamp visiting, marriage, and sexual liaison. Aboriginal organizations have strenuously argued that the Warlpiri camp should be upgraded, better houses and facilities provided to replace the tin sheds, blocked taps, and latrines that have characterized the camp. Despite the origin of the camp as a "transient" facility, the Warlpiri presence in Katherine will not disappear.

In my first three years in Katherine, from 1976 to 1979, I not only spent time in the Katherine camps, but also at Barunga, former Bamyili settlement, to the east of town, and at Elsey Station on the Roper River to the southeast and some of its neighbor stations off the Roper Highway (see map 1). Many of the Gorge campers and some people at Mayali-Brumby had close relatives who lived at Barunga; there was a continuous flow of people between these camps and the settlement. People from Elsey Station, too, made infrequent trips to Katherine town and had a few close kinsmen and countrymen with whom they could stop in town.

Conclusions

My aim in this chapter has been to give a view of the diversity of Aborigines' relationships to the town. This has been presented at a variety of levels, as it was presented over time to me: at one level, in terms of Aboriginal people's usage of concepts of large-scale socio-territorial identity (Jawoyn, Wardaman, Mayali, summarized for the region as map 4); and at another, in terms of my developing acquaintance with individuals and families of those regional clusterings who came forward in their particularity, sufficiently confident, open, and hospitable to undertake long-term interaction with a person like myself, neither insider nor stranger. While there tends to be close interaction and kinship among many of the residents of any given camp, no camp is entirely self-contained and independent: networks of kinship and connection extend outward from all camps to other locales. But there is always a dense clustering of ties between certain locales and others that Aborigines can encode and summarize in terms of socio-territorial identity (as, for example, people can speak of Bunjarri camp as "Wardaman mob," though its residential composition is more diverse, and can see both Bunjarri and Rockhole as having a "western-side" orientation, despite diversity and change in the actual composition of the camps' populations). To give another example, relatively dense ties exist between individuals and families at the Gorge camp, and others at Barunga and Beswick to the east; but such interconnections between regular residents of the Gorge camp and Wardaman people wherever they are currently living, whether at the High Level, Bunjarri, or elsewhere, are relatively weak. Terms of socio-territorial identification (like "Wardaman") thus continue to be part of a significant framework for understanding the social and spatial orientation of persons, where they are likely to live in and around Katherine, and with whom they are most likely to associate. Nevertheless, the clarity of such orientations is constantly revised and rendered less simple by changes of patterns of intermarriage and other forms of social interaction (perhaps most notably among the young) and by innovations on the social scene (such as the arrival in numbers of Warlpiri people, who now interact with others and increasingly are found co-resident in other camps besides the Warlpiri camp).

As a researcher, a person with recognizably intellectual interests in their languages and social practices, I tended to cultivate shared interests of these kinds with persons of middle to older age and their families and to develop my own associations along lines of kinship connection that such relationships opened up to me. The people with whom I formally worked most closely—Elsie Raymond, Alice and Peter Mitchell, Sandy Barraway, and others—tended to be regarded as prominent and knowledgeable individuals within their own networks of kinsmen and countrymen. Over the years, they have thus also tended to be among the people most sought after as participants in the growing processes of consultation (on matters of land claims, town camp development, the boards of Aboriginal organizations) as representatives of regional Aboriginal constituencies and viewpoints rather than as people with "modern" skills of literacy (all these being completely illiterate), management, or the like. Though by no means absolute, there was and is still a certain enclavement of such prominent Aboriginal people within regional clusters of kin and countrymen. This enclavement (and also the cultivation of some wider ties) has been supported by land rights and other developments of the last twenty years which, I argue in chapter 5, have sought to incorporate by imitation what have come to be understood as Aboriginal forms of sociality.

It is useful to draw back from some of the details sketched in this chapter and to see Katherine town as having developed in a borderland, or as a meeting place, between two long-term settlement ecologies, now undergoing further transformation. The difference between these has had great influence upon the colonial and postcolonial experience of Aboriginal people historically linked to each.

On the one hand, I have mentioned the escarpment that rises to the north of the township. The gorges on the Katherine River form part of this, stretching away as what the Jawoyn call *bat guyangguyang* (high cliffs) of the river system into Arnhem Land. On the other hand, Katherine town is at the approximate northern extreme of what early became exploited as pastoral country, even if sometimes only at marginal viability, first with the development of Springvale and later the constellations of Manbulloo, Willeroo, Delamere, and the large stations of the Victoria River district to the south and west (Makin 1987, Rose 1992).

The dissected high country along the northern Katherine River was seen to have little pastoral potential. The history of Aboriginal people affiliated with the upper Katherine was strongly shaped by mining exploration and development to the west and south of them: for instance, the mining boom and development of gold reefs at Pine Creek from 1873 to 1875 (Eylmann 1908), toward which many Aborigines moved from the Katherine River catchment. Katherine itself lay at approximately the southern extent of that prospective country: gold was discovered in 1887 at two locations in the vicinity of Maude Creek (near present Jodetluk camp), and there followed six to seven years of fairly intensive exploration, mining, and processing operations, including the establishment of a significant township complete with hotel, before the closure of the crushing works in 1891. Newspaper reports of the early 1890s tell of "natives" implicated in thefts and housebreaking at Maude Creek and their trial by Justice of the Peace Alfred Giles of Springvale (e.g., *Northern Territory Times and Gazette*, December 2, 1892). Today, with new technology, fields have been reopened in this area. To the east was Maranboy, which drew to it hundreds of Aborigines from the southern Arnhem fringe and the major rivers east of the Katherine. The town centers of Pine Creek and Katherine, and numerous other, mostly short-lived mining centers throughout this region, constituted main foci for people indigenous to the Katherine River and some adjacent river systems.

As compared with this, and despite the violence of pastoral settlement to the south and west of Katherine, pastoral stations like Delamere and Willeroo became established after tenuous beginnings and persisted as centers around which remaining Aborigines of the region managed to reconstitute their lives. They established patterns of work, social interaction, and travel, always within heavy constraints of their connections with the stations, but resulting in the kind of vivid association with country characteristic of some Wardaman people as the main spatial framework of their lives into the 1970s.

This contrast, which I have exemplified by comparing Jawoyn and Wardaman, began, with the passage of the Aboriginal Land Rights (Northern Territory) Act 1976, to take the shape of one between Aboriginal people who could make land claims to country because it had remained vacant Crown land, historically outside technologies of settler occupation and development and in which no person besides the Crown held an interest, and those, like the pastoral Aborigines from the south and west, who were unable to make such claims because their country was not "vacant," having been subject to pastoral lease from early settlement.

The town, then, has been a particular mid-zone between these two settler ecologies. Aboriginal people have converged upon it from further afield under the conditions of racialized inequality and formal exclusion for many years that I sketched at the beginning of this chapter. Partly, it would seem, because of this convergence, senses of socio-territorial difference and differential connection to hinterlands have been relatively strongly maintained by those who have come in, even as direct experience of these hinterlands fades for many (see chapter 3). But what of the center, the town area itself?

From the account in this chapter, what stands out most clearly about the "Rockhole mob" is that a core of its residents had a former association with CSIRO. No particular or distinct socio-territorial identification (such as "Wardaman" or "Jawoyn") has local currency as characteristic of this mob. The "Rockhole" as sociohistorical entity emerges in the main as the product of the wartime history of compound formation, later reshaped by CSIRO in the project of creating exemplary Aboriginal workers and families who could live acceptably in the town context. In the immediate postwar period, this concept of Aboriginal workers living as families and kin groupings in town was unprecedented. It may have partly conformed with the aims of Native Affairs Branch in providing managed Aboriginal labor, but it also sharply contrasted with the branch's policy of regularly breaking up families and kin groupings and sending the unemployed away from town. The CSIRO managers involved were criticized to some extent by other (white) townspeople as "social engineers" and "missionaries."[15]

The Rockhole camp has continually varied in its detailed composition, with some residents who do not share the CSIRO background, but always with a core of earlier residents remaining who do. These people are seen by themselves and others as belonging to Katherine. In chapter 4 another aspect of this is brought into focus: that the postwar CSIRO camp comprised a core of people whose socio-historical affiliations appear to have been to the range of country (including the town) identified (today, mostly by Wardaman people) as Dagoman. With the growth of the town as a regional center at the border of two settler ecologies, these people tended not to be drawn far from it, but to develop their livelihood around Manbulloo Station and the town itself. Today, they tend not to look out to hinterlands, but to identify with the town in a mode no longer securely embedded for them within a framework of Aboriginal socio-territorial identities.

The long-term association of CSIRO people with the town raises the multifaceted question of the sustaining of "difference" at this center in Aboriginal terms. As the maintenance of socio-spatial difference in certain of the earlier Aboriginal terms became more and more difficult around the town, modes of social and spatial identification were constituted in new and changing ways among those principally oriented to it.

Two

From Place to Town

JULIE WILLIAMS, whom I call "mother" in the Aboriginal way, and I were standing on a street corner in Katherine on a hot, wet-season day in November 1991. At my request, she was showing me where something had happened that she and a number of other Aboriginal people in the town had mentioned several times over the years I had known them: the removal of a rainbow serpent from its former lair underneath the pavement where Julie and I were standing. We were at the intersection in the town (photo 1) of the Stuart Highway, the main north-south highway through the Northern Territory, and the Victoria Highway, which runs from Katherine through the relatively flat Manbulloo country to the terrain of sweeping tablelands of Willeroo and the sandstone cliffs of the Victoria River valley to the southwest (see map 1).[1]

Neutralizing Difference: The Rainbow's Cave

The corner where we were standing used to be known generally to Katherine residents as "March's corner" and is still called that by some, especially white old-time residents and Aboriginal people who are slow to convert their earlier, particular knowledge of the town in terms of associations between

Photo 1. March's Corner (buildings on right) and the Stuart Highway–Victoria Highway intersection, part of Katherine's main street in the 1990s.

people and places to a system of more abstract reckoning by which that corner is now commonly known as the Vic Highway intersection (see location 6, map 3). Julie explained:[2]

They been have'im cafe here blanga old Eric March
and im been run'im taxi rank here, yeah, old Eric
this the place been have'im hole
and they been get'im little *bolung* [rainbow serpent] gotim dynamite
take'im out pull'im out
take'im this way and chuck'im la rubbish.

(There was a cafe here belonging to old Eric March
and he ran a taxi rank here, yeah, old Eric
this was the place with a hole
and they got a little rainbow serpent with dynamite
got it and pulled it out
took it this way and threw it in the rubbish dump.)

I could not resist the pursuit of dates then, but will come back to *sequence* as shifts in networks of interrelations between person and place, much more important in Julie's reckoning than such abstract chronology. When I asked Julie when the event had happened, she answered,

Hm, I don't know what time now, long time too muchy, I don't remember, my mother been workin for Cox's [store] then, my stepfather
and pull'im, drag'im out, no street been here then
TODAY this bitumen, been dirt road . . .

they been pull'im that *wang* [animal] now, *bolung*, pull'im right out outside
from here now been pull'im
take'im this way now, they been take'im this way
this way now *bu-wukanay* [they took it]
langa [to] whatchacallim, whannim this'un now
two and a half mile they been have'im rubbish dump
two and a half mile . . .
rubbish dump out that way, and they been chuck'im THERE *narnbay bolung* [that rainbow].

(Hm, I don't know when, long time ago, my mother was working for Cox's then, and my stepfather
pulled it and dragged it out, there was no street here then
this bitumen is RECENT, it was a dirt road
they pulled out that animal, that rainbow serpent, pulled it right out
from right here
took it that way, they took it that way
that way, they took it
to whachacallit, what's the place?
they had a rubbish dump at the Two-and-a-Half-Mile
the rubbish dump was out that way,
and they threw that rainbow serpent there.)

The rainbow was red in color, a "young one," according to Julie. Another similar incident had taken place in "Army Time," during the war, and had resulted in the extirpation of an even larger rainbow, the "mother one" in the Katherine River that flows two hundred yards or so to the west of March's corner:

JW: That way la that bridge there, you savvy that old bridge
FM: Old bridge, yeah
JW: There now they been kill'im that *bolung*, mother one, *ngan-berndak* [big one]
kill'im, they been pull'im out again take'im away
I don't know what they been do, might be use'im for oil . . .
FM: That's in army time
JW: Army time
FM: They been pull'im out
JW: Yeah, like my mother was telling me, that old woman

ngal-gagak-nginygu ngan-jungay [your grandmother told me][3]
from there they been pull'im out take'im away
FM: Where they been put that one?
JW: I don't know where they been put'im
might be take'im la army camp keep'im there *oil-wu* [for oil]
first time they been use'im bout oil blanga rainbol [rainbow].

(*JW:* There at the old bridge
you know that old bridge?
FM: The old bridge, yeah
JW: They killed that rainbow right there
the mother one, the big one,
killed it, pulled it out too and took it away
I don't know what they did with it, maybe used it for oil
FM: That was during the war?
JW: Wartime
FM: They pulled it out?
JW: Yeah, as my mother told me
old lady, your grandmother told me,
they pulled it out of there and took it away
FM: Where'd they put it?
JW: I dunno where they put it
maybe took it to the army camp and kept it there for oil
before, they used to use the oil of the rainbow serpent.)

Two older, close relatives of Julie's, Sandy Barraway and Nipper Brown, had mentioned to me the army time killing of the rainbow near the Katherine River railway bridge. They did not have a great deal of detail to offer, especially since (Sandy said) they had been out of town, doing stock work. They had more to say about the rainbow presence at other locations farther north, in what they regarded as their country of origin.

Progress: Katherine Street Drainage

Julie's story about the rainbow, like much of her sense of Katherine town,[4] rests upon the specificities of the attachment of people to place (old Eric March to March's corner) and their activities in those places (running the cafe). There is no explicit comment in her telling on the different social positioning of people like Eric March and her mother; they are all people on the scene, with familiar and understandable jobs or things that they do. Contrasting with known people in her story is the unfamiliar white man who is pulling the "rainbol," as Aborigines of Katherine say, out from the hole in the road.

Though Julie told her story in a very matter of fact way, we sense that it might be saying much more about her feelings for the world around her: about the "rainbol," her sense of changes in the landscape, and the purposes of whites, among others.

Julie was born during the war years, at an army compound on the Ferguson River north of Katherine (see map 1). The story of the first removal of the rainbow serpent from under the Katherine railway bridge, which Julie's mother had told her about, evidently dates to "army time." This seems to have been a period of especial reorientation and wonder for Aborigines about whites' activities, partly in terms of the changes the whites were making to the local landscape. Local white townspeople recount that the cage under the bridge in which, Aboriginal people say, the rainbow was entrapped, was part of a water pumping facility.

After the war, civilians began to return to the town, and businesses were reestablished. A town Progress Association, which had been formed in 1937, was reestablished in the town from 1948 (Lea 1987). But despite the efforts of this body, Katherine, in the view of many white townspeople, failed to progress. They attributed this failure to their territorial status, to the lack of local control, and to what they perceived as the mismanagement of their affairs by the Commonwealth, from Canberra. In Territorians' eyes, it was Canberra that was remote, not they. There was always deep suspicion that administrators were making flawed and perhaps even corrupt decisions concerning the development of the north.[5]

I got a feeling for prevalence of disappointed hopes from Henry Milton Scott, a long-term Katherine resident who was generous in sharing with me his extensive knowledge of Katherine town, which spanned the period from the Second World War until his death in January 1992. A South Australian, Scott first came to Darwin in 1941, as acting line foreman for the Postmaster General's Department. Describing what he considered to be the continuing disappointments of the postwar period, Scott said, "Well, actually Katherine went into a period of doldrums whereby there wasn't any development here whatsoever, not until 1960. So you had a long period there where we only had three or four hundred people, and . . . they all worked for the government, building roads." After this, he added, there were two important, related developments: the construction of beef roads so cattle could be carted to Katherine from the Barkly Table-

Photo 2. Katherine's main street under water in the 1957 flood (Pearl Ogden collection).

land (see map 1) and elsewhere in the Territory and the arrival of an "airfield construction crowd" who built the Royal Australian Air Force (RAAF) base Tindal, east of Katherine (see map 2), from 1963. He was also pleased about the redevelopment and expansion of Tindal that had taken place much more recently, from the mid-1980s, and about mining potential in the area, both of which over a few years had resulted in the near doubling of Katherine's population to its present size of about ten thousand.

In discussing the significance of the Katherine River, Henry eventually talked about the limestone cave under the sidewalk at March's corner. He noted that the underground cave had been part of the limestone system that underlies much of the Katherine area. Growing down into it had been a large banyan tree. He and several other people mentioned that some townspeople had disposed of garbage there. There was no connection, he averred, between the "peculiar system" of limestone caves and the river. His recollection was that the cave had been filled with tons of reinforced concrete in 1957, the year of a big flood that put much of Katherine town under water (photo 2).

However, Dan Darben, who was district engineer from 1965 to 1974, has told me that work on the main street was prolonged and that the capping of the sinkhole occurred later.[6] In memory, Scott linked the capping of the cave to the severe flooding of 1957. Darben, more authoritatively, placed it between 1968 and 1971, within a series of planned changes. For Julie, perhaps the most notable aspect of the work on the limestone cave was that it was the occasion of the rainbow's extraction. Since for her the event was not centrally a particular phase of the roadwork, it is not possible to go behind her account and attempt to place a precise date on the extraction. She sees its timing in terms of the intersections between her mother's and stepfather's working at Cox's store, her own time of life and ties to others, and the extraction itself. I think that this is more likely to have been about the time of the flood of 1957 than at the later time of the extensive roadworks. Using her criteria, we know that Julie was a young, unmarried girl when she, together with her friend Margaret Katherine, saw the rainbow—and that is consistent with the earlier, rather than later, time period.

In any case, central to Henry Scott's account of the roadbuilding is the filling of the empty space of the limestone cavern to strengthen its load-bearing capacity. This might be taken as exemplary of many of the things he cited as part of the sequence of town development: the building, the filling up of the landscape, and the modifications necessary to permit development, such as changes to the limestone system, the building of the abattoirs, the development and redevelopment of Tindal, and the growth of Katherine East. Scott's account of the town consists of events unfolding through time that find a place as waypoints in a retrospective history of "development" or progress: expansion and the increasing complexity and sophistication in the town's services and functions with respect to its residents.[7] The evaluative dimension in Scott's account of Katherine's modest early efforts to modernize and progress are immediately apparent. It is unlike Julie's story, in which the sense of place is constituted by a back-and-forth relationship among people and between people and places. His story ultimately has the character of a pioneering narrative featuring the one-way transformative relation between settlers and locality. Julie's story has a different character. It is not clear that her story moves toward an end. Hers is a story of changes to place that is nevertheless kept familiar through human relationships and by the building up of a sense of shared experience of town life and belonging to it. Her own experience of having seen the rainbow drawn from his cave was in some sense made more familiar by her mother's account of a similar episode having occurred during "army time," despite the unusual character of both events. In Julie's story, because the meanings associated with places are importantly given in, and transmitted through, the active relationships among people at a given period of time, there is (as we shall see further) a substantial opening in her account for persons, both socially distant as well as close, both white and black, to play a part in those processes of definition.

The evaluative dimensions of Julie's story are probably less clear to most readers than are Scott's. Something that belonged to the ground was torn from it, and then what? Chucked on the rubbish heap or maybe used to run the white man's machinery. Questions seem to be latent in these stories: Are familiar creatures and powers efficacious in new ways? Are there consequences to tearing things out of the ground? Is the deracination final?

We might be tempted to see these as stories of white destruction of local Aboriginal culture, with perhaps an element of speculation about the possibly empowering, or perhaps simply destructive, redirection of the rainbow powers to be used as oil. But why is it that Julie seems to let no clarifying word enter her account, to tell us what she feels about the events she narrates? When I have sometimes asked Julie and others why they think the "army" or others might have done such things as removing the rainbow, the answer is simply, "I don't know." Are the images simply powerful by themselves, capable of interpretation in a variety of ways? At the limestone cave in town, the uprooting of the rainbow seems to have been complete. But efforts to remove rainbow from some other places, to which I refer farther on, are said to have been unsuccessful, and the creature remains dominant and dangerous, driving strangers away.

Julie told me another story of a rainbow appearance, which by her own account occurred about the same time that Katherine was seriously flooded when she was a girl (1957). A rainbow was reported by Aborigines to have been seen on the road from Bamyili (now called Barunga, the Aboriginal settlement established after the Second World War east of the town). Julie had heard that the rainbow

> been lift'im out that *yoyn* [earth], been come out
> im stand up, you know,
> look around country, and go back again.
>
> (lifted up the ground, it came out
> it stood up, you know
> looked around the countryside and went back in.)

This story depicts the animal in its usual mythic condition: as of the earth and water, as the monitor of events, as a force that often makes itself felt in the form of rains and winds and even floods like the one that deluged Katherine in 1957, about the time of this sighting, probably also about the time of the removal of the rainbow from its cave under the street.

The difference between Julie's stories of the rainbow and Henry Scott's account of roadworks leads to consideration of the partial synchronization of social relationship between Aborigines and white townspeople. "Scottie," as many Aborigines and other townspeople referred to him, would have been one of Katherine's residents best known to Aboriginal people, and especially to those who were employed at the Postmaster General's Department and the soft drink factory, which Scott and his wife ran. But it is clear that he did not know stories of the eradication of the "rainbol," even though a number of Aborigines were working for him in 1957 and even though he was directly concerned with the living conditions of people working for him then. Such differences in perspective and gaps in communication between whites and Aborigines beyond immediate matters of living and working conditions should not be a surprise: they were commonplace. They make possible, and are aspects of, Aboriginal marginality in other townspeople's accounts of the past. For most white townspeople, the limestone cave was a negative space, impeding development of Katherine's main street; it needed to be filled. I have already intimated, however, that whites are less peripheral in accounts of Katherine such as Julie's: they cannot be excluded from narrative space any more than they can be seen as peripheral to the town's spaces and its activities. They are central to the way Aboriginal people define places, and their relation to them, within the town. This asymmetry is an aspect of domination, of the unequal relationships between black and white.

Therefore, in seeking understanding of Julie's rainbow stories, we must reach for an account that can illuminate these asymmetries and the openness of Julie's narrative to a cast of characters that includes black and white. It must be the sort of account that can restore the sense of person-relative space of Julie's story and enable us to place it in relationship to Scott's progress- and chronology-oriented one. To gain an understanding of Julie's social experience and the possible meaningfulness of the rainbow stories, we must find the ways in which the two accounts are a joint product, as well as the ways in which, at the same time, they are unequal in the manner and extent to which whites and blacks fit into each other's accounts.

Dimensions of Town Experience

How does Julie, in this story and in other accounts of herself and her life, constitute a relation between the present and the past? Within those accounts, what is her presentation of the ways in which Aborigines and non-Aborigines interact? To answer these questions and eventually gain a better understanding of the rainbow stories, I will tack back and forth between some things Julie had to say at other times about herself and her relationships to other people and to the town, and then return to the rainbow. I want to place in relief what I have understood to be some dimensions of her social experience within the town.

Julie's story of the rainbow rests very much on the specificity of her relationships with other people and the understandings they gave her. It was her mother and another older relative, we learn, who provided her with a way of understanding what she and her friend Margaret Katherine (surnamed after the town, the name commemorating her early years here; see chapter 3) had seen at March's corner. Not long after she had told me the portion of story given above, I asked her:

FM: But this time they been pull'im out of here, you were here?
JW: Yeah, that I been little girl
FM: You been look, they been pull that body, and it was red one?
JW: Red one, yeah, young one. Pull'im out chuck'im away.

(*FM:* But when they pulled it out, were you here?
JW: Yes, I was a little girl then.
FM: You saw it, they pulled out the body and it was red?
JW: Red, yeah, a young one
Pulled it out and threw it away.)

There is already a hint in Julie's saying she was only "little girl" that the act of seeing was distinct from understanding. Julie went on to say:

You know that March's cafe
well me and Margaret been walking down from Cox's
walkin down
go to that Neal's shop get some ice cream
when we come out from there we seen that one white man eh?
pull'im out that rainbol from that hole
pull'im out right out la road
all right, take'im away now

take'im this way two mile, two and a half mile
and then when we been see'im
me and Margaret been go back
then old Rubbish Dump [man's nickname] been workin there langa Peterson, old man
all right, go back home now
we been go tell'im, my mother
and HER mother, Margaret's mother
went back home, tell'im
and they been tell we that RAINBOL they been pull'im out.

(You know March's Cafe?
Well, me and Margaret were walking down from Cox's
walking down
going to Neal's shop to get some ice cream
and when we came out of there we saw one white man
he was pulling out that rainbow from the hole
pulling it right out on the road
OK, it was taken away
taken that way to Two, Two-and-a-Half-Mile
and then after we'd seen it
me and Margaret went back
old Rubbish Dump was working there for old Peterson
OK, we went back home
we went and told my mother
and HER mother, Margaret's mother
we went home and told them
and they told us
that's a RAINBOW they pulled out.)

In keeping with Julie's life experience, and the shaping of her character in its terms, there is no questioning of the old women's identification of the thing as a rainbow. Julie's experience was such that knowledge was not to be severed from the conditions of learning and knowing. In such matters as the identification of a thing like the rainbow, she assumes the authority of "old people." Her mother's identification also occurs against the background of a previous incident briefly alluded to, the pulling out of another rainbow in "army time" from underneath the old railway bridge: "like my mother was telling me, that old woman, yeah, *ngal-gagak-nginygu ngan-jungay* [your grandmother told me], from there they been pull'im out take'im away." While the authority of old people who have been around, and as they say, themselves "been catch'im up old people," is assumed, in Julie's versions of Katherine-area social history there is no special glorification of old people as "elders" in the manner that has occurred more recently, particularly in the heat of political debate and mobilization of the land-rights era. "Old people" straddle the border between present and past, but they seem not to have been an especially privileged group in any clear social sense. In a way, as they pass away into memory, the most touted achievement is that of the present generation who can say that they "been catch'im up" and can present what they know, when required, as backed by the authority of that encounter.

Thus, faithful acceptance of the word of older people on such matters as the particular meanings of place is characteristic of Julie (and many others of her age and background). The existence of the rainbow is not queried as improbable, fantastic, or mythical—a "fairy tale," as some younger people whose experience differs from Julie's might say.

Accepting those terms of nurturance and authority, Julie evinces the self-assurance of the person who belongs locally. Julie speaks of herself as a person on the scene, familiar with Katherine town and able to walk around it without problem, given the personal relationships that anchored her and kept open to her over time a range of campsites where her relatives and other close countrymen were living, usually working for whites or in close association with a camp of people working for white employers.

Julie's sense of the town is a person-relative one, in which the associations of people with place form the basis for differentiation of locales within the town. Her kind of representation of Katherine makes present kinds of spaces that, increasingly, are excluded from dominant narratives. The personal history that she tells is an account of shift from one locale to another, the main rationale (even in her account) usually being employment of her family members by one white person or another.

For Julie at this period, her mother's presence seems to have been definitional of where she belonged, of home. Also important to her was a man named Bamjokjok, her "second father" (whose English surname, Williams, Julie and, much later, her husband assumed). He is a significant but backgrounded figure, her mother's companion, a respected but not completely intimate familiar person. Julie defines "home" or "camp" in a traveling mode, as a succession of movements from location to location, in the company of a selection of such familiars. This movement kept the entire town open and familiar to Julie, partly through the continuing intelligence that Aborigines in town shared with each other about their work and their employers.

It is glaringly clear from an outsider's point of view that there was no semblance of equality between Aborigines and their white employers and that the Aborigines' conditions of employment were often materially meager, sometimes generally oppressive. Hence it is all the more interesting that many people like Julie tend not to comment on that situation, or to have a distinctive vocabulary of inequality. Theirs is a condition in which the traveling mode of experience and knowledge cannot be separated from their interaction with whites, generally with white employers. This is a critical moment of whites' insertion of themselves into Aboriginal lives. Aboriginal representation of it, frequently, is in terms of whites' directives having a surprising coincidence with, and meaningfulness in terms of, the Aborigines' own projects and sense of imperative. In Julie's accounts of the past, this feeling creates and preserves a sense of separate but convergent intentionality.

Thus, for example, in a portion of personal history narrative (preceding but continuous with the rainbow story), Julie represents her mother's agreeing to camp at a certain place as a directive given to her mother by one employer-boss, a doctor, who told Julie's mother how she had to organize herself. In this representation of what was said, the critical feature is the doctor's reportedly enjoining Julie's mother to stay there *with her:*

JW: What he been tell'im now, tell'im my mother, you have to stay now. "Ginny," him say, "Ginny you got to stay with your daughter here." [We] been camp bat [about] somewhere . . .
FM: Who been tell you?
JW: That doctor now . . . doctor
FM: Doctor Fenton?[8] or 'nother one?
JW: 'nother one . . . him been savvy, that doctor now . . . now been camp langa [at] oh, down langa river, you know la [at the] hospital.
FM: Right down la river, la hospital way?
JW: Ya, I was camped there . . .
FM: Got'im somebody? [Were others there?]
JW: Yeah, there was big mob old people . . .

As older Katherine Aborigines know, the "hospital camp" was in theory the place for hospital workers and for the very young and old who might need medical attention. Julie represents the doctor as giving her mother a directive that realizes and confirms Aborigines' own frequently given reason for living near the hospital: you have to stay with your daughter here.[9]

Other parts of Julie's accounts of herself illustrate her and her family's movement from one place of employment to another, in traveling mode:

JW: Next week, coupla weeks, right, Mum been go work na, langa [for] one of them, might be Daisy, Daisy Angus . . . the other side, you know, la [at the] bridge . . .
FM: This side, toward this side now, toward Corroboree Hostel way?
JW: Yeah, them first houses, in front, middle one, middle one.
FM: Nother side of that mango tree? Where you been show me one time, that side?
JW: We been workin there, been livin there, Dad and Mummy, but that old man Na-Bamjokjok, he been workin for Scottie [Henry Scott], lemonade. Lemonade business there, workin there, this old man reckon, Oh, I think we'll have to siddown [stay] . . . Mum and that old man been siddown now, old man Na-Bamjokjok, work for Daisy finish, mefella been leave'im Daisy now, we been start workin for Mr. Dumigan, Mum and Dad, Mr. Dumigan, just in front that house, la that mango, that old man, cuttin wood . . .
FM: He was railway worker wasn't he? Or what that Mr. Dumigan?
JW: Him been driving train, used to drive train, from Mataranka, might be come back Katherine or go langa Pine Creek, and one upstair house, you know where that library is? Upstairs there, well, nother train driver been there too, Angelo, old Angelo, good old man him, might be Indian bloke . . . Mrs. Dumigan never let me go school, that old woman.
FM: What for?
JW: Keep me langa [in] camp.
FM: You and you mother and nother one your father, Na-Bamjokjok, any more been there?
JW: Only three-fella . . . little bit of house they been givit, you know, like big tank, you know them big tank langa water . . .
FM: Did that Mrs. Dumigan pay you money?
JW: Yeah, that old man been get'im three pound, three pound a week, and Mum used to get three pound a week, like that, those days bread been cheap you know, only twenty cents, like two bob we used to call'im before, two shilling.[10]

FM: And you used to buy rown [your own] tucker [food]?
JW: Yeah, we used to get rown [our own] tucker, here, from that butcher shop, baker shop here, ol baker shop before, you know where that um, that Uralla meat fella . . .
FM: Yeah.
JW: Well just next door . . . we had to work hard to get them, my mother and father they used to work hard, get to buy tucker, like bread, and m eat, like that beef.
FM: And when you fellas had little bit of time off, where did you go?
JW: Go langa, what this place here, ol Pascoe. Go langa Pascoe, like other Jawoyn mob been workin there too, old Degan.

Pascoe's was a farm along the Katherine River north of town (map 5). Julie mentions that they went hunting and fishing there, sometimes with Mayali people who had come to town from hinterlands to the north. She mentions a sawmill that operated in town, where some of her close relatives, including her close classificatory brother, Roy, worked: "like him, like mefella been all level, you know level [of similar age], him, me and Margaret Katherine." She mentions that her mother and father "been shift out" from Dumigans' to work for Cox's store, but "not much money, that money been coming up too, not too far, right, Mum reckon we'll have to go work for . . . old Mr. Phillips and him wife."

This is the Phillips who managed the Aboriginal camp at CS, as Aborigines call CSIRO for short, then the sole Aboriginal camp permitted in town. Again, Julie evokes the people who were there: old Henry Brumby, Ivy, Cookboy uncle, "all been there CS."

Finally, Julie herself got a job.

JW: Me I been workin la welfare lady . . . over here langa this street now, Stutterd Street [see inset, map 3], that first house I been work . . . I been work for myself, got money for my rown [of my own], get pay five pound.
FM: What kind of job you used to do?
JW: Look after all them kid, little baby you know, for her. That ironing, mind'im that picaninny [kids], till that lady come back from work, well once they been ready to leave now, reckon that lady, you know, come with me, down south, Sydney. No, I don't want to go, I got my family here, I'm not going, I been reckon la him . . . She had one little one, 'nother mob been growin, go school, other mob kid. She used to tell me, you can stay here, live with me, she

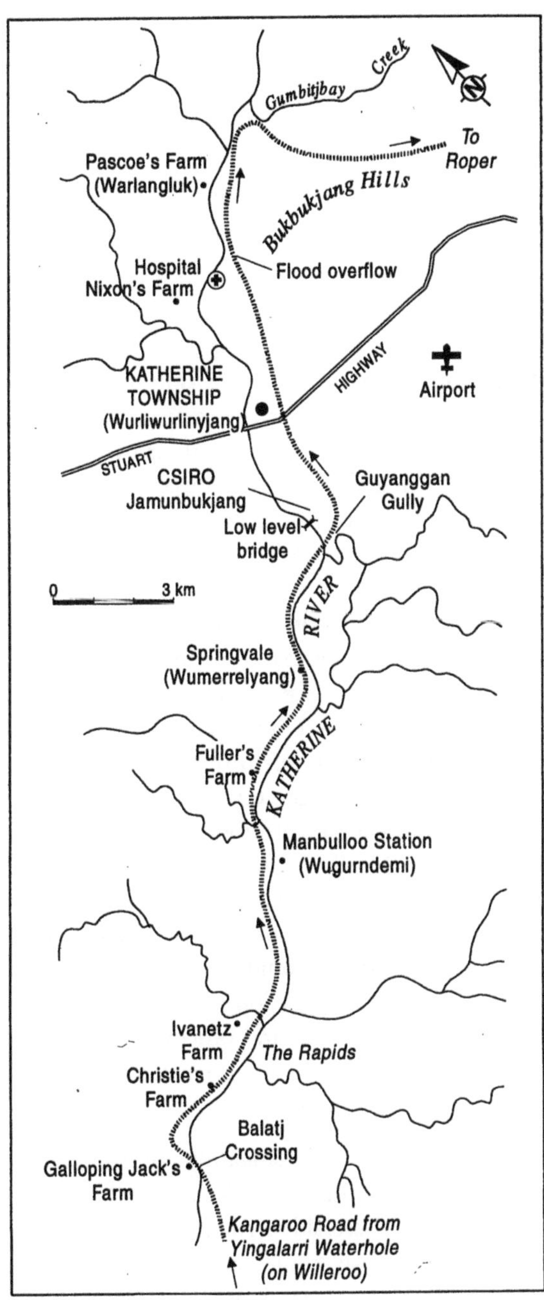

Map 5. Locations on Katherine River North and South of Township

used to tell me you know. One day I stopped there, I camped there, one day and I went back home.

FM: Why?

JW: I didn't like that. No good, thinking about family, granny you know, we used to go fishing that way langa Low Level.

As the last part of this personal history in traveling mode relates, there are some shifts, certain organizations of people and place, that Julie would not countenance when she was old enough to decide for herself. In her personal history "work" is the dominant reason for being in a particular place, though as I have noted, Aborigines often explained such work in terms of white directives intersecting with their own purposes and concepts. But the prospect of a living situation that makes of "home" just an abstract or mere work space is unacceptable. "One day I camped there," Julie says of her employer's offer to her to stay with her; then, "no good, thinking about family."

A more problematic conjunction of place, purpose, and people for Julie was the school to which she was taken when she was still a "small girl," maybe eight. She describes having been picked up by a welfare man, Oscar Ryan. He was an Aboriginal man (but not a local—he had originated from western Arnhem Land, far to the north of Katherine town). He worked for, and was surnamed for, Katherine town's resident welfare officer, Ron Ryan. (Julie explained Oscar's acquisition of the surname thus: "Welfare bloke, this Mr. Ryan now, Mr. Ryan, for that old man, right, they been call him Oscar RYAN.") Julie had recounted that she used to go to Pascoe's farm to "walkabout" and was picked up from there. (There was an official welfare policy that "native" children should be schooled at Bamyili settlement east of Katherine.) Oscar came "got long socks" (wearing the knee-high socks characteristic among officials and officeworkers in the tropics) and told her, "You gotta go school." They put her in a car "no mother and father." I asked how she lived at Bamyili.

> No more dormitory, been sleep langa my family, I think it was . . . not Aunty Sarah, them all finish [they've all died] . . . stop there that mob, for a while, come there, siddown, siddown, I been runaway, me and Margaret been run away, come back this way. . . . We been sneak in from Barunga. "What you two doing here?" come back from that place, too many, no use staying there, my mother reckoned, no good, might get killed, go back home again, siddown there, allright, that old

> woman reckoned, you mob gonna have to go school here now, go this school, now, you two, we go this school first for a little while.

Although the people at the settlement school were "family," they were not close and familiar; in any case, they are "all finish" now. The time there was an endless round of "siddown siddown." Eventually she and Margaret ran away, back to the Katherine life with their familiar people. Probably under some compulsion, their mothers said then that they must go to school in Katherine. But that was interim, another period of "siddown siddown" and "go school go school," finally punctuated by a brief return to the settlement and then "my father been la Darwin . . . ah, have to take you la Darwin."

Even when discussing her daily life, Julie represents her exploration of place in a traveling mode. It is probably no accident that when her parents were employed in Cox's, the main general supply and grocery store in town, and she herself was able to earn small amounts there, she and her friend Margaret Katherine (whose parents also worked at Cox's) bought themselves bicycles. With her friend Margaret, Julie was able to visit the length and breadth of Katherine town. The two girls, and sometimes others of their age, could "make up" the money with which they bought the bikes by helping out, uncrating produce. Julie noted that they used to ride their bikes all around, "only us two, but no traffic in those days, nothing." Interested in the novelty of her acquisition, especially for those times, I asked her,

> *FM:* Only you mob been have'im bike I s'pose?
>
> *JW:* Me and her, she had blue one, I had green one, lady bike, alright, we go fishing with it, sometimes picnic with it, langa hospital, or from Clyde Fenton [school, map 3], down the river there . . . walk around . . . I been single girl, me and Margaret . . . brother they used to come out there, humbug [bother] mefella for bike, ride'im, sometime we used to fight, we used to tell'im you go way you man, you boy, only us two gonna ride this bike, girls' bike . . . and then I used to go lookin' for that crab you know, billabong crab, this other side from that BP [location 9, map 3], other side motel . . . take'im back now, billy can, and *jalwak*, you savvy *jalwak?* . . . little round one, like a potato, all right, I dunno how many year I been stop there.

Julie's story includes the longer periodicity of movement from one work location to another and the shorter cycles of daily movement, the means by which she and Margaret continued to reaffirm their place in the network of town camp connections. There is a sense in which those kinds of mobilities are the conditions of what she knows, or thinks it worthy to report. Her sense of interim periods, like her time at school, is largely a function of immobility, often relayed in her narrative by a summary such as, "We been siddoooown, right up" or "We been siddown there little bit long time." In her narrative of the past, places where activities took place are sometimes described with reference to structures that were not there at the time, indeed in some cases (as with the mention of Clyde Fenton School or the BP service station, above) have only recently been built. Unless I explicitly asked her questions about the difference, Julie did not usually attempt to distinguish our shared visual knowledge and experience of Katherine from her own earlier experience of it. Instead, she often sought to make the past intelligible by clarifying details of place in terms of present spatial organization.

Periods of time are primarily defined by connections between people and place, and the mode of knowing about them is the traveling mode. This means that the organization of time is not governed by an abstract chronology. When, for instance, I had asked Julie "Which time this one?" that the rainbow had been killed at March's corner, she had refused my formulation of the question, but then answered it: "Hm, I don't know what time now, long time, too muchy, I don't remember, my mother been workin for Cox's then, my stepfather."

The Social Distribution of Memory

Although whites could come to be at the basis of the Aborigines' sense of relationship to those locales where they were employed, the episode involving the extraction of the rainbow has a somewhat different character. It concerns a place in the town not represented as associated with anyone in particular, white or Aboriginal. In Julie's story, the extraction is being performed by an unknown, someone who is not recognized and is spoken of only as "one white man." Rather than supplanting other significances with his own, the white man is furthering uniformity: following the removal of the rainbow serpent and the sealing of its hole, this place will be less like itself and eventually just another part of the town.

That this process is well advanced is shown by the fact that the story of the rainbow is not widely known among Aborigines who live in Katherine now. Nor are the details of what was formerly there—the limestone structures—widely remembered or remarked upon by Aborigines or other townspeople. But a cohort of Aboriginal people in Katherine do remember and associate the limestone cave with rainbow serpent stories, though not all of these are exactly the same. The social distribution of these stories is significant, for it indexes a subset of Aboriginal people in Katherine who regard themselves as having closer ties to the town and its environs than others. At their core are people whose identification around a submerged and now obsolescent socio-territorial identity still subtly differentiates them from others less closely connected to the Katherine town area. They are people who, like Julie, lived mainly or at least periodically at the CSIRO camp after the war.

A small grouping of people fairly closely linked by family ties, including Julie, tell a similar story about the rainbow extraction. Within this grouping, others besides Julie are some people of her generation level and the one above hers, relatives on her mother's side. The Katherine rainbow story is also known to some members of Julie's former husband's extended family, the senior members of which are her ex-husband's close "father" Nipper; her ex-husband, Peter Jatbula; and his half-brother, Sandy Barraway. But their stories mainly concern places to the north of Katherine town, from which they originated.

There is another extended family grouping, in earlier decades probably primarily affiliated with an area to the southwest of town on the King River (see map 1), to which specific family attachments are now rather vague. In keeping with that earlier localization, members of the family spent long periods working at Manbulloo Station just outside the town on its southwestern margin and later worked and lived at CSIRO. Some members of this family vividly remember what the old March's corner used to look like and associate it with a rainbow presence, but their story is different from Julie's. They say a rainbow emerged from the hole at March's corner, traveled east where it came out at another place in the limestone system known as Cutta Cutta caves (about thirty kilometers southeast of Katherine town; see map 1), and then went north toward Edith Falls, a place with a large plunge pool at the base of steep sandstone cliffs. This is the kind of place that Aboriginal people who know that country associate with the rainbow serpent; and indeed this is one of the places about which certain of Julie's former husband's family tell stories concerning the army's efforts during the war to extirpate the rainbow there.

There are a number of families of mixed descent, Aboriginal and other, who have been around the town for many years but who had a different socioeconomic position from people like Julie and a correspondingly different residential and spatial relation to the town. Some, for example, formerly worked in regular jobs for the railway and lived in railway housing along the south bank of the river within the town ambit. Some members of these families have told me that as children playing around town, they were told by their seniors that there were "devil-devils" in the limestone cave, and they should stay away from it. That none of these people has mentioned any rainbow association to me points to distinct circuits of ideas about place between themselves and some of the locally residing Aboriginal "fringe" families, like Julie's, who were integrated at a quite different level into the town's economic life.

The striking limestone cave was woven into the stories of Aborigines who lived well away from the town and only came to visit occasionally from rural areas. In her book *Dingo Makes Us Human* about the Victoria River district, Debbie Rose quotes one of her informants, an old man from Yarralin, far to the southwest of town (see map 1). Old Tim Yilngayari and his wife Mary Rutungali told Rose about Tim's father's death, which apparently occurred while he was visiting Katherine, presumably at an early period before the town's focus had shifted from Emungalan to the south bank:

> *Old Tim:* They been put him on the gravy [in the grave], I'll tell you. You savvy that big hole? That big hole right longa store, Katherine store? You been look?
>
> *Debbie Rose:* Yeah.
>
> *OT:* That's the gravy [grave] belonga my old man.
>
> *DR:* Oh, true?
>
> *OT:* And him been, him been get up Rainbow now.
>
> *DR:* Him been get up Rainbow?
>
> *MR:* Yeah. Get up.
>
> *OT:* That my Daddy longa Darwin now, alive.
>
> *MR:* Him there now.
>
> *OT:* Him there longa Darwin la buffalo shooter, Marrakai [Station]. I was been there. My old man still alive. Him been dead there [Kather-

> ine], and that thing been come out, Rainbow, and him fly up. Him been there too, going longa Darwin. You know my old man too fucking clever. Really clever. (Rose 1992:70–71)

In Old Tim's story, the cave is far from a negative space that needs to be filled: it is a place of revitalizing power, from which his father arose as from the dead and reappeared in Darwin.

The extraction of the rainbow, as these various Aboriginal perspectives show, removed the particularity that underlay the varied inventions around the theme of a dangerous or deference-demanding locality. It is a move toward making the place merely a part of a larger space within its vicinity of street and storefronts, no longer a source of difference but a part of the "whole" central commercial area of town.

Such processes fragmented the landscape, contributing to the creation of a broad difference between the increasingly homogeneous space of the central "town," and the outlying, ever less intricately defined "country." The attenuation of linkages among places across the countryside is part of a wider set of processes of socio-spatial change on which this book provides perspectives.

The Rainbow Serpent

Much that has been said about the northern "rainbow serpent" complex focuses on its arcane and even secret and sacred associations with gleaming objects, with pearl shell, and even with semen (see, e.g., Radcliffe-Brown 1930a, Robinson 1956, Maddock 1970). These associations suggest themes of fertility and regeneration and tend to be linked with a high culture of ceremony. The rainbow serpent is generally thought of as combining male and female properties. But in the Katherine area, the most widespread ideas of the rainbow serpent have to do with its aversion, as a native of place, to the foreign sweat and smells of people it does not recognize[11] and its stormy response to incautious intrusions into its localities.

In the Katherine area, or more precisely all along the southern Arnhem fringe and into western Arnhem Land (see map 1), the rainbow is strongly associated with pools of water, especially deep and dark blue ones like the plunge pool at Edith Falls. People are not supposed to "bogey" (swim, bathe) in such waters. To do so there is to risk making rain clouds come up and raising high winds that can "chuck" everything down. If the rainbow captures a person who ventures into its domain, it may try to swallow its victim. Aboriginal people also often speak of the rainbow as sometimes displaying its victim to other people before taking him or her into the deep for good. There is also a notion of the possibility of final cataclysm, a "last day," when the greatest rainbow, who lives in the sea, will put all the people on her back and carry them to doom.

What arouses the rainbow? The serpent is sure to become incensed if it does not recognize someone's sweat, if strangers come into its midst without cautionary introduction to local waters by "watering" of their heads. Those venturing into new terrain should have their heads watered from pools or other water bodies by locals who belong to the area. In this process, the baptizer generally takes a handful or mouthful of water, rubs or sprays it onto the newcomer's hair, and then rubs it over the head. At the same time, the local person speaks to the serpent, telling it about the person being watered, and asking it not to harm the newcomer. The local water makes a known person of one who was originally "different," or unfamiliar: it neutralizes difference.[12]

Perhaps the reader can now better understand the image of the uprooted rainbow. The rainbow is an autochthonous force that assaults the unfamiliar. Dangers associated with it can be avoided only by making oneself familiar, and in any case by circumspection. Older Aborigines of the Katherine area emphasize that they have seen, or felt, the historical transformations that have brought so many outsiders here in this century. They say, "Never been whitefella before." Sometimes they add something like "Only been old Charlie Peterson here." In other words, in the early days local outsiders were few enough so they were known as individuals, despite general, gross inequalities between black and white. At least part of the force of the extraction of the rainbow from March's corner is that here the anonymous stranger uproots and destroys the native force that was the guardian of the difference between "countryman" and "foreigner." One of the suggestions of this image is that anybody can be here now, without fear of reprisal. This is not necessarily to be interpreted as an unmitigated disaster, since people fear and are constrained by the destructive potential of the rainbow serpent.

Katherine-area Aboriginal people know a number of Arnhem plunge pools where the rainbow serpent is still believed to reside, such as at Edith Falls north of Katherine (see map 1). These places were little frequented by whites until some were used as army recreation areas during World War II. This and some other places where a rainbow is still thought to be present are now widely frequented by tourists, who swim in the deep-sided pools without caution. Older Aboriginal people, seeing this, conclude either that outsiders have no intelligible "law" in relation to such things or that they have brought with them an era of "new law" that somehow weakens or displaces the old constraints. An implicit indeterminacy arises: to whom does the "new law" apply? to everyone, or just to non-Aborigines? Rather than asking this question directly or reacting to it categorically by rigidly observing or flagrantly ignoring constraints, Aboriginal people live the indeterminacy, sometimes swimming in the shallow water, sometimes fishing at the pools' margins, but always with an awareness of the rainbow's dangers and often repeating that, in the old days when people were walking the country, they never would have camped within close proximity of these plunge pools, as white people do now.

Of a large Arnhem plunge pool, Gunlom, well to the north of Edith Falls (see map 1) but still within country to which some Katherine Aborigines (including Julie's in-laws) consider themselves affiliated, Aboriginal people say that, in the old days, they camped well away, on the South Alligator River. Since the early 1950s, however, when there was uranium exploration and mining in this area, increasing numbers of whites have used the pool. In 1975 Gunlom was incorporated as a recreation reserve, and since 1987 it has been part of Kakadu National Park. Though the shallow water is thought not to be too dangerous, a rainbow serpent is thought to live in the deeper part of the pool, into which a waterfall drops from the high cliffs above. The rainbow can still bring storm and winds if incensed, and I have known people to attribute unusual, gusty storms to the rainbow's anger at such extensive use of the pool as is now common. But, curiously, on other occasions it is said that greater tourist use of the pool may have helped to make the rainbow "quiet," to make it "settle down." A feeling—nothing as definite as a clearly formulated idea—is perceptible among Aboriginal people that outsiders settle and defuse the power of the rainbow, so that it reacts in its accustomed manner only to the difference between known and unknown Aborigines. This notion, as I say, has not become routine or universal. But it is not simply an extension of a "traditional" thought: it is a tentative reformulation of ideas about the behavior of the rainbow in a changed situation. Elsewhere, as at Edith Falls, occasional tourist drownings are directly attributed to the rainbow serpent and are the occasion for comments by Aboriginal people that outsiders do not know or understand the country.

Given local understandings of the rainbow serpent, the image of its extraction at Katherine suggests removal from the ground of a power that discerned difference and required that one take the precaution of making oneself known. Although one may wonder whether this is suggestive of an intercultural struggle of deracination, most storytellers (like Julie herself) do not draw an explicit conclusion from these stories about changes in the nature of Katherine town, beyond the comments of "old people" that before, "no whitefella been here, been nothing this town." Nor, as I have said, do they usually give opinions about the motives of others, including of the white man in extracting and dumping the Rainbow. And although the extraction of the rainbow is generally thought to be definitive, storytellers do not moralize about it. Their attitude seems to be that, as is true of all complex processes and events, only time and the unfolding of other events will show the significance of what happened, or maybe reveal alternative interpretations of it, or even shed a quite different light on what the earlier event might have been.

Conclusions

One conclusion we must draw from all of this is that, whether or not they put the matter to themselves in just this way, Aboriginal people like Julie now live with a diversified consciousness of the possible meaningfulness of country and places. Myers (1986:57) insightfully discusses Aboriginal conceptions of the place-world at dual levels of the impermanence of "camp," or lived locale, and the enduring quality of "country" as mythopoetic creation. Just as "camp" is associated with people who made it and lived there, so country is associated with enduring Dreaming presences that made it and are felt to be perennially in it.

For people like Julie, some places and areas are strongly invested with mythic significances, along with the other dimensions of meaningfulness that arose in the processes of former practical association with that country. Other areas and places have no clear mythic significances but may be meaningful as "home" places in which people have lived, with the mutuality of person-place relationship that this implies for many of them. In such places, there is always the possibility of the "discovery" of existing but newly revealed and interpreted significances, whether or not these be clearly attributed a mythic dimension (see Myers 1986:64–66, and this book, chapter 7). And some places and areas are said to be "just country," by which people sometimes mean that they assume that mythological associations exist but they do not know them, or more flatly, that there are none: "no Dreaming." This process of divisions within the landscape—

more exactly, people's development of a consciousness in which country and place are experienced as meaningful in a variety of ways—has not just begun; those of Julie's parents' generation doubtless lived with certain unevennesses in the landscape, perhaps particularly around the town.

Clearly, through direct occupation, settlers could insert themselves into the middle of Aboriginal relationships to places, for however absolute the "Dreaming" significances of places may seem, they were always constituted (as various authors have shown, e.g., Bell 1983, Rose 1992, Povinelli 1993) within and through the range of practices that linked people with places—hence the inherent permeability of Aboriginal accounts of place, such as I have illustrated through Julie's stories of herself as a Katherine girl, completely accepting of the proximity of a rainbow serpent to Neal's ice cream shop and movie theater on the main street but also aware that the activities of whites worked toward its removal. Whites activities also had considerable transformative effects on both temporal and spatial dimensions of Aborigines' relationships to places through work, modifying some of the sensitivities for relationships to places in the earlier Aboriginal mode.

Some other sociohistorical inflections and implications of these processes require explicit comment. The destruction of the limestone cave was understood differently by Aborigines who related to it as a storied place and by whites who saw it as a natural feature now inappropriately in the middle of what had become the town. Insofar as the rainbow's extraction from March's corner is believed to have been definitive and the roadworks to have homogenized the place with the area around it, possibilities of independent Aboriginal interpretations of this as distinctive "place" have been foreclosed upon. The outcome has rendered the area serviceable in terms of dominant ideas of appropriate use. Even its vitality as currently shared memory has been attenuated by continuing change in the relation of Aboriginal people and others to Katherine, and in the town itself. A former "place," almost definitively, has become part of town space, no longer a significant focus for Aboriginal objectifications of identity, either in general or more specific terms. But this has also occurred in the context of some Aboriginal people's managing, under difficult circumstances, to sustain and refashion an organic relationship to the town as the principal focus of their place-world. In chapter 4 I consider the relation of the filling and covering over of the cave to a long-term trajectory of shifting objectifications of socio-spatial identity *among* Aborigines around the town and in relation to it, "internal" changes nevertheless directly related to the history of outsider occupation of this area.

The evanescence of the rainbow's cave as bearer of meaning is part of the processes of neutralizing difference at the center of an area originally both differentiated and continuously interconnected in Aboriginal terms. Aboriginal people, whose lives were drastically changed as the town was established, later converged upon it; thus conditions were shaped for the erosion and considerable dropping out of earlier Aboriginal terms of difference at this center. The situation has been historically complex in that such earlier terms have been differentially maintained among Aboriginal people who have come from hinterlands into the town yet continue to look out upon those hinterlands and to have varying relationships to them, including involving periodic employment, continuing attachment to areas and their people outside town, and to return there for a variety of reasons.

To conceptualize present differences among Australian towns, one must develop a comparative sense of the particularity of historical conditions around them. The social history of the much larger town of Alice Springs in Australia's center, for example, has been different from Katherine's. Alice Springs developed in the homelands of widely distributed congeries of indigenous occupants who, at one level at least, share an identity as Arrernte (Spencer and Gillen's 1899 "Arunta" and Strehlow's 1947, 1970, 1971 "Aranda"). On stations established around Alice, whites gave social recognition to the mixed-race children of Aboriginal women and to consequent domestic units over time (see Briscoe 1991). Thus, despite the existence of exclusionary regulations in Alice Springs such as the Prohibited Areas Ordinances as around Katherine, these stations were reservoirs of people who, to a considerable extent, could retain Aboriginal language and a sense of local connectedness and who, with some background of occupational and formal education, were able to play a considerable role, first, in the region's pastoral industry and, second, in the rise of a nationally fostered Aboriginal organizational politics over the last two and a half decades.

Katherine is more appropriately compared to Australian towns historically characterized by more profound precolonial fault lines of social and linguistic diversity and by the establishment of a town that more radically depleted its local population. Also involved was the creation and maintenance of an unbridgeable social gulf between most social strata of settlers and between remaining and more recently arrived Aborigines. Many towns are more comparable in these respects to Katherine than to Alice Springs (cf. Kolig 1981). Their social trajectories remain to be more completely compared.

What are some of the conclusions to be drawn concerning the Katherine situation from a generational perspective?

Julie has conveyed to her own three daughters some particularities of their relationship to Katherine town and its environs, such as showing one of them the tree under which she was born near Nixon's farm (see map 4) where the family was working, talking to another of her place of spirit emergence as a crocodile caught by Julie's father at a place remote from town in high country that fringe-dwelling Aborigines used to frequent, and showing all of them old campsites in and around town where they lived as children.

In general, stories of the rainbow serpent do not have currency within her children's generation. Nonetheless, Julie has an evident sense of attachment to "Katherine," and of herself as a person who, along with certain others to whom she is linked in specific ways, has a long-term identification as a local Katherine Aborigine. She sees this as distinguishing her from outsiders, both white and Aboriginal, with whom her personal history is bound up and partly overlaps; and this identity shapes the terms of her interaction with others, including her children, and therefore their own orientation.

Nevertheless, over the recent twenty years of land rights activity, the attention of Julie's family and of most of her close associates has been focused on lands to the north of the town, to which her husband had strong attachment, some of which he had showed to Julie as they moved around within the region, especially early in their married life. Given the generally successful outcomes of claims to areas to the north of town, the attention of this family and others is likely to be focused on this northern area and their sense of it in "traditional" Aboriginal terms to be much livelier than their sense of Katherine in such terms, though they are much more likely to live in Katherine than distant from it and to engage more fully in place making in relation to the town than outside it.

For many of those who continue to look toward hinterlands, relations to them have become increasingly past-oriented as life situations have been much altered over the past decades. The next chapter is concerned with this perspective upon socio-spatial relationships.

Three

We Useta Walk Around, All the People

IN THIS CHAPTER, I explore ways in which Katherine-area Aboriginal people's relations to hinterlands have tended to become specialized and rarefied, increasingly particular to individuals and small groupings of especially older people, as the relevant places cease to be a part of everyday living space. Although processes of this kind are occurring with respect to all the hinterlands from which Katherine's Aboriginal people have come in to town, here I focus in particular on those who have come to town and outlying settlements from the north and east. These are regions in which what has become known in Australianist anthropological literature as "clan" organization was apparently universal, the wider area being associated with the higher-level socio-territorial identity known as Jawoyn. (Map 4 shows relative locations of this and other similar socio-territorial identities referred to in this chapter.) Also relevant is that these people have had a contact history of the kind briefly described at the end of chapter 1, dominated by the existence of mines (especially Maranboy) and towns at or beyond the peripheries of their countries of origin. Theirs was not, by and large, a contact history of pastoralism.

Lefebvre (1991) pioneered discussion of the ways in which social space is "produced." Rejecting views of space as either natural or conceptual abstraction (and thus the whole Newtonian and Kantian a priori, absolute, and infinite space, as does also Casey 1993), he argued that particular forms and understandings of social space are created only in social practice and that the capacity to shape space is also a capacity to influence the processes of social reproduction. Although some Aboriginalist accounts emphasize the meanings ideally associated with place, they leave contemporary spatial practices, ways of living in place that are vitally relevant to its ongoing construction, insufficiently examined. Myers' (1986) discussion of the double-layered character of place, as transient camp and enduring Dreaming, gives us a way of exploring what happens as the density of everyday life and practice become separated from places that people hold in memory as significant and in terms of which they conceive of certain kinds of sociocultural categories. The pulling away of such ideal concepts of place or person linkage from the everyday experience of places is also related to changes in the forms in which personhood is experienced and attributed. In particular, this chapter begins by exploring changes in socio-spatial categories that may be called "clan" identities in relation to changes in the ways in which Aborigines live in places. Experience and practical knowledge of living in places is generationally differentiated, as one might expect given considerable change in the forms of Aboriginal life. Among the young, certain places have an increasingly historicized character.

Changing Ways of Life

In latter 1976, having spent some months in Katherine, I moved to Bamyili (Barunga). People from southern Arnhem Land (including many who identify themselves as Jawoyn), were numerically predominant at this settlement, but there were also some who consider themselves to come from more northerly areas of Arnhem Land (including Ngalkbon, Rembarrnga, Mayali people, and others). Although many of my new acquaintances were close friends and relations of people at Katherine Gorge (and many of the latter had spent periods of time at Bamyili since its beginnings as a wartime compound), the tenor of settlement life was different in many respects from that of town. For some town-dwelling Aborigines, the settlement has always stood for the loss of freedom and mobility. Given the communal dining arrangements and other features of the wartime and later assimilation era, it has also stood for unwelcome forms of control and communal organization. For many settlement-dwelling people, the town is a specter (as well as sometime attraction) of abandonment to alcohol and loss of regular participation in the communal ceremonial life of Bamyili and neighboring Beswick settlement. Generally, town is seen as offering an unregulated and often alcohol-focused life that, although it may be one of greater liberties, is also seen by many Aborigines to be characterized by continuous (even if diffuse) influences of the surrounding, numerically-dominant white presence. In the settlement context at Bamyili I met numbers of people who had, in certain ways, retained greatest distance from outsider influences upon their current daily lives and social arrangements—people like Fanny Birlamjam, about whom I write below.

Not least among the influences that Aboriginal people of the Katherine region have experienced has been the recent period of land claims. In 1978 the Northern Land Council (established under the Aboriginal Land Rights [Northern Territory] Act 1976) lodged a claim to areas of vacant Crown land to the north, east, and south of Katherine town, including areas in the immediate vicinity of Bamyili. This claim would eventually come to involve many Aboriginal people in town and at Bamyili, Beswick, and other places. By 1980, preparation of the claim was still not very far advanced, and I was asked by the land council to help, as by that time I had already spent the better part of three years around Katherine and knew many of the potential claimants. I also had considerable experience of the nature of many people's relationships to country in the Katherine/Bamyili area and of their sense of connection to more-distant hinterlands, which preparation for the land claim required us to visit. This experience contributed greatly to my understanding of Aboriginal people's current relations to country, and of "clans" in terms of which only a relatively small number of older people involved in the claim continued to relate to places. It also provided insight into the ways in which, through their relationships with outsiders, Aborigines had come to live centralized around towns, mines, and stations. This centralization resulted in changes in their socio-spatial practices and pulled them away from intimate and far-ranging contact with wider country. The Katherine Area Land Claim was a lengthy process (lasting from early preparations in 1980 to the land commissioner's final report of 1988). The success of the claim over the area of Katherine Gorge National Park (now Nitmiluk National Park; see map 1) has had major implications. It has resulted, for example, in the formation of an incorporated body called the Jawoyn Association to develop and manage the relationships of the successful claimants with changing park structures. Here I focus on the claim insofar as material produced for and in it illustrates the nature of relationships to country that are the central subject matter of this chapter and illuminates the issues of changing consciousness and generational difference.

Clans, Totems, and Country

The concept of the "clan," patri-clan, or sometimes, patrilineal totemic clan, emerged as the centerpiece of Radcliffe-Brown's (1913, 1930b, 1931) discussion of Australian social organization. Radcliffe-Brown thought of each clan as a separate unit, territorially grounded, totemically distinguished from other like units, and the basis of political society. Later anthropological perspectives that characterized Aboriginal societies as hunting and gathering in their mode of subsistence, with their focus upon human relations to resources, tended to present clans as ideal groupings rarely realized in actuality except perhaps in ritual, as compared to on-the-ground "bands." Marxist perspectives had less to say about clans as a particular kind and level of Aboriginal social categorization than about domination as something exercised within Aboriginal society (with religion as an important source of gender-differentiated and largely male-dominated powers; see Bern 1979), as well as upon Aboriginal society from without. From this perspective, religion (and its clan-based apparatus) became an important form and substance of politics.

Certain more recent perspectives upon clan have emphasized the territorially, mythologically, and ritually negotiable nature of this kind of unit (Keen 1994, Tamisari 1995). Such views revise earlier, rather more-structural and solid-seeming notions of clan and clan territory (and are an instance of wider, poststructural rethinking in anthropology of notions of "group"). In those terms, regional contrasts had been suggested, for example, of the allegedly more fixed social forms with apparently more fluid ones of the Western Desert (see, e.g., Myers 1986:293–296 who contrasts Warlpiri and Western Desert in such terms).

In the region north and east of Katherine about which I write, the clan is named and is usually of numerically limited membership that can be quite definitely specified in terms of a principle of recruitment through continuous links in the male line. One belongs to one's father's clan. The Jawoyn word for this kind of social unit is *mowurrwurr*. Clan organization is also a way of relating people to places. Clans for which such information is still known are associated with one or more focal places, as Girrimbitjba (clan) with Wetji Namurrgaymi (place), Bagala (clan) with

Melkjarlumbu (place), and Jambalawa (clan) with Wubilawun (place). In each place inheres at least one focal creator entity that clan members consider their own (sometimes referred to in English as "Dreaming" or in Jawoyn as *ngan-jarang-ngayu*). This is a particular regional form of the Australian integration of place-person-totem (Maddock 1982).

Sarah Andrews, now "old people," was then a middle-aged, socially and ceremonially active and competent woman with a family of three adult children and increasing numbers of grandchildren when I first met her at Bamyili. During the land claim, she was asked by counsel for the Northern Territory government (who opposed the claim) to clarify a statement in which she had identified herself with a place, Wetji:

I thought you used a name like Wetji. What is Wetji?
Sarah: Wetji that emu Dreaming.
Emu Dreaming?
Sarah: Me Wetji now.
You are Wetji?
Sarah: Yes.
Was your father's country Wetji country?
Sarah: Yes, my father. (KALCT 1982:603)

Similarly, counsel for the Northern Territory asked Phyllis Winyjorrotj, similar in age and recognized as a central person within Bamyili because that was part of her father's country, with its inherent Dreamings:

Did Bamjuga [established to have been her father's father] tell you which places in the old time were very special for your *mowurrwurr*, the ones that your *mowurrwurr* looked after in the old time when Bamjuga was still alive?
Phyllis: Yes.
Which places were they?
Phyllis: Waterfall [a specific local designation].
That is out on Beswick?
Phyllis: Yes. (KALCT 1982:692)

Such links as these among place, totem, and person constitute an individually and collectively cherished socio-territorial identity. Though there is strict bounding of inclusion in any particular clan by the principle of patrifiliative recruitment, this form of organization also, in Aboriginal practice, implies differentiated connection of other people to it in which those people's membership in other, similarly constituted identities is relevant.

For older people, at least, connections reckoned as ones among clans are an important dimension of social relatedness and kinship. During my research for the Katherine land claim, I collected the names of forty-two such *mowurrwurr* groups that were said to be Jawoyn (see chapter 4) and was subsequently told of one further group, making forty-three in all. I will refer to this kind of group generically by the Jawoyn word for it, or by the word "clan." Of the forty-three, twenty-five had no living members at the time of the claim (in some cases, the alleged last member or members of a group were remembered by older people; last members of several others have died in the years since the claim).

This form of organization into small, patrifiliatively recruited groups is still common in Arnhem Land and may have been universal in southern Arnhem Land. Consequently, some people also know many group names and their personnel, which they regard as not Jawoyn, but as associated with other large-scale socio-territorial identities with which some of their settlement co-residents are identified, such as Mayali, Ngalkbon, Rembarrnga, and others. The identification of lower-level units as participating in one or another high-level identity is part of fluent social knowledge in this area. Thus people who are members of Wurrkbarbar clan may also be identified as "Jawoyn mob," while people who are Wurrparn will also be recognized as Ngalkbon or Mayali (for there is more than one distinguishable lower-level unit of this name). Around Katherine, the usual practice of people who know about this level of organization is to talk about each lower-level group as identified with only one high-level identity; thus, Wurrkbarbar (the clan with which I became identified) is Jawoyn, and not anything else. However, there are a few instances of lower-level groups that people think of as having had a dual higher-level identity, and they may refer to such groups as, for example, "Jawoyn-Ngalkbon mixed."

As this discussion has implied, older Jawoyn people adhere to the idea that *mowurrwurr* are, or should be, place linked. But in the present, only a few people still have the sense of inherence of clan in place and the knowledge of connection between clans and particular places; in some cases, such information is diffuse or vague; in others, completely obscure. I will illustrate with a range of contemporary cases.

Consider Wetji Na-Murrgaymi as a place within an area to which the feeling of inherent belonging is preserved in memory and in sensibility. This, as we have seen, is the area that Sarah Andrews considers her own, by virtue of her being Girrimbitjba. Sarah and some of her kinsmen and contemporaries lived for a number of her formative years around Maranboy, the tin-mining location near present-day Barunga; the mine began operations in 1913 and periodically attracted miners and several hundred Aborigines of the southern Arnhem fringe. Sarah's family at Maranboy did not have as much access to whites' resources there as some others who held down long-term, plum jobs as police trackers and the like. Thus not firmly held at Maranboy and drawn by continuing attachment of their elders back to Wetji Namurrgaymi to the north and east on the Mainoru River, Sarah and close relatives including Fanny Birlamjam (see below), spent time there as girls and young women. Sarah speaks of a number of named places around Wetji that form a cluster of sites, most of them semiotically integrated as parts of the body of emu. Downstream of Wetji, to which emu ran from farther north, is a place Jarnngurrayn, and even farther is Niborna-wern.go. Here, Sarah told me, the bubbling water is the emu's heart pumping, and some standing paperbarks are its throat. Because of the continuity of human experience of this area, beloved and constitutive of the sense of who one is as Girrimbitjba, I take these as kinds of significances that would have been found in many locations if we still had this kind of information about them and if the effects of settlement had not been as great upon Aboriginal people and their connections with places.[1]

The clan identity Yurl'mayn provides another illustration of the certainties that remained, and the uncertainties that had arisen, with respect to clan-level identities as part of spatial practice. The person whom I knew best of this group was Fanny Birlamjam, known to her camp mates as Duljuwuk (lit., "short body") and frequently, too, as "Shorty." (She was of noticeably shorter stature than many other local Aborigines, but I had met a few individuals of similar stature among people from western Arnhem Land and the Arnhem plateau.)

Fanny was already an old lady when I first met her, in her camp near Sarah's at Bamyili, but still lively and active. She was reticent around whites and sometimes was reduced to confusion in their presence, so that some whites (for example, among the staff at Bamyili) thought that she was silly and discounted her. Her camp mates thought nothing of the sort; they appeared to have every respect for her everyday competence and her personal experience, though they fronted for her in encounters with whites.[2] She lived much of her life around Maranboy, Beswick (started up as an Aboriginal pastoral training station postwar), and Bamyili. She had had one daughter by a white miner on the Maranboy field, but the daughter had died, leaving two granddaughters, who lived with Fanny. Though Fanny's life had revolved around the mine fields for quite a while, she saw her clan,

Yurl'mayn, as associated with Wetji Namurrgaymi—the same focal place, in fact, that Sarah Andrews identifies as Girrimbitjba, that of her own *mowurrwurr.* Fanny had walked around there for considerable periods when young, with Sarah and with other members of both their immediate families.

It is not implausible that, in the past, both Yurl'mayn and Girrimbitjba partook of the same focal place, Wetji—for shared relationship to place on the part of two or sometimes several groups is otherwise attested around the Mainoru River area. But to me the notable thing was that Fanny, while a woman who had lived completely within a certain Aboriginal lifestyle and who was regarded as knowledgeable about traditional things, showed some uncertainty about the nature of Yurl'mayn's connection to Wetji. She, like Sarah, was of Emu Dreaming—that was not to be doubted. Fanny almost always referred to her Dreaming as *durrk ngurrurdu* (emu) in Jawoyn and then Ngalkbon, the two language areas through which her Dreaming moved. She would say the phrase in a kind of sing-song, a way of referring to the creator figure and intonation pattern that she shared with a few other older people. This identification with her Dreaming appeared to give her a sense of completeness: she *was* emu, and this was an anchorpoint of her sense of self. On getting up at her camp in the mornings she would sometimes stretch herself and say, in the manner of some of these older people upon first rising, "Go-go-go Wetji lerr-ngaku" (Oh! Wetji my country!), an outward projection of an inner-centeredness and centering as the resumption of sociability.

But for someone who had been steeped in feeling for completeness in terms of the inherent connection among person, Dreaming, and place, Fanny sometimes seemed puzzled about the relation among them. Yurl'mayn was emu, she was both Yurl'mayn and emu, Wetji Namurrgaymi was Emu Dreaming, Sarah Andrews was all of these and they had been in the past, and were still, extremely close. But perhaps emu (though still identified strongly with Wetji) had come to Wetji from somewhere else that was Fanny's place as distinct from Sarah's? Was her emu the same as Sarah's, or was Yurl'mayn connected to another emu place? Puzzlement was fueled by some persistent hints that Fanny's family attachments lay farther north or elsewhere, as I describe below. In other words, her orientation to country was combined with some sense of oddments that could not now be referred to anyone more authoritative because, as she sometimes told me, "Your uncles [by whom she meant, her father and his brothers, since she considered me her cross-cousin] all been die too quick." That

Fanny could entertain such ideas showed the continuing force of a principle of difference between groups in terms of their being "different place." On a few occasions Fanny concluded that whether Girrimbitjba and Yurl'mayn were "same place" or not did not matter too much: she and Sarah were "same." This conclusion shows the countervailing force of social closeness between these two, who had spent much time together over the course of their lives with Sarah as a younger woman in the orbit of Fanny's practical experience, in dispelling the issue of difference that their being different *mowurrwurr* nevertheless signified to both of them.

Part of Fanny's difficulty was evidently linked to the fact that other places had been made significant to her early in her life by, among other people, her father—who had died before she got to know how he might have dealt with the relations of Yurl'mayn to other places, Dreamings, and clan identities.

And apparently nobody else of her father's generation imparted such understandings to her in those years when much energy seemed to have been directed simply to eking out a living on the fringes of the Maranboy mining field. Her father had, for example, told her about a place, Barrmang, where he said he had been born. Was this place near Wetji? Sometimes Fanny spoke as if the two were proximate, as in this reminiscence to me about her country, which she had seen when a child, and in which she specifically included Barrmang and Wetji:

> Jitjwarr nga-bolk-wongayn . . .
> nabay ngarrk nga-garayinay lerr-ngaku-luk . . .
> na-ganya-nginy.gu-wa bu-ny-joyoyiyn . . .
> ngan-yorrorn nyiyarrkurlung lerr-nyiwu
> gilkan ga-bolk-butjbutj-mar ga-dul'dul-mamang
> ngayewun yutyut-may nyirranggurlung nawarnbay Wetji.
>
> (Poor thing, I left my country
> me, I grew up in my country
> all your uncles had died [this to the writer, i.e., my "uncles" being her "fathers," as we were cross-cousins]
> *yorrorn* [high riverine country] is [our and my] country [again she honorifically identifies the writer with herself]
> "inside" [in the interior] the country smokes and lightning flashes
> it [her Emu Dreaming] ran that way, Wetji is our [exclusive] place.)

The last line refers to the main Dreaming, emu, of the Wetji area; and the possessive pronoun here becomes exclusive (i.e., includes those who belong to Wetji, but not the writer). This poeticization of memory is achieved in part through the imagery of haze, a kind of smoky fog that hangs over the Arnhem landscape under certain weather conditions as it now hung over Fanny's memory of these places, and the piercing of that haze by occasional lightning flashes. From that country, which was now for Fanny a space of distant imagination rather than of physical immediacy, her Dreaming perhaps came. The poeticization transcends the locational obscurity of Barrmang in relation to Wetji and pronounces the inherence of emu in Wetji and of self in both.

But Fanny was also aware of the store of things said about one of her brothers, known as Joe Yirrpinyjo, who had mostly resided in and around Mataranka, a small town due south of Bamyili on the Stuart Highway (see map 1), for some years past. He had worked carting timber when the Maranboy sawmill was operating, apparently taking the name he bore as surname, Yirrpinyjo, from one of the places of timbering and milling activity. Sometimes Fanny, but mostly other people including some younger members of her wider family, give Yirrpinyjo as one of the places of Yurl'mayn *mowurrwurr*. But this is far from Wetji and most likely represents the association of the clan name with this place as a result of Joe's long-term presence there for work and his having used the name Yirrpinyjo as English-style surname as a result. Or maybe he had also been born there and taken the name of his place of birth, as Jawoyn people frequently did (see further)—but this was unclear. In any case, Yirrpinyjo as Yurl'mayn place was inconsistent with the location of the clan at Wetji.

There was at least a third perspective on the location of Yurl'mayn. A federal government inquiry was established to investigate the conditions under which uranium mining might most acceptably take place near the border of Arnhem Land. A town, Jabiru, has subsequently been built as a service center for the Ranger Uranium mine. In 1976 the Fox Inquiry, as it was known, commissioned a mapping of Arnhem clans allegedly of that general area with a view toward establishing "traditional countries" as a basis for estimating the potential social effects of mining and including Aboriginal people of the region in any benefits flowing from it. In that mapping (Australia 1977), Yurl'mayn is shown high up in the Arnhem escarpment, distant both from Wetji on the Mainoru River and from the sawmilling operations at Yirrpinyjo out of Maranboy. One might conjecture that the Fox Inquiry mapping relates to another Yurl'mayn, not the one to which Fanny and Joe were affiliated (for there are, as an earlier example has shown, cases of the same name attaching to what are otherwise considered distinct clans). But one need not resort to this explanation, for certain family ties suggest that precisely Fanny's Yurl'mayn is meant.

Fanny had had a considerably older sister (whom I never met), known by the nickname Jatjmuya (Hurt Leg), who was married to a Mayali-speaking man of a clan called Garnditjbal. The two of them lived in the vicinity shown on the Fox Inquiry map as Yurl'mayn—and not fortuitously, Garnditjbal clan country is shown as adjacent to it. I knew Fanny's nephew, her sister Jatjmuya's son, in the early 1980s. He was already an old man, who at some stage had been given the ridiculous-sounding name Maginnis McGee (after a character in "The Bush Christening," a poem by Australian balladeer Banjo Paterson, in which the christening of Maginnis is achieved when a bottle of whiskey is thrown at him.) Maginnis was of the same diminutive stature as Fanny. His locations of Garnditjbal, his own clan's country, were permeated by the same sorts of indeterminacies that I have sketched for Yurl'mayn. As far as I know, though he had wide-ranging practical experience of this northerly region, he did not have a concept of a focal Garnditjbal place and Dreaming in the way Sarah Andrews does for Girrimbitjba. The Fox Inquiry mapping of Yurl'mayn and Garnditjbal had, as far as I can see, seized upon fragments of information, expressing a particular marriage relationship as geographical proximity of the "clan territories" of the spouses.

Most of the clearer clan-level attachments to places still recognized by Jawoyn people (as in the case of the link of Girrimbitjba to Wetji) are in areas well away from the major towns of Katherine and Pine Creek. One closer to town is Julie Williams' connection through her father (actually, her close "second" father, Fortymile), to a large, open, wind-swept swampy area between Maranboy and Katherine called Leech Lagoon, or Wubilawun (map 6). This place is a Turtle Dreaming, connoted by her *mowurrwurr* name, Jambalawa. Women from the Gorge camp asked me to take them there several times to hunt turtle lying underground in the mud, and so we went, with Julie, who always took a keen interest in these visits. For the most part, though, notions among Jawoyn people of clan-level attachments to areas closer to Katherine seem not to have long survived the Second World War period. Alice Mitchell had the most definite and highly elaborated concepts of clan-level links around the mouth of the Katherine Gorge. For example, she referred to a clan-level identity called *ganybarrakbarrak*[3] as linked to a place Barrakbarrak-luk in the Gorge. She identified this as the Dreaming and country of a certain man, Peter Barrarndila, who according to official records died in 1971. What is less certain is that,

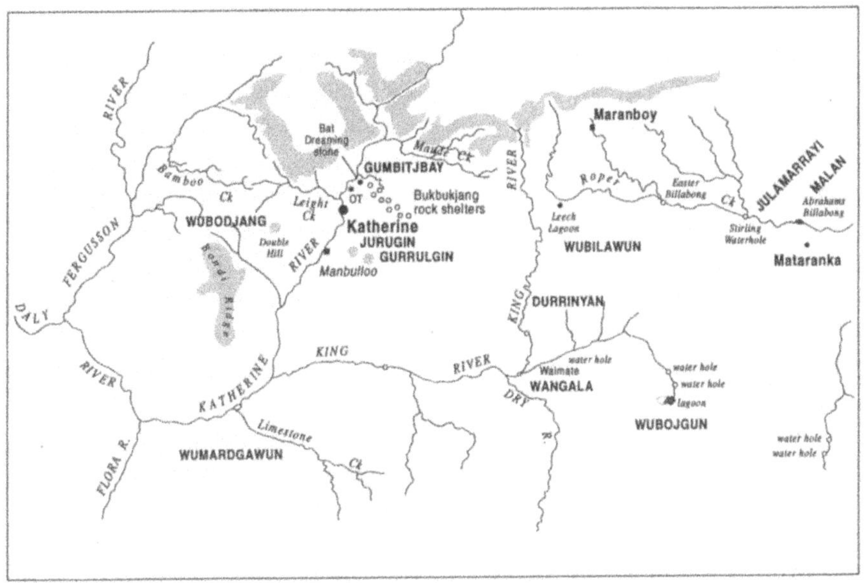

Map 6. Dagoman and Adjacent Country

in his lifetime, he was primarily or exclusively known as Jawoyn; but that is part of the story of chapter 4.

Julie Williams, too, was aware of her own mother's specific attachment to a place near the mouth of the Gorge called Bemang-luk (blanket lizard place), part of a low, jagged set of foothills at the edge of the escarpment. Her mother's *mowurrwurr* was in fact called *gany-bemang*, with blanket lizard its totemic animal. Julie always expressed her own attachment to Bemang-luk by referring to it as "my mother's place," rather than in terms of her own connection to it directly. In the next chapter, I return to consider how these facts appear to be pieces of a puzzle of evidently long-term attachment of her mother's father's family to the immediate Katherine area and to the odd way in which her grandfather, who died long before I ever came to Katherine, has turned out to be one of my main sources about the nature of socio-territorial identifications in the Katherine area earlier in this century.

Given the obsolescence of clan identities in the vicinity of Katherine town, the question becomes how it was that a few have persisted. The tie of Bagala to the Barunga-Beswick area is instructive, but I think unique. The Maranboy mine operated under conditions of Aboriginal numerical superiority and intense sociality where they carried on, among other things, a thriving, perhaps even intensified, ceremonial life. Although settlement significantly affected Aborigines' lives—miners consorted with Aboriginal women, purveyed methylated spirits, made use of Aboriginal labor, and generally heightened the dependence of Aboriginal people upon the mine field—the size of the white population, and related development, did not continue to expand. After a boom period, mining declined and most of the whites moved away. The few who remained did so partly because they had made an accommodation with a particular bush lifestyle and with Aboriginal people (some having taken Aboriginal women as long-term partners). By the postwar period, Native Affairs took the decision to develop Beswick Creek/Bamyili, and also Beswick itself, as Aboriginal settlements, partly because they would serve as living areas, training grounds, and above all, rural holding pens for Aborigines whom Katherinites and the authorities wished to keep from town.

Phyllis Winyjorrotj is locally recognized as principal traditional owner of Bamyili (Barunga) and Beswick by virtue of her being of Bagala clan. Phyllis was born at Maranboy, and with Sarah Andrews and their extended families, spent her early years there. Members of their families worked in a bakery and brewery and had extended the use of kinship terms to at least the principal storeman who was there for many years, Dan Gillen. Phyllis' father worked at Maranboy as a well-regarded police aide, accompanying police expeditions into Arnhem Land in the 1930s. Phyllis' grandfather Bamjuga had carried mail through the Katherine district. There was a family history of relative prominence and adaptability in the context of white settlement.

It was my good fortune that Phyllis took me under her wing at Barunga in 1976–1977. She and I call each other *jarmunggin*, ([cross-] cousin). She was painstaking in teaching me Jawoyn, and generous with her time, help, and the family contacts she extended to me. When I first went there, her brother was president of the Bamyili Town Council (but he passed away not long after I moved there). Because of the practice by Arnhem Landers of brother-sister avoidance (see Warner 1931, Maddock 1970, Cowlishaw 1982), which Phyllis strictly observed, she used to send me to him when she thought it would be useful to me to talk to him, but she would not come along herself. Her own large immediate family, her children and grandchildren, were welcoming. Phyllis has remained a widow since her husband, a Ngalkbon man, died many years ago.

As a young woman during the war, Phyllis went from Maranboy to

Mataranka with some members of her family. Her eldest son was born there. Like Sarah and others, she spent some time working around Katherine and experienced the disruption as well as the excitements of the war period, which she spent in a compound near Mataranka. After the war she moved with her family to early settlement locations and eventually the permanent site of Bamyili.

During the land claim, Phyllis talked about the effort involved in building up the new settlement at Bamyili, where much of the evidence was being taken: "My father been doing really hard work along [at] this place and my mother." Records concerning the founding of the Bamyili settlement shows that Phyllis' father threatened to leave at least once because he objected to decisions that were being taken by the superintendent. Aborigines at the settlement clearly regarded him as the head man for the Bamyili area, and it is notable that his resistance is recorded in settlement documentation.[4]

During the land claim, when Phyllis was asked where she would like to live, she replied, "Maranboy"—the area where she spent her early years. Despite her stated desire to move, she is still at Barunga today. Since her brother's death, she has been regarded as the central and senior person there because of her family attachment to the area. Although she is advised by younger people around her who are more directly involved in administering Barunga, she is often consulted and asked to go to meetings about most major developments and issues reviewed by the council. She also is on the executive of the Jawoyn Association, based in Katherine (as Julie and Sarah have been). Although she would be the first to say that it is proper that she should be consulted about all these matters, it is not hard to understand why—having been through the establishment of a settlement and subsequent changes culminating in the formation of a Local Government Council in 1986, concerns relating to the running of a cattle project at Beswick Station, two major land claims (the Katherine Area Land Claim and, more recently, another land claim on behalf of some Jawoyn people to former Gimbat Station northeast of Pine Creek, the southern part of the shaded area of Kakadu National Park; see map 1), and the setting up of Jawoyn Association and ringed around by resource, telecommunications, roads and other development proposals, and Barunga community consultations—she sometimes threatens, "This my last meeting. Can't go any more meeting after this."

In Phyllis' case—despite her own and others'understanding that her father's father, Bamjuga, originated from west of Pine Creek, and gradually became integrated through marriage, ceremonial activity, and the daily round of life into the southern Arnhem community gathered around Maranboy—a firmly established collective sense of clan-level connection to the Beswick/Barunga area, now at least attributed both to her father's father and her father, has conferred upon her all the trials as well as the recognition of authority. Hers is an unusual case in which Bagala clan identity may be said to have been modernized in the context of the development of the settlement. Not only does a sense of Bagala connection permeate the Beswick and Barunga area, for those who understand this kind of thing in clan terms, but the recognition of her family's prominence, which extends to many forms of structure and activity within the settlement, is even more widely shared across the generations. It also extends to Phyllis' family broadly speaking, not only to those who, like herself, are formally Bagala clanspeople. Any changes that may occur in the political life of the settlement will, in some ways, have to take into account the position of her family.

Of the forty-three Jawoyn *mowurrwurr* I was told about in the early 1980s, attachments to specific places, or even regional locations, could be confidently established for only a few. In only a limited number of cases, like those discussed, could one be fairly certain that clan identification with place was of long term, rather than a reembedding of *mowurrwurr* identity in place deriving from the significant relationship to the locality of individual *mowurrwurr* members during their lifetimes. An example is useful here.

A case that I came to understand as this kind of reinvesting of a clan name in place concerned an old man named Shorty, also called Jarlung (King Brown [snake]), of Diny'mi *mowurrwurr*. In travels around Eva Valley Station east of Katherine (see map 1), I was told that a striking hill called Gunyjangnekay (Mount Felix) was Diny'mi clan and belonged to Shorty. On other occasions, however, those who knew him best noted that he was *na-biral*. This term is applied to people from the far northern Jawoyn area who, unlike those farther south, did not circumcise, and on that account were known in this way, as was Shorty. This version of his origins seemed consistent with his self-accounts of considerable youthful experience around mine sites and other locations well to the north of Katherine. If Shorty originated from country far to the north, how could Gunyjangnekay be his clan place? Shorty himself did not consistently say that Gunyjangnekay was Diny'mi country.

My collecting of life histories eventually helped me to see that the reference to Diny'mi in regard to Gunyjangnekay focused upon Shorty himself, as an individual who was a member of that group, and not upon the clan as a whole. Strong association of him with Gunyjangnekay had arisen from his having camped in the area with certain members of another clan, called Barang, with whom he had had (and realized) an arrangement of marriage promise. In the apparent absence of any other, persisting identity at this place, it was identified with Diny'mi as a function of Shorty's membership of that clan combined with his occupancy of it. Rather than Diny'mi identity being inherent in place, as in the normative mythototemic scheme, there was every indication that the place had acquired this identity recently through Shorty's being in this place. Unusually for this area, a fairly detailed creator story attaches to Gunyjangnekay, of which the transparent meaningfulness (for the Jawoyn speaker) of the place-name (*gunyjang* [devil], *nekay* [trod]) is an indication.

Such processes of reembedding of clan-level identity in place may have always gone on in some form and been a dynamic source of revision, renewing clan-level attributions of country identity in terms of lived relationships to place. However, here change was clearly more thoroughgoing, and what had happened had to be seen in the context of widespread dissolution of clan-level systematization of country as a result of the thinning of lived experience of it. With the loosening of *mowurrwurr* from locality as a matter of collective identification had also come an attenuation of place-specific clan-level Dreaming associations. Although the best informed "old people" could supply a clan dreaming (usually one, sometimes two or several) for most or all known clans and considered such identifications a normative aspect of clan identity, there was variation concerning particular ones. Although this too might have long been the case, the notable fact was that even for those best-informed people, some clan-level Dreamings of this sort were not localized, despite the persistent feeling that they must be and that someone ought to know where. They remained part of the identity of the clan, the present membership of which could still be clearly defined by knowledgeable "old people," but with diminishing confidence, or quite variable accounts, concerning the location of many clan places.

Not surprisingly, all those clan-level identifications with places that appear to be collective and (unlike Shorty's case) of longer term are found with regard to clans with members still living, or members whose life spans overlapped significantly with those of people now living.[5] The general decline of this level of relationship to and knowledge of places was, as one might expect, generationally strongly differentiated.

At the time of the Katherine Land Claim, relatively few people had wide-ranging and fluent knowledge of clan identities; among the Jawoyn, these were all older people. And of those, an even smaller number had vital concepts of clan-level identities as a systematization of the relationships of people to country, in other words, of clans as *territorial*. The extent to which older people saw clans as territorial tended to vary directly with their way of life in their younger years, particularly with the experience of having walked or, in some cases, particularly for men, also having ridden on horseback, over a considerable range of country. Age alone was not necessarily associated with such close bodily experience of country. Two of the oldest Jawoyn women at the time of the land claim lived at Beswick and were "mothers" (mother and mother's sister) of two men with wide-ranging knowledge of country and a strong propensity to identify places in clan terms, Peter Jatbula and Sandy Barraway. Both men had experience of country gained in the course of stock working from "young time" in the northern Jawoyn area and in the course of long-distance footwalking with family in small "mobs" while not in the immediate employ of whites—on one prolonged occasion, when they fled up the Katherine River after the Japanese bombing of the town in 1942. In contrast, the two old women—their surviving mothers—having lived closely around Maranboy and then, postwar, at Beswick, are unfamiliar with wider stretches of country and do not identify country, near or remote, in clan terms. They have an easy familiarity with the use of clan names as social identifiers, both among Jawoyn people and among other Arnhem people, such as Rembarrnga, with whom they have long resided at Beswick. They are uncertain, however, of the places and locations associated with most of them, including the area they presume to be associated with their own clan, Bertbert. They think it is quite distant from Beswick and high up on the Katherine River, an extremely general indication.

Clan organization remains an ordering of country, and of people in relation to it, to those for whom the grounds of this order were made sensible through experience. What remains more intact for them than for others is the feeling for differentiation of the landscape and of the inherence of Dreaming and personhood in particular places. Such experience is the ground for their feeling for, and insight into, a vaster reality that Aborigines call the "Law." Though the Law is greater than people and in some ways (as Myers 1986 has emphasized) treated as external to ordinary forms of interaction, it constitutes a ground of human subjectivity in this particular clan-level form of ties between persons and place, giving rise to a feeling for a differentiated landscape with multiple anchoring points that can be felt and dealt with in practice as clan constructs. Stanner (1965:231) depicted the feeling for completeness and the disposition to take this conjunction as a clue or a symptom of some vaster reality when he figured the reaction of an Aborigine asked *what* is in the place, his country, that his father had showed him, and his father before him: "We do not know. *Something* is there. Like my spirit . . . ; like my brother; like my Dreaming. . . . Something is there; we do not know what; *something*."

The anchoring of subjectivity in the linkage among person, place and Dreaming—not only as a matter of one's own sense of self, but also as a general scheme of reference—is rendered vivid through presence and founded in close experience in differentiated country with similarly oriented others. The firm setting of this conceptual and emotional foundation seems to make it possible for Aboriginal people who have lived this to continue to experience themselves as part of distant places and milieux, despite considerable remove; thus, the familiar image of the Aboriginal person who is possessed by the feeling "My country!" and also "My uncle!" "My granny country!" and so on, though miles and a mode of life away (see Munn 1970:158 who writes of the mode of experiencing the world in which ancestral objectifications are "constantly recharged with intimations of self"). But this feeling for continuing psychic presence in distant places, on a basis of sometimes long-term absence rather than simply presence (contra Giddens 1990:101–102) can only be felt once it is established as a ground of subjectivity. If it is not established early in the individual's formation through close experience, not just of the country but of it in the terms of differentiated human relationship (one's own and others'), to it, attachment must be psychically on a different basis.

Though Sarah Andrews' children know their father's clan was Derkorlo, there has never been, on anyone's part, a clear sense of its location; nor is their mother's Wetji country, at least clearly locatable, familiar to them. One of their strongest senses of attachment is to the King River area, between Barunga and Katherine town (see map 1), where Sarah worked for many years and where they lived as children.

For Fanny Birlamjam, the clan-level person-place-Dreaming link remained experientially significant, despite the indeterminacies I have discussed arising from her own early separation from what she continued to consider her country. But for younger Jawoyn, who have lived always in the shadow of Katherine and under settlement or town conditions, concepts of clan territoriality exist in different ways and in many instances are no longer recognizably clan-level identifications, though they may have arisen from one or another aspect of clan-level identity. A few—typically, older children of the well-traveled, former footwalkers—are able to identify their *own* clan and one or a very small number of places with which they believe their parents to have been closely associated.[6] That is, they know of places through family ties, rather than through experience as a person of a certain mytho-totemic substance, like Fanny. Frequently, too, place is generalized and designated in terms of the most salient or proximate European settlement site or name of a pastoral property.[7]

In my experience, those people most disposed to talk of country in clan terms do not ordinarily do so in terms of a perimetric model, that is, in terms of boundaries at which one clan's area ends and another's begins. They tend instead to identify clans in terms of their focal places (sometimes extending these to include a range of country).

What seems to have undergone great attenuation is not some disposition to bound clan areas, for which I see no clear evidence, but people's sense of the distinctness and differentiation of places in the landscape as ongoing anchor points of human and dreaming activity and subjectivity. The semiotic character of places and the extent to which places continue to be distinguished vary with the nature of human relationship to larger areas, including settler occupation. One notices, with some exceptions, a general attenuation of the storied aspect of country, alongside some continuing differentiation (and naming) of places in the landscape. Places now known as named country are not randomly distributed: many of them tend to be along watercourses or have some significant relation to settler roads and sites. Others are not along "whitefella roads" (strategically situated with respect to water sources), but along "walking tracks"—"blackfella roads"—that Aborigines used to travel cross-country, to and from settler destinations.

Older Jawoyn people, talking of the foot-walking past, report that their elders, after having spent time in the bush away from settler sites and therefore away from large concentrations of Aboriginal (and other) people, would say, "*Nga-beng-gapony-jiyn!*" (I'm tired of this!)[8] And they would propose going to Maranboy or other locations, ostensibly for rations and tobacco, but undoubtedly also because Aborigines gathered in such places. Mobility through country became more focused on certain places and trajectories, largely ones of settler development (see Stanner 1958); many other places were frequented less and less.

Transformation of the meanings and purposes of traveling around is reflected not only in the attenuation at many places of Dreaming story, but also by the absence or thinning of a sense of connection among places as part of a Dreaming track. Although some older Aborigines have a sense of linkages among places in this mode, in many cases places are principally related for them as locations along roads and walking tracks, with "Dreaming" associations having become much attenuated since the settler presence.

Similarly, some change in the conceptualization of places must be seen in contemporary practices of applying place-names to very broad areas—for example, up and down a lengthy stretch of river or to all of a given section of country. Although I assume that place-names may have been used in this inclusive way before, especially perhaps with reference to certain kinds of topography (such as vast, seasonally marshy uplands north of Katherine), I also assume that the contemporary extent of such usage reflects a reduction in the differentiation of named places and of connections among them. I assume that the identification of particular topographic features as focal aspects of Dreaming at specific places (compare the specificity with which parts of the emu's body are identified as particular features of places around Wetji Namurrgaymi) has also declined. Such reductions are forms of homogenization of place within larger areas (some of which are still relatively well known and actively frequented) and reflect the contraction of Aborigines' reliance upon places differentiated in this way as their total life-world and the expansion of place-linked dependence upon outsiders.

Despite the general lack of connection among places as storied, Aboriginal witnesses in the Katherine Land Claim nevertheless evinced a clear sense of custodial responsibility for particular places as Dreaming, and for certain ones more than others. Areas around major settlement sites, such as Maranboy, are dense with places meaningful to Aborigines mythologically and as well-known camping places. Similarly, there were places of significance near the Katherine Gorge. Frequently, an element of attachment to places *as Jawoyn*, and as sentient in their Jawoyn identity, was explicit here. Peter Mitchell said about looking after Wun.gurri, a Bluetongue Dreaming on the Katherine River near the Gorge, "We got to talk—tell something—help from him. Him understand my language. That's where he going to be, that water—rainbow" (KALCT 1982:706).

Explicit in Peter's words is the concept that the place is sentient, that it will listen to appeals made to it in Jawoyn, the language of this place, and that this kind of relationship (between people and Dreaming place) must be invoked to get "help" from the place in the form of fish and other bounty.

Witnesses in the land claim also emphasized a practice protective of persons: keeping newcomers to country from harm by watering their heads. Margaret Katherine recalled her father having done this on a weekend trip to the Gorge for Cyril Cox, his employer at Katherine Stores. She represented him as having said, "Cyril, I have to put some water on your head so that the rainbow don't smell you and you get sick" (KALCT 1982:754).

Jawoyn people spoke of some places as still dangerous and capable of releasing enormous destructive power if disturbed. The most feared places of this kind are within Gimbat Station, quite distant from Katherine (see Merlan 1991a). Bolung, the rainbow serpent, was also mentioned as awesome at a number of places. And at some places that had been extensively frequented by whites there arose some of the same conceptions of change in the rainbow's powers as mentioned in chapter 2. Peter Mitchell on a few occasions spoke of the "freeing" of certain places from the rainbow and its destructive power. Of Edith Falls, he said, "That's free, Edith. Been bad before. . . . He been very dangerous, that place." When counsel asked if the place was still dangerous or not dangerous," Peter replied, "He's all right now. All the tourists can just go there, have a bath. He won't touch them; he's gone. They been putting gelignite; army been putting gelignite. Bomb kill him" (KALCT 1982:707).

In reference to the rainbow presence in deep waters in the Katherine Gorge, an old woman named Queenie Morgan said, "Anybody go, even Katherine Gorge. Him been danger, that water. Now this time white man bogey [swim]. They got boat, everything" (KALCT 1982:727).

Places are most differentiated, and their features most intimately known, in areas that were intensively occupied and traveled. For some decades past, such intensive occupation tended to be related to white settlement. Clan-level identification of places has become attenuated: that system of categories arose and was sustained under conditions of high mobility across wider stretches of country. But, as these last examples show, profoundly felt significance still inheres in many places despite the general trends of disconnection of places from each other and the attenuation and simplification of country as storied.

Names

In a study of interaction between Cree Indians and whites in a small Canadian plains town, Braroe (1975:123–131) shows that continuity in Cree naming practices is not only central to distinctively Indian concepts and the practical constitution of personhood, but is an aspect of social practice that Indians conceal from whites. Braroe considers this "covering" of difference as one of the ways in which Indians reduce their visibility to and negative valuation by whites, who deny any continuity in Indian customs.

Stanner (1937:301) has written that Aboriginal names "are thought to partake of the personality which they designate" and that they are "verbal projections of an identity." For Aboriginal people of the Katherine area, including Jawoyn, major forms of naming persons were place linked, and thus an important aspect of spatial practice. As part of change in socio-spatial practices more broadly, patterns of naming have changed significantly and are still changing.

The concept of the identification of an individual with his or her place of birth is designated *mangal* in Jawoyn. This word means "*woomera*" (spear-thrower). Because the *woomera* is so strongly emblematic of male productive activity, hunting, this may suggest genderization of the concept of place of birth. It may metaphorically imply linkage through the father or be based on the expectation that one's birthplace coincide with notions of one's "father's country" in clan terms. However, alternatively interpreted as metonym (as suggested by personal appellations of a form beginning with *bam-* [head], illustrated below), the usage may imply projection from the womb, or the launching of the child into the world. In any event, it is common for older Jawoyn people to bear the names of their places of birth. Sandy Barraway was named after his birthplace in Katherine Gorge. Fanny Birlamjam was so called after her birthplace, Birlamjam, north of Beswick Station.

Another common Jawoyn pattern of naming amounted to a kind of snapshot of the moment and circumstance of birth at an even lower level, that of the surrounding vegetation. Births, of course, took place on the ground, and (usually, no doubt) in some chosen, protected location. Many older people were and are known by the generic name of the particular kind of tree or shrub near or under which they were born. Thus, a woman named Topsy Stevens was Ngal-Warawitj (billy goat plum); Nipper Brown's older brother Paddy was Na-Danak (commemorating his birth under a particular tree of this kind, common in the Gimbat uplands). Often, too, people are known by a compound birth name consisting of the relevant gender prefix, the word "*bam*" (head) which alludes to the birth or physical emergence of the child, and the term designating the plant or tree near which the birth occurred. Thus, one man born near a plant from the roots of which red dye can be extracted *(Haemodorum coccineum)* is known as Na-bam-mulupirndi (red dye head). The noun stem *bam* may also be productively combined with place-names, to designate "born at such-and-such place" (e.g., Na-bam-Worreluk). With the birth of children in hospital now nearly universal, no younger people are known by designations of this sort. The use of these patterns of naming presupposes more or less bush conditions of birth, as well as indigenous language proficiency.

A few names of this pattern, however, make explicit the condition of birth in a non-indigenous or outsiders' setting. The giving of these names indexes a period transitional between the autonomy of the bush birth and the hospitalization characteristic of contemporary birthing. One man who was born on one of the Katherine River peanut farms, near the rows of peanut plantings, was known as Na-bam-binat (peanut head), the last part based on the English word "peanut."

As the English model of first name and surname became more widely adopted in the postwar period, some older Jawoyn people began to use as surname the name of their place of birth (e.g., Sandy Barraway). Other examples are the name Nancy Marndarrpa, the last the name of the rocky area near which the old Katherine airstrip was built; and Nancy Manyala, where Manyala is the name of a place near Eva Valley homestead. Many Aborigines used to camp in these areas, and so births also occurred there. People known in this way may also be called by a form of name, consisting (for Jawoyn people) of simply the appropriate gender prefix (*na-* for a man, *ngal-* for a woman), and the place-name: Na-Barraway, Ngal-Manyala, and so on.

Once places in the landscape began to be known by English names, or sometimes by both English and Aboriginal place-names, some Jawoyn people were given foreign place-of-birth names. The innovation consists in the explicit designation by a name in a nonnative language. Many such names, however, sound like native-language words and indeed were incorporated into the speech of Aboriginal people. With some knowledge of places and past Aboriginal movements, one can establish their English-language origin. Such names, in general, tend to have an auxiliary character: they are applied to people who also have standard, first name–last name combinations. For example, one woman is known as Ngal-Gadin, after the English word "Garden." The place commemorated, otherwise known as Joe's Garden, was a location to which women were moved during the Second World War period by Welfare from the nearby tin mining center at Maranboy, where it was feared there was too much "interference" with native women and too much illicit grogging. The woman who is known as Ngal-Gadin otherwise has a standard English-sounding first name, Violet, and a surname, Smith, adopted from "old Jack Smith," a miner around Yeuralba (Mt. Todd) and elsewhere in the Katherine region, who employed her and her husband. Another name of this kind is that of her daughter, Ngal-Wulpum, after the English word "wolfram." The woman known by this name was born at a wolfram (tungsten) mining site, and also is known by a combination of English first and second names.

Commonly, one of a child's relatives—often but not necessarily the mother—would identify the child well before its arrival, in the form of some unusual natural phenomenon. Julie Williams told me that, when she was walking around in the bush north of Katherine, her eldest daughter was recognized as a crocodile by her father, Merengbet, as he wrestled the animal out of the water.[9] The specific event, however, leaves a trace in the form of the commemoration of the relation between the person and the place of appearance.

There were also death names, or necronyms, of place. Among the Jawoyn, as among most Aborigines, the recently dead are not referred to by name. One way of creating a term of reference to a person recently dead was to prefix *-mulu-* to the name of the place where he or she had died, the term preceded by the appropriate gender prefix. Thus, a man who had died at Yurmikmik was Na-mulu-yurmikmik, a woman who had died at Yerreljirriyn, Ngal-mulu-yerreljirriyn.

Today, some Aboriginal people of the region have surnames that commemorate the locale in which they grew up or lived for a long time. Though a few people are surnamed "Katherine," the use of this as a surname is not widespread: if the name were used as widely as it now might be, it would have no differentiating value.[10]

Many older Jawoyn (and other Aborigines of the Katherine area) at some point in their lives adopted, or had applied to them, the surname of a regular employer or boss (who sometimes also was a short- or long-term partner for a woman), to yield a combination of first name and European surname. Some older people have English first names, commonly given to Aborigines in that past, that would rarely have been used as first names of white people. These names were possibly suggested to Aboriginal parents for their children, or given directly in everyday usage, by whites. Illustrating such a combination of typically Aboriginal first name and employer's surname was the English name of an old northern Jawoyn woman, Topsy Stevens. Stevens was the name of one of her long-term employers, who ran a butcher shop in Pine Creek. Other commonly found, "Aboriginal-sounding" first names (even if not all seem as condescending as "Topsy," and some might occasionally have been given to a white child), include Lulu, Molly, Fanny, Kitty, Maggie, Rosie, Ruby, Elsie, Magnolia, Maudie, perhaps Violet, for women; and Tiger, Sambo, Tarpot, Pannikin, Nipper, Nuggett, Pharlap (a famous Australian racehorse), and a few names of the famous and despotic, including Kaiser, Hitler, and Mussolini, for men. Such names are also a general indication of the age of their bearers: most are in their fifties, sixties, or older. Nowadays, such names typical of an earlier era are rarely given by Aboriginal parents to their children.

In the early period, the relation between (what those accustomed to standard naming patterns in English-speaking countries would see as) first and last name was not always preserved as names were bestowed or adopted. Sarah Andrews' first husband had worked for Clyde Fenton, a famous flying doctor, who used to land his plane on Katherine's main street. Sarah's husband's English name was George. In time, as Fenton's assistant, he became known, in full, as Doctor Fenton George, a name which he evidently used proudly and that had some of the honorific quality of a title.[11]

Some of the practices described above show the ways in which naming constantly evoked place and was an aspect of the constitution of personal identity in relation to place. Centralized and less mobile living has not been conducive to the retention of many of these ways of naming, and there have been changes in ways of manifesting personal specificity through naming.

Nowadays, creativity is evident in many Aboriginal parents' naming of their children, and some names sound rarefied or downright unusual: Shay-Leigh, Martika, Zarak, Nevron, Demetrius, Finicole, Deleneon (cf. Braroe 1975:124, who remarks on Cree preference for exotic-sounding English names, and Mencken's 1947:523 discussion of American blacks' "reaching out for striking and unprecedented names"). Some parents create alliterative names for a set of siblings, so that all the children's names, for instance, begin with "M," the initial letter sometimes being that of one of the parent's names. Some go farther, creating whole sets of alliterative first *and* last names.[12] Such patterns are of course not unique to Aboriginal people and at one level at least represent the adoption by Aborigines of patterns they have observed in use among whites. But at the regional level, such patterns as this have come to be typical or at least common among Aborigines and thus may to some degree be a new kind of expression of distinctively Aboriginal identity, as well as specific family identity. Interesting, too, is that older children and young adults often write out their full given names on the walls of houses, sometimes individually but also, typically, in family and friendship groupings of those "running" together at any given time, followed by a date or other sign-off: "Daniel James John Roberts, Clifton Wayne Lippo, Clarissa Levina Wesley, Mary Anne Baruwei, Only 1992!" These are young people's inscriptions.

Whereas many kinds of personal names were aspects of personal relationships with place (and also Dreaming), earlier schemes of place-linked naming have largely given way to wider use of more standard English patterns. Adults of the Katherine area now almost universally have first and second names, some second names having been adapted from earlier common patterns of place-commemorating forms of naming, generally (for Jawoyn people) reflecting an individual's place of birth or of long-term residence. Some of those names are now transmitted in families (for example, Barraway is now a family surname, whereas it is one of the Aboriginal names of the father of this family) and so no longer express attachment to the place specific to that individual. Whether Aboriginal people will continue to understand such names as signaling ties to place or whether they will become emptied of such significance remains to be seen. Whatever else happens, it would seem that this form of surnaming will not predominate as long as many families prefer to adopt standard-sounding English surnames and Aboriginal names become Anglicized. The preference among parents now seems to be to give a child one, and now frequently two, first names, and I have already noted that many of these show a flair for distinctive naming of children individually and for giving patterned names that distinguish people as members of what, through such patterning, are increasingly constituted as familiar "family" structures. Though there is variety in naming patterns, a significant shift has occurred from forms of naming that index relationships with place toward naming of persons as the creative marking of individual and collective identities largely freed of specific reference to place.

Settling Down

Evidence taken during the Katherine Land Claim provides some insights into a profound social and cultural demarcation between those people who had lived in some form of traveling mode when younger, moving from one camp to another in ever-shifting mutual definition of place and people, and those who had grown up in more fixed locations. For these latter, place tended to be defined much more clearly in terms of a central attachment to a home base; and emergent characteristics of the person were shaped much more by the institutional possibilities that place offered. Other differences appeared to pattern along these lines. Those who had lived a life or at least some formative years of close, foot-walking experience of country tended to speak of country in ways that narratively modeled that experience, telling stories that involved the recounting of movement from place to place, while those who had not spoke of their relationship to country more in terms of visitation for specific purposes. Those who had lived the traveling mode of life tended to speak of knowledge as gained from observation, imitation, and internalization of ways of doing things from encounters structured by the differences in status between authoritative senior and submissive junior, rather than from explicit pedagogical exchange between them. On the other hand, those who had lived in a more sedentary way around settlements and other centers showed a greater tendency to extend the notion of culture to both black and white domains, to produce relativized objectifications of "blackfella" and "whitefella" culture, and generally to endow "culture" with an abstract quality that makes both black and white forms seem equally teachable.[13] Finally, those who had lived in traveling mode showed little disposition to treat the possible outcome of the land claim, which they spoke of as "getting country back," as separable from a return to living in that country.

Some Aboriginal people, as we saw in chapter 2, lived in traveling mode around the town: in those times, and under prevailing conditions, life in and around town was not stationary. Needing the support of an employer to live, Julie's family moved from place to place. Since Aboriginal people and family were dispersed over work locales, sustaining contact with them, as well as getting bush foods, required movement. Julie's family had nothing and accumulated nothing; the only resources on which they could rely were the direct return for a period of labor generally already performed. The interdependence associated with this way of living helped support the value of immediate proximity to family over any recommendations made to Julie's relatives—for example, that she and her age-mates should go to school. Yet Julie did see the inside of a school and absorbed from the experience a sense of its importance for her own daughters. After Julie married, she and her husband Peter walked around country more distant from Katherine toward the Edith River system (see map 1), and Julie gained familiarity with it in a way that built on her experience around town.

Conversely, rural living did not necessarily involve high levels of mobility, especially following the growth of compounds and institutions of the postwar period. After the upheavals of the war years, Phyllis' family seems to have lived relatively fixed in the Beswick and Bamyili areas. This is not surprising, given the family's sense of attachment to this stretch of country, in which two major settlements grew up immediately after the war.

With the more mobile lives of Sarah, Fanny, Peter, Julie, and others, we may compare the self-account given in evidence by Raymond Fordimail. At the time of the land claim, he was thirty-eight years old (slightly younger than Julie). Raymond was aware of his chronological age; Julie does not tend to give her age in such terms (although she had a greater degree of familiarity with such age reckoning than did, for example, Fanny Birlamjam). Ray had then the status of a prominent man at Barunga and in Katherine and was increasingly in the public eye as a "Jawoyn leader." The task of representing Aboriginal people, and Jawoyn in particular, often fell to him, particularly during acrimony and media coverage leading up to the land claim. Asked to summarize his life's history during the land claim, Ray said:

> I was born at Maranboy and at the age of five or six years I went to Tandangle school. There was a bad water supply so we moved into Bamyili. I went to school and left school at about fifteen years of age and started work with the government, welfare. I was working there for about five or six years, then left and went to work for Shepherd's sawmills at Maranboy, near the police station. I worked there for a while, about four years, and then came back to Bamyili and worked for the Department of Aboriginal Affairs. . . . I worked for the Department of Aboriginal Affairs, carting garbage around the place.
>
> *Counsel:* Whereabouts?
>
> *Ray:* Here at Bamyili. Then I was employed as an Aboriginal community adviser. That was about three years.
>
> *Counsel:* How long did you have the tractor driver job for?

Ray: Quite a while, but I don't remember whether it was five or six years.
Counsel: Then your employment with DAA was for four years?
Ray: Yes, then I resigned and worked for the community council as executive officer.
Counsel: How long was that for?
Ray: That was about four to five years.
Counsel: Your title as executive officer, what did that mean in terms of Bamyili?
Ray: It was a sort of accountant clerk position, I think, and then I resigned and moved into Katherine. I was president for about three years—president of the town council.
Counsel: When was that?
Ray: That was from 1975 to 1979. (KALCT 1982:782–783)

Ray's responses show an easy familiarity with institutional structures and with Western measurements, which emphasize the conceptualization of experience in terms of fixed chronology (rather than, as is the tendency in Julie's account in chapter 2, upon persons in relation to place as an experiential frame). The nature of his answers contrasts strikingly with the responses of Dick Gararr. Dick was enough older than Raymond so that he was bypassed in the postwar intake into the settlement school; in fact, he was already a big lad when the army created the compound at Joe's Garden to get Aboriginal people away from Maranboy in 1942. It is perhaps relevant to seeing the differences between them in Aboriginal institutional rather than solely chronological terms that Dick was married for a time to Raymond's mother when she was relatively old and he a younger man with some possibility of perhaps gaining a younger wife in the future. Dick responded to questions from counsel for the claimants without elaboration, showing in his answers a very differently oriented personal history from Raymond's:

Now Dick. Dick, where were you born?
DG: Back of Eva Valley.
When you were a young fellow where were you living?
DG: Maranboy.
Where was your first job?
DG: Joe Garden.
Any name for that?
DG: Yes, Guymanluk.

What sort of work were you doing there?
DG: Growing up vegetables.
Were you still single then?
DG: Yes, I was a boy then.
What did you do after Guymanluk?
DG: I went and got a job at the sawmill.
Where was the sawmill?
DG: At Maranboy.
After the sawmill where did you go?
DG: Bamyili.
What sort of work at Bamyili—any?
DG: Housing.
What sort of work was that?
DG: Fellow out there got a contract putting these up.
Referring to the building we are in at the moment—or are you talking about the things out the back?
DG: No, this one and the supermarket. I worked with Bob Nolan.
After housing where did you go then?
DG: Other housing out to Beswick.
After Beswick where did you go?
DG: Into Katherine.
Whereabouts in Katherine were you staying?
DG: Working at the council, labor.
How long did you do that for?
DG: For about a year.
What did you do after that?
DG: Went back to Bamyili again.
What did you do back at Bamyili?
DG: Work.
What sort of work?
DG: Hygiene.
What sort of work is hygiene? What do you do for hygiene?
DG: Picking up tins and papers and all that. (KALCT 1982:782–784]

A concise account was given by Robert E. Lee, who was for some years Barunga town clerk. Between Barunga and Katherine schools, Robert had gone through year ten. He is now much involved in tourist enterprise development at Eva Valley, is on the Jawoyn Association Executive, and has been chairman of the Nitmiluk National Park Management Board. He and Ray were about the same age. His father had been a white miner at Maranboy. Asked to tell about himself and his part in town management, he periodized his life briefly in the following categories: "Born here [Bamyili], grew up here, went to school here, start work here." (KALCT 1982:797).

Larry Ah Lin's account showed a different, but still highly institutionally influenced, life history. His extended travel outside the Katherine region and his familiarity with world geography set him apart from most of the claimants. Larry was about fifty-five at the time. His mother had lived at Manbulloo and on the Katherine fringe. Asked for his life story, he recounted that he was taken away from his mother at about five years of age as a "half-caste," along with his sister. He went to school in Alice Springs, then worked in central Australia and studied in Sydney. He was later employed in a variety of jobs in different parts of Australia. He enlisted in the army, at Brisbane, in 1950, serving, as he said, "five years with the regular army and eighteen months operational with the spearhead battalion, third, first, and the second—eighteen months operational in Japan and Korea" (KALCT 1982:793–794).

Correlated with these different forms of experience are noticeable differences in the way witnesses spoke about place. Those who moved over the country in close relationship to it, walking and shifting camp, frequently structure their accounts of themselves and their personal histories in terms of movement over country that shows the same sort of sequencing typically found in some accounts of the travels of Dreamings over country. Sandy Barraway, asked where he went hunting and fishing as a young fellow, gave his answer as a narrative of travel among proximate places, reproducing the sequence one might easily follow in walking around this area:

> Bilkbilkbam [a plunge pool near the mouth of the Gorge], getting kangaroo, looking for sugarbag sometimes and porcupine. Go down to Nitmiluk [at what is now the Katherine Gorge's main tourist center, about three miles], fishing around there with wire spear . . . looking for goanna and turtle and anything like that. Camp one night there, maybe two nights looking for fish, goanna, sugarbag. Look around and maybe camp or something like that with a wire spear, camp two night or maybe three nights—no fishing line; fishing line today. Look around with a spear. Come back to Blue Tongue Dreaming [Wun.gurri, downstream from Nitmiluk], camp there four days; go down other place, anywhere. We used to go down to Jodetluk [Gorge camp, at the mouth of the Gorge] and camp over there sometimes; go back to Marlunba [junction of Maude Creek with the Katherine River, downstream from Wun.gurri] and camp maybe three days or one night, go down

Yerreljirriyn [slightly farther downstream], camping out there, killing kangaroo with a spear or goanna, like that, turtle, you know that crocodile. (KALCT 1982:812)

Raymond Fordimail had had some childhood experience of walking over country: he spoke of going "from Bamyili to Marlunba [Maude Creek junction with the Katherine River] through King River, and we camped there. There was a camp at Knuckey Junction and that is where we went from, pushing upstream" (KALCT 1982:912). It is unlikely that someone of Sandy Barraway's age and particular experience would talk about movement between such distant places as Bamyili and Marlunba without referring to other, intermediate places, as in Raymond's account (above). At another time, Ray discussed foraging, in terms of visits (mostly by vehicle) to places conceived of as good spots in the landscape, rather than in terms of their relationship to each other. His kind of account thus differs from Sandy's precisely in being grounded in a different experience of movement between and among places. Thus Ray's account of landscape is more often in terms of visits to discrete places, whereas in Sandy's account, places appear as a function of human movement through them, in which terms Sandy conceives of their relation to each other. Larry Ah Lin spoke of moving around in yet a different style, referring to his interest in prospecting and his "living off the land practically" (KALCT 1982:814) in that context.

Paralleling these experientially different formulations of country, concepts of knowledge and its transmission varied among the claimants, too. In the claim, counsel for the claimants frequently asked questions about teaching and learning, and about continuity of knowledge in general, insofar as it was part of their case that rights to country, and knowledge of country, had been transmitted to them from their Jawoyn forebears. But witnesses answered such questions in different ways. For the most part, older people relied upon two interrelated concepts. First, they implicitly assumed the largely informal acquisition through experience of the kind of knowledge they understood to be relevant, with the result that they sometimes refused suggestions put to them of anyone explicitly having taught them about certain things, such as about the nature of particular places. Second, they relied upon notions of typical relationship between senior and junior in which deference from the latter toward the former is expected, and there is little direct questioning: learning is expected to occur by observation and imitation.

Illustrating the consequences for their answers upon the first concept, learning through experience, is the exchange between counsel for the claimants and Peter Mitchell. After he had been asked about a number of specific places, he was asked, "Who taught you that those places belonged to Jawoyn?"

PM: Myself I know.
Did somebody tell you that?
PM: I know. I'm Jawoyn. My father Jawoyn; my mother Jawoyn; myself Jawoyn.
Did your father teach you any place-name?
PM: No, my father never teach me. (KALCT 1982:705)

Illustrating the second emphasis is what seemed to me a pointed remark made by Sarah Andrews. In answer to questions that constantly focused on who had "taught" her, she and many other witnesses had spoken with feeling about hunting, foraging, and collecting food from the land. Asked yet again about who had "taught" her to make artifacts, Sarah replied, "My grandmother been telling me 'You do this one, that one and that one now.' I used to be sit down quiet and watch my grandmother" (KALCT 1982:972). Sarah's answer politely and subtly rejected the assumption implicit in the stream of questions, that teaching amounts to a direct exchange and transmission of knowledge. Her answer instead was an insight into the importance, for her, of the instructional situation as a step toward coming to "know" by oneself or within oneself, sometimes expressed by these same Aboriginal people as a process of coming to *understand* (see Harris 1984).[14]

Raymond Fordimail and some other Aboriginal witnesses who had had experience of formal schooling found it easy to make a different move in answer to questions about teaching, talking of it as an explicit instructional dimension that can be applied both to European learning and to Aboriginal culture. The remarks of some older people like Sarah at least implied (as in her remarks quoted above) that Aboriginal and white instructional styles are quite different. Some of her other remarks showed that she held strong ideas about imitative learning by younger people from seniors as the preferred and appropriate learning style. Raymond, on the other hand, spoke as if teaching could be applied across Aboriginal and white content in the same manner. He assumed both were important, and both might be learned in a more or less formal manner:

I think it is very important that we should not stop teaching our kids our traditional culture and things and to cook kangaroo the proper way. Nowadays the kids come back from Kormilda [a college in Darwin]. They use a frying pan on an electric stove, and not the traditional way to cook. I think that is wrong. I feel we should teach our kids what to do out in the bush, how to make fires with a fire stick and to cook in the ground and that sort of thing, to use paperbark and things like that—traditional cooking. I think it is [also] important to get an education the white fellow way. There are some jobs these days you have to be qualified for. I think that is important also. What should be happening is that we teach our kids how to do things the traditional way, take them up to the ceremony when they get older, tell them what should be told to them and warn them not to talk about sacred business outside of the ceremony ground. (KALCT 1982:819).

Differences were also discernible among witnesses in their variable emphasis on the relation between content—on what it is important to know—and the conditions of its transmission. Peter Jatbula, who has only daughters, expressed a strong sense of the importance of gender division when asked about transmission of knowledge: "That's all up to Julie. If boy one, I learn him different way—getting kangaroos, goannas, lizards, and something" (KALCT 1982:823).

In a response that emphasized "two way" learning (see Harris 1990, McConvell 1991), Robert Lee said,

Firstly, white man school—that is all right for long term with our kids, administration and learning about European, health workers and all that sort of thing. They have to read and write and be able to understand the problems about administration of their own books and money affairs and that sort of thing. The other thing that is important to us is our survival and culture. We definitely don't want to lose the Aboriginal side. We want to still continue the Aboriginal ceremonies and survival—how to hunt and just live out in the bush—and to show our kids what our grandfather used to do or our father, what they used and so on. It is important to them [the children] both ways really. (KALCT 1982:817)

These examples show, not surprisingly, that exposure to Western schooling, gained in the postwar period marked by residential centralization and institutionalization for many of these people, brought greater familiarity with Western institutional structures. It was also associated with a tendency of claimants to talk, not as some older people often did, in terms of there being different cultures belonging to whitefellas and blackfellas respectively, but in objectifying and relativizing terms about the possible coexistence of these two cultures, generally viewed as discrete domains of content and action, but both ideally available to Aboriginal young people through instruction conceived as the direct transmission of knowledge between persons (see further chapter 7).

Especially the young and more sophisticated were able to talk about "getting country back" as a result of the land claim and about various long-range possibilities for perhaps going back to country, but perhaps starting a business, or both. As Geoffrey McDonald, a Barunga man of about Raymond's age, said, "You never know. My kids might want a place of their own. You never know. They might want to do something if we get a place like that. They might have their own farm" (KALCT 1982:821).

To people of Queenie Morgan's and Fanny Birlamjam's age and experience, however, the idea of "getting the land" was not to be dissociated from an idea of returning to the land to live as they had in their younger years. When asked whether it was "important for you to get that land," Queenie understood this not as the questioner meant it, as about the importance of gaining formal recognition of title. She took it to imply reestablishing practical ties to country and living as she had years before. But she could not envision a return to country under the conditions of her youth, especially without the social support of family. She therefore answered in a qualified way that indicated her personal conditions on any return: "Yes, might get him. Somebody come and stay with me, or I get him, as long as somebody come up and stay with me" (KALCT 1982:720). Of similar age and background to Queenie, Fanny also assumed that the prospect of "getting the land" meant returning to live on it as before. She even saw in questions put to her (by her own counsel) about where she intended to live, thinly veiled coercive suggestions that she must return from Jabiru, a town well to the north of Katherine where she had been staying, to what she had declared in the course of her answers to be her own Jawoyn country. Given how she understood the line of questioning, and her sense that in this situation, at least, it might be more or less possible to parry or mitigate omnipresent and immediate directiveness on the part of whites that she had often experienced, she tried to secure for herself the option of returning to Jabiru for the time being when the hearing was over: "I get'im swag first time, isn't it?" (I'll go get my bedroll first, won't I?) (KALCT 1982:74).

Larry Ah Lin's answer to the question about getting the land back was the most multiperspectival and the most complex of all in his expression of we/they and traditional/modern boundaries: "I'm happy for my people getting their own country back. I'd have to put it down; I'd say 75 per cent of it commercially is bad cattle country, 25 per cent of it is all right. It's going to take a lot of money to put it on a real production basis, if we're going in that way; but as far as people living there, it's all right. They can have a community of their own out there, like our ancestors. If I were a geologist, I'd jump at the chance. Thank you" (KALCT 1982:857).

Conclusions: Transformations in Spatial Practice

At the beginning of this chapter I focused upon the dissolution of clan-level organization. I also considered generational differences in people's relations to the landscape, particularly in terms of the widening obsolescence and vagueness in that specific kind of relationship to country. Later parts of the chapter showed that not only has change occurred in clan-level organization, but that change there is part of larger processes of shift in the ways that relationships with country are made and are personally and socially constitutive.

Discussion in this chapter of shift in the formation of identities at the level of "clan" has shown, I hope, how an earlier mode of conceiving landscape characterized by multiple centers, and practices anchoring person and Dreaming to such centers as points of subjective grounding became reorganized as a framework of places along settler travel routes and at sites of incipient development of a built environment. Aboriginal relations to place came increasingly to be defined by and reoriented to settler presence. Aboriginal people extensively redefined their daily lives and practices in relation to the place-dominating character of settler presence and projects, though without necessarily representing this to themselves as the grounds of their actions. This redefinition was accompanied by a reduction in density of places that Aborigines identified as such in the landscape, in the kinds of meanings associated with them, and by changes in Aborigines' sense of interrelationship among them, especially in the attenuation of the dreaming mode of making relationships to place and among places: by degrees of homogenization and dissolution of specificity within a formerly intensively socialized landscape. Names of prominent places, senses of their physical character, memories of travels through them, and more or less detailed concepts of human relationships to these places at "clan" and other levels—these are the traces of earlier patterns and styles of movement through country that Aboriginal people recount from their present locations in such places as Jodetluk, Katherine, and Barunga.[15]

It was convenient to begin this chapter with discussion of change in clan-level organization because this form of social categorization is, in some respects at least, easily perceptible, salient (to older Aborigines, at least, as well as outsiders), and organizationally neat (e.g., in the clarity of the recruitment principle). But in beginning with this, I do not endorse a Radcliffe-Brown model of Aboriginal social organization as a collection of clans, nor even identify the clan as a fundamental "structure." The more appropriate view, I believe, is that the regional specificity of forms of clan-level organization rests on more general conditions and social orientations that were common to Aborigines over the Australian continent. On these bases developed particular regional forms of organization that, as Sahlins (1976) would remind us, can never appropriately be seen as fully "determined" by particular material or other, apparently objective conditions. Nevertheless, there seems to be a view in the Aboriginalist literature that clan organization, with its bounding recruitment criterion, was common to better-watered areas, where resources were more predictable, as opposed to desert environments (where Myers 1986 remains the most revealing discussion of the multiple and comparatively open range of social criteria by which people conventionally claimed attachments to places in this more extreme ecological setting).

Despite some acceptance of this generalization, earlier views of clans as strictly socially and territorially bounded have been considerably revised (Hiatt 1965, Keen 1994), replaced by more sophisticated ways of understanding clan-level organization as a cultural form of human relationship with country. Realization has grown of the ways in which even clan territoriality (which Radcliffe-Brown took as a given of group difference) is less absolute and more highly negotiable than previously thought. It is part of a larger and diverse system of relationships grounded not in "land" as mere physical reality, but in a landscape interpreted and mediated through a complex and politicized mythopoeisis.

Recognition that even highly salient-seeming clan organization is only a particular kind of expression of relationships with country and is underpinned by much more general conditions and social orientations allows us to reject any simple equation of such organizational forms with "culture" and thus also to reject any view that Aboriginal culture "falls apart" when clan-level organization dissipates. The conditions and orientations that underpinned it have complex continuities in, for example, the way that people like Julie "found" their children at places, the naming of people after birthplaces, and even in very ordinary socio-spatial dispositions, such as the ease many Katherine Aborigines display in sitting on the ground and not feeling themselves out of place. However, the dissolution of clan-level organization *is* a symptom of a much more general process: changes in the form of life such that landscape recedes in importance as an experiential medium. From being a primary medium of personal and social reproduction, human relationships with it have become less immediate, less complete, and much less a primary source of imaginative life.

And this brings us back to the beginning of this chapter: to the recognition that the dispositions in terms of which clan-level organization was lived have become attenuated and changed as experiential remove from country has deepened. Much remains distinctive in Aboriginal ways of relating bodily to places, despite the advanced dissolution of previously highly articulated forms of place-based organization. These, however, were clearly central to the way in which Aborigines constructed a sense of regionality. Along with their attenuation, the sense of landscape has become disjoint and reduced in intensity; and some areas where Aboriginal people know their forebears to have lived are now practically unexperienced by people of today.

What have been some of the implications for people? For older individuals, such as Fanny Birlamjam, the feeling-complexes and assumptions that underpinned clan-level organization were still vital and personally felt as inherent, despite years of absence. Even in her receding experience of country and her uncertainties Fanny always unhesitatingly and feelingly spoke of Wetji as *lerr-ngaku* (my country), neither historicizing nor relativizing her relationship to it.

Younger witnesses in the land claim hearings, in contrast, were able to produce a discourse of possibility concerning their occupancy of country in a way that people like Fanny were not inclined to do. Their sense of country had been shaped at least as much within a framework of developing Western institutional influences as in some awareness of the socio-spatial experience of their elders. Implicitly, one of the dimensions that shaped their discourse was recognition of "land" as utility, as a potentially productive force external to them that they could "do something with," even if this were limited to expressing an interest in going back there to live. Like Fanny, many older people could not recognize any pressures or incentives toward the production of such discourse. Younger people, in contrast, could to some extent relativize relationships to country and, since country was no longer embedded within an imaginative life-world, could abstract and objectify it as a possible element in a way of life under construction.

Four

Tribes and Town

THIS CHAPTER is concerned with shifts in socio-spatial identities in relation to the town area of Katherine. Processes of change can be shown to have occurred over a period of decades as Aboriginal people converged upon the town from different hinterlands, building and intensifying social relationships with others already there.

In the last chapter, I focused on relationships to hinterlands north and east of the town at the level of "clan." While such relatively small-scale identities as "clan" are one important level of Aboriginal relationship to country, they are not the only one, as the omnipresence in the last chapter of a wider notion of "Jawoyn" identity will have suggested.

In this chapter, I look at changes in relation to the town largely in terms of socio-territorial identities of this more inclusive sort, widely known to non-Aborigines as "tribe."[1] I think that much confusion has existed, in popular and anthropological conceptions, about the nature of this level of identification, and a portion of this chapter is devoted to discussion of its character in the Katherine region.

The chapter also undertakes to examine similarities and differences among popular, anthropological, and Aboriginal representations and practices of identity at this level by focusing on the issue of "tribe" as this came to preoccupy a CSIRO agronomist and amateur ethnologist, Walter Arndt who, discerning that change was occurring, interested himself in the relations of Aboriginal people to the Katherine area in the postwar period.

Arndt's material has been important to my own understanding of the situation on two counts. First, it is the only substantial historical evidence concerning the distribution of Aboriginal social identities around Katherine in the early postwar period. Second, in some ways his understanding of the situation participates in ideas that informed both popular and early anthropological views of Aboriginal social organization and therefore serves to highlight some of the conceptual problems involved in understanding these dimensions of Aboriginal social identity and issues concerning the ways in which change may occur. I will show that Arndt's notion of tribe as a fixed group rather than as a way of formulating social identity restricted his understanding of the kinds of change taking place among Aboriginal people in relation to the town. I attempt to give a perspective upon these changes more in keeping with my understanding of this level as a way of making identities rather than as bounded social forms, both by consideration of what is presupposed by Aborigines' identifications of persons and places as "Jawoyn," "Wardaman," and the like and by exemplifying how these identifications play a role in the lives of individuals through whom change occurs.

Arndt's Discovery

Walter Arndt came to Katherine after the Second World War, serving as experimental agronomist for CSIRO from 1948 to 1959. A Queenslander of German extraction and scientific bent, he took great interest in the archaeology, rock paintings, and Aboriginal prehistory of the Katherine area. He investigated all of these things with the help of Aboriginal people—particularly certain older Aboriginal men—who after the war lived and worked at the CSIRO station at the southern end of town.

It was in this camp that Julie Williams spent much of her childhood. And it is through the information that Walter Arndt gleaned from people in this camp, as well as by reinterpreting this through the self-accounts of people like Julie, that we can trace the shifts in Aboriginal identity that were taking place in relation to the town area. One of Arndt's most knowledgeable informants was Julie's mother's father, a man named Nolgoyma. Arndt became heir to forms of Nolgoyma's understandings of Aboriginal identities and places in a way no one else did, because he was the only person posing questions of a certain kind during the 1940s and 1950s.

In seeking to gain information from Aboriginal informants concerning the Katherine district's numerous rock paintings and stone artifacts (of which he made a considerable collection), Arndt found that he made "disappointing" progress with informants from the CSIRO camp who identified themselves as of Djauan (Jawoyn) tribe,[2] even though locally the latter were reputed to be the Aborigines of the town area and had been identified as such by no lesser authorities than Spencer (1914), Elkin (1964), and others. Arndt eventually found that "specific questions could be answered by a few individuals who claimed to be Tagoman people and the rightful heirs to the district"—of whom Nolgoyma was the recognized elder.[3]

One of Arndt's purposes in pursuing his work around Katherine then became to present adequate evidence, and have this recognized by academics, for Tagoman (my spelling, Dagoman) as the people of the Katherine area. From his personal papers, it is clear that he wrote many drafts of a paper quaintly entitled "The Recognition of the Previous Existence, Industry, Mythology and Art of the Tagoman Tribe in the Katherine District, N.T." He thought of his findings as a "discovery" (at least in relation to the writings of Spencer and Elkin), but this sense was rendered somewhat problematic at the local level by his recognition that some Aboriginal people continued to regard themselves and others as Dagoman. What was a discovery to him, was not to them.

Arndt noted that one couple, among the twenty "members" of the tribe he identified at CSIRO and Manbulloo Station, were "raising a family of four or five who have little prospect of finding Tagoman partners." He did not suggest what might happen if and when they found *other* partners. He did not suspect that those children might grow to maturity, as they have, and their children after them, unfamiliar with even the name "Dagoman"—but still, with particular and locally recognized forms of continuous attachment to the Katherine town area. Arndt's "discovery" presents us with the problem of morphological thinking about identity, which makes it difficult to imagine how robust forms can "disappear" except through "extinction," the ethological terms in which he tended to phrase the situation.

However, Dagoman people who identified themselves as such to him were physically there, unlikely to disappear in any complete or sudden biological sense. Despite this, Arndt thought in terms of the impending "disappearance" of the "tribe," as against the previous "existence of a whole tribe." And while it cannot be doubted that Aboriginal people in the vicinity had suffered enormous loss of numbers from the early period of Katherine settlement—there is an objectively physical dimension involved in the changes that had occurred—Arndt came to know the situation at a time when the issue was no longer simply one of biological reduction of human numbers, but of more subtle, subsequent processes of social re-identification of those who had survived this early period as they gradually integrated into their number Aborigines from farther afield who were making the town their home.

In a word, Arndt was concerned with understanding Aboriginal ties to the Katherine town area in terms of "tribal"-level relations to it. He thought of "tribe" as a bounded entity with a specific membership, and persons (such as the ones he knew as Dagoman) as having fixed identities. He concluded that the "tribe" of the Katherine area was disappearing and had for this reason (combined with inadequate inquiry) gone unrecognized in most of the expert literature on this area. His "discovery" was that the "tribe" had existed. In some ways, by this time Arndt's kind of ideas about "tribe" as fixed, substantial groups would best be seen as more like popular conceptualizations, rather than like contemporary anthropological ones, which were beginning to question such views.

From early settlement, "tribal"-level names were seized upon by colonizers, later by ethnologists, in the attempt to place "Aboriginal groups in a geographical landscape" (Povinelli 1993:74). But Australianist anthropologists, from the time that social organization was explicitly theorized by Radcliffe-Brown (1913), had had to begin to deal with the problem of the seemingly evanescent and *in*substantial nature of groupings among Aborigines. This was difficult, perhaps, to square with popular imaginings of a much more concrete nature, as well as with administrative demands for fixity. In view of apparent difficulties involved in conceptualizing Australian social organization in the structural terms emerging and pioneered by him in this era, Radcliffe-Brown (1913, 1930b, 1931) sought to establish clarity by proposing that concreteness and fixity did exist, but at the narrower level of the "horde," or totemic clan, which he envisioned as stable through time in its patrifiliative mode of recruitment and thus as a structural building block. Proceeding from what he conceived as most empirically real to most diffuse, Radcliffe-Brown attributed to higher social levels fewer and fewer determinate functions, the physiological correlate of forms. The "tribe" in this view was a bounded cluster of clans, distinguished from its neighbors "by possession of a name, a language, and a defined territory" (Radcliffe-Brown 1913:144), neither a political unit nor an economic one, but nevertheless a homogeneous unit, its members sharing customs and cultural traits exclusive to them. In part, this is what Arndt also assumed, at least with respect to the distinctiveness of "tribe."

Warner's classic, *A Black Civilization* (1937) was fraught with unresolved tensions over the nature and mode of existence of social units in northeast Arnhem Land. Though he assumed that the notion of tribe had some kind of descriptive utility, he nevertheless wrote that this was an almost "nonexistent unit" (p. 9) among those he treated collectively as the "Murngin," that "tribal membership" is often uncertain, and that people may insist that they belong to more than one tribe (p. 35). Following Radcliffe-Brown, Warner's first and last word on the subject of social organization was that clans were "of basic importance . . . the largest units of solidarity" (p. 5).

Sharp (1958:4), who had worked in Cape York from the 1920s, derided the notion of tribe as "cookie-cutter modelling" in the "stereotyped ethnography of aboriginal Australia," opting again for the solidity of "clan" (see also McConnell 1930, Thomson 1939 for this view, and Sutton 1978:58, von Sturmer 1978:245–246, and Keen 1994 for alternative positions). In doing so, however, Sharp left the character of larger-level, named regional groupings in Cape York inadequately examined. In a later review of anthropological treatments of the tribe in Australia, Berndt (1959:106) concluded that there might be little advantage in treating them as "empirical" entities; "tribe" might be better seen as a "conceptual" construct.

Countering these tendencies, for some time, anthropologists and ecologists with strong interests in population biology, ecology, and spatial modeling made a vigorous defense of the applicability of the notion of "tribe," asserting the stability and boundedness of such units (see Tindale 1925, 1974, 1976; Birdsell 1953, 1970, 1976). But in their development of models of language and other differences as necessarily constituting social barriers to communication and interaction, these views are problematic as ways of conceptualizing regional organization for Australia, with its well-documented degree of multilingualism (Sutton 1991) and its clusterings of large- and smaller-scale differentiated groupings within which inter-marriage and interaction regularly took place.

Recent reconceptualization of the issues involved suggests that a more appropriate notion is one of the products of relations of representation in which social practice is immersed, a notion I encode in the phrase "socio-territorial identity." Carter (1987:163) writes of boundaries that are not barriers; and Rose (1992:222), writing of the Victoria River district, conveys the relational nature of the Aboriginal use of the term "boundary," its inherent "shifter" quality, in describing it as an "angle of perception." (See also Myers' 1986:28–29 useful discussion of Pintupi identity.) It is as part of a set of ways of making social differentiations, rather than as names for social groups that exist as brute facts, independent of how they are identified, that we need to understand designations like "Dagoman." Relevant questions are What sorts of social differentiations do such terms presume and make possible? and What sorts of empirical reference do Aboriginal people understand them to have? And how, as Arndt's contemporary observations in relation to Dagoman might have been put, can these identities "dissolve" but still leave sociohistorical traces that influence subjective orientations?

Katherine Socio-territorial Identities

Aboriginal people of the Katherine region use terms such as "Dagoman," "Wardaman," and "Jawoyn" with reference to people, to a more-or-less neatly definable stretch of country, and to a language they consider to be associated with that country. Let us consider all three dimensions and the interrelation among them.

Affiliation

One may hear someone say, "Me really full Jawoyn" or "Really proper Wardaman, me" or hear someone referring to another as "Mayali bastard." Sometimes such a description may be amplified: "My mother Jawoyn, my father Jawoyn, me really full Jawoyn." That is, these terms are commonly understood to construct identity in terms of a link through one or both parents. In the event that the parents are differently identified, one may also hear "Me Jawoyn-Rembarrnga mix" or "My father Dalabon, my mother Jawoyn." Self-attribution to more than two identities, one via each parent, is not usual among people of the town camps.

Julie Williams, for instance, says that she is Jawoyn, because her mother Ngetngeta and her father(s) were "really Jawoyn." A designation like this makes possible a wider construction of commonality or community (and, as we shall see, ties to places and to a wider stretch of country encompassing them) beyond immediate kinspeople in a narrow sense. It suggests a community of people who interact with each other on the basis of an understanding that they share this kind of identity. This gives a sense of people broadly connected as "countrymen," linked to a common area.

It would appear that marriage among people who considered themselves to be affiliated with the same identity of this kind was previously more common than it is now. Genealogical documentation in preparation for the Katherine Land Claim of all those people considered Jawoyn showed a much greater proportion of Jawoyn married to partners also recognized as Jawoyn in earlier generations, as compared with more recent marriages. Changes in marriage frequencies mean that older people tend to have a well-established identification with a sole identity at this level—Jawoyn—to a greater extent than do younger people, who are more likely to cite dual (or more complex) identifications.

During the claim, Dick Gararr was questioned about dual identity. Dick had identified his mother as Jawoyn, his father as a Dalabon[4] man of Wurrparn *mowurrwurr* (a Dalabon clan). Attempting to draw negative implications for his participation in the land claim, counsel for the Northern Territory asked, "Your father's country, that one who passed away was Dalabon. Is that right?"

> *DG:* Yes. . . .
> Do you take country from your father? Do you take some country over that way?
> *DG:* I take mother's country now, Jawoyn.
> Why do you not take your father's country?
> You have been living most of your life in Jawoyn country. Is that right?
> *DG:* Yes. . . .
> Is there a Dreaming for your *mowurrwurr*, that Wurrparn?
> *DG:* Yes, emu.
> That is the Dreaming that goes with that *mowurrwurr*?
> *DG:* Yes. Emu gave me that *mowurrwurr*. (KALCT 1982:904)

In fact, I knew Dick as a person who effectively did maintain attachments to both his Jawoyn-side and his Dalabon-side relations, viewed over the long term. The former tended to live around Katherine and Barunga, the latter around Barunga, Beswick, and Bulman to the north, on the fringe of Arnhem Land, in what is recognized as Dalabon country. At the time of the land claim Dick was living near Katherine with some of his Jawoyn-side relatives. His father had died at Barunga in 1976. His own marriage to a Mayali woman had ended in alcohol-related disaster some years earlier, and he had served a jail term as a result. He probably did have a stronger sense of Jawoyn-side ties at the moment he was called to give evidence. But he, like many others, could have been questioned in a way that revealed genuinely lived social links both ways, to mother's and father's side. For him, attachment to country was a choice among various living sites, recognized as in Jawoyn country or elsewhere in or near Arnhem Land, which he was seen to be able to legitimately exercise on the basis of family ties, parentage, siblingship, and at least potentially, marriage.

Proliferation of socio-territorial affiliations might seem to be a possibility for any individual at each generation level. That is, it might seem one could claim attachments through parents, grandparents, and the like, so that from any of these forebears who were different, one could claim affiliation to a wide range of identities. But although this kind of accumulation of social identities is a logical possibility—as in the common Western practices of recalling ethnic or national diversity as far as it is known at upper generation levels in tracing connections to the multiply endowed "individual" at the bottom level of a family tree—such was not the practice among the claimants. Each older person knew of his or her parents as having one, or at the most two, affiliations of this kind from grandparents that formed the basis of a strong sense of linkage to country. And each person seemed to think of himself or herself as having an effective choice of following mother, father, or sometimes, both. People did not approach dual affiliation as an issue of the dilution of personal identity, but rather as the question of whether one follows mother, father, or both.[5] There were at least two assumptions implicit in this attitude: first, that for either side, a unitary identity that determined identification prevailed at the previous generation level; second, that every such identity was grounded in a stretch of country, more or less known or knowable, and that this gave the identification an inherent and practical "ground."

The extent to which summary social identifications are unitary, or sometimes dual, rather than multiple, has seemingly been bound up with the extent to which these identities have been grounded in a territorial dimension, realized and actualized over the course of a lifetime in terms of principal attachments within one area or another. Dick Gararr's remarks indicated that he could choose to follow up his dual affiliation and take country through his (non-Jawoyn) father. But he said he didn't have "much family" that way—that is, his effective choices in that regard were presently limited. Thus, at each generation level, choices that might seem to exist in hypothetical terms were simplified.[6]

From the perspective of younger generations, older people are recalled as having been of a particular, unitary identity (even if their own ties as traced through parents may have earlier been more complex). Clearly, that such identities have a territorial dimension has been central to how they signal affiliation between people.[7]

Country

Aboriginal people also use these labels to designate broad areas of country as well as specific places within them: Jawoyn country, Wardaman country, and so on. At any given time, there is a widely shared view among Aboriginal people (with some variations) about the distribution of socio-territorial identifications in relation to countryside of the Katherine region and town. Map 4 represents such a composite view, the outlines of which were generally reproduced and confirmed by most Katherine-area Aborigines of middle age or older when I began research around the town from 1976. One point on which there was great difference among some older people was whether they had a concept of Dagoman country as being around Katherine town and to the southwest, or whether they thought of the town area as Jawoyn, as other than Jawoyn, or as of indeterminate identity.

Many Aboriginal people designate specific places or areas to which they considered themselves and their families to have ties (such as Julie's tie to Leech Lagoon through her father) or alternatively speak of these specific attachments as within a broader country to which they express affiliation. In the Katherine Land Claim, one old man, asked what was his "father country," replied "Maranboy." Later asked whether Pine Creek and Edith Falls were part of his "father country," he replied (after having said they used "to walk around there everywhere from Maranboy, backward and forward, right up to Pine Creek and coming back again"), "Yes, still all the Jawoyn country" (KALCT 1982:621). He was able to move from an answer in terms of specific and focal attachments, which the question about father country first elicited from him, to a notion of the participation of specific place within a broader socio-territorial identity, Jawoyn. This kind of move from specific place to more inclusive area, from part to whole and back again using the high-level social-identity term, is an aspect of social fluency concerning country that older people assume and control. It is underpinned by broad consensus among older people concerning which places are Jawoyn (or of some other identity), which are not, and generally, where the broad expanse of country is. Not everyone, however, would feel equally confident if asked to provide an overall description of the extent of country at this level without assistance. In general, younger people would find it more difficult to do so, a hesitancy that doubtless reflects the narrower experience of country that most people of the postwar generation have had.

For older people who continue to think of country as "put," "made," or "named" through travels of creator beings, those travels are often themselves the context in which differences appear as ones between different socio-territorial identities. A creator kangaroo may travel a long distance, making places considered to be Jawoyn, and then pass on into Ngalkbon country. It is his passage that makes the difference appear. Certain places may be said to be where Jawoyn people, or traveling creator figures, "hand over" to Mayali, where Jawoyn and Mayali "meet up." Places in their physical character provide a topographic basis for the construction of the relationship as one of simultaneous sameness and difference (different identities on the "same river").

Because of this tendency to express difference relationally, certain places in the Katherine region have stood out as noteworthy to me in that Aboriginal people have indicated boundaries as precisely pinpointed by some specific physical feature. In these cases they have sometimes used the word "boundary," which has no simple lexical equivalent in any Aboriginal language I know. Older Aboriginal people may have learned the word in the course of rural work. In a few (but not all) cases, the proximity of this marker to a settler-built place or site has suggested that the designation and particular significance of an object as boundary has emerged with reference to that built environment as Aboriginal people readjust their spatial definitions in relation to it.

On Elsey Station to the southeast of Katherine along the Roper River, people point to the course of Salt Creek as the north-south boundary between what they identify as Yangman country to the south and west and Mangarrayi country to the north and east along the Roper River (Merlan 1986b; see map 4). They are not concerned to further define a complete perimetric boundary of either Yangman or Mangarrayi, though they have quite widely shared concepts of which specific, named places as well as broader areas are included within each one, along major waterways as well as elsewhere.

To the south and west of Katherine town, older Wardaman people have frequently pointed out to me an access road that leads to Scott Creek, off the Victoria Highway, as the boundary between Dagoman country (which runs back toward Katherine) and Wardaman country (extending to the southwest). Reference to this fixed point as boundary must derive from times in which travel along the main road had become a common means of getting back and forth between Katherine town and Willeroo and Delamere Stations, where most Wardaman lived.

During the time I lived at Bamyili (Barunga) in 1976, Gordon Bulumbara,[8] then council president (and Phyllis' brother), asked me to give him a lift into town. When we got near the King River he told me to stop the car, and we got out briefly so that he could illustrate some of the things he had been talking about. Pointing upstream where the King River crosses the road and waving his arm to indicate the area north of the road, he said that the highway was the Dagoman boundary, that Dagoman country had been to the north, Yangman to the south of it.

Language

Radcliffe-Brown considered language a criterion of tribe, understanding this as a common speech form shared among tribal members (and conversely, he understood that speech form as bounded, its distribution coinciding with tribal membership). In taking such a view of language and its distribution as a criterion for defining social units, and in not considering indigenous ways of understanding language difference and its social significance, Radcliffe-Brown's model was clearly inadequate. The distribution of language *proficiency* does not correlate in a simple way with personal identification as member of some particular tribe or other kind or level of identity.

The relationship among land, language and person has subsequently been understood in terms that more closely approximate the ways in which Aborigines use such labels.[9] A multilingual speaker of Arnhem languages, for example, may say, despite his fluent command of several, "My 'rown [own] language Jawoyn" or "Jawoyn my proper language." Of himself he says, "Me full Jawoyn." And in respect of the "Katherine area" he will (if provoked) declaim, "Mayali bastard got nothing to do, this country blang [belong] to Jawoyn" (in other words, the Mayali do not belong here, have no business here).

As this suggests, Aborigines of the Katherine area tend to define personal relationship to languages in terms of ownership rather than proficiency (see Sutton and Palmer 1981). That language in relation to which one declares oneself ("my language really Wardaman") is conceived as inherent to an area of which one is entitled to say broadly that it is one's country; and usually, within country thus broadly defined, individuals will also cite more specific entitlements and give the basis for them ("from my father that place, blang to [it belongs to] Wardaman country").

The crucial point is that in indigenous thinking, and especially that of older people, there is a concept of a direct relation between a particular language and a tract of country. Sometimes the instantiation of this relation by extraordinary creator figures is explicit. During the Katherine Area Land Claim, Peter Jatbula spoke of the creative and differentiating activities of the crocodile creator Nabilil, in traveling the Katherine River: "Old Nabilil been carrying up that fire stick, *mogurrgurr* [clan] and all those places name. Fire stick for name, we call him *meya*, fire stick. You call him matches. . . . He been got him up water and fire stick all the way from sea. He been come to different relation now, different country, like say Wardaman and Nangiomeri, then come to Jawoyn country. . . . Jawoyn language belong to this place, Katherine, all the area" (KALCT 1982:845-846).

The travels of Nabilil were the process through which occurred the differentiation among Jawoyn, Wagiman, Wardaman, and other high-level identities. With each is associated a "language" as indigenously conceived.[10] Socio-territorial difference, of which language is part, is primordial, going back to the creative formation and differentiation of the landscape and grounded in it.

Rumsey (1993:204) has summed up the grounded character of language, and thus its particular territorially anchoring potential as a dimension of social identification, in the following terms:

> Languages . . . are directly placed in the landscape by the founding acts of dreamtime heroes. From that point on, the relation between language and territory is a necessary rather than a contingent one. People too, or their immortal souls, are similarly grounded in the landscape, in the form of spirit children . . . associated with specific sites, and via links through their parents to more extensive regions.

But the languages were already placed in those regions before any people came on the scene. The links between peoples and languages are secondary links, established through the grounding of both in the landscape.

Placement of language in the landscape may be more or less explicit in indigenous conception (cf. Rumsey 1989:25). But whether or not this element is explicit, the concept of enduring grounding of a (particular, indigenously recognized) language in country, as part of the essential nature and difference of that country, is pervasive (see Sutton 1991).

Language inheres in country, which is sentient, and is part of the "difference" country senses between familiar and unfamiliar people. These presuppositions underlie Katherine Aborigines' concept that one should talk to country in its own language to get it to yield up its produce (Merlan 1981, Povinelli 1993:153ff.). The notion that people are right for country—that they belong there and the country knows them and they know it—underlies Aboriginal people's diffidence about going to country where they are "wrong one," mere strangers to it, where any untoward event—lack of success in hunting, fishing, or relating to other people—will cause them to say, "This country no more savvy [doesn't know] me."

Where language is not a contingent but a constitutive and grounded element of difference in this way, boundedness may be signaled by the seemingly involuntary shift on the part of a story character from one language to another as he travels: language wells up, as it were, from the country. I have already mentioned that among Aboriginal people of the Katherine region (and elsewhere; see Strehlow 1965:133), this kind of grounding of language as a dimension of identity is made explicit by the fact that characters whose travels are recounted in mythic narrative are made to change language as they pass through countryside associated with one language into countryside associated with another (see Merlan 1981, Rose 1992). But the focus is not solely upon difference as an expression of discontinuity. Mythic travel between one area and what becomes recognizable as another is the agency through which primordial difference appears in a landscape also linked and made continuous (Myers 1986:60) by those travels.

Transformations of Socio-territorial Identity

For older people, the citing of a socio-territorial identity as one's own is usually an expression of where they consider their country to be. Parental affiliation is the normal basis for such self-identification. Thus, this kind of identity is understood by Katherine Aborigines as inherent, not something that can be assumed, taken on, or put off.

However, I have encountered cases in which individuals themselves, as well as their current campmates and close associates, have come to regularly give for themselves identities of this kind that reflect marriage and long-term consociation with people who are not their original countrymen. In some cases I knew, this identification had resulted from thoroughgoing social relocation, in which a person had established ties to people and country quite different from those to which he or she was born.

Bobby was a man well into his fifties when I first met him in the late 1970s at his camp at Bunjarri, on Manbulloo Station, with his Wardaman wife. The dominant social identity of people associated with this camp was Wardaman, but some residents were also affiliated with a range of other identities, mostly of the Victoria and Daly River areas: among them were Nungali, Ngaliwurru, and Jaminjung. A few camp residents were recognized as having Yangman affiliations. The Yangman identity is generally associated with country just to the east of Wardaman, extending to Elsey Creek and Warloch Ponds near Mataranka. One Bunjarri family retains specific attachments, patrifiliatively transmitted, to a Dog Dreaming along the Dry River within Yangman country.

I had been inquiring whether anyone knew the Yangman language, and Bobby was recommended to me as Yangman by some Bunjarri people. This interested me, partly because Yangman identity is hardly cited by any Aborigines in Katherine nowadays, with the exception of members of the family, mentioned above, who have a specific and locally well-known paternal link to a place associated with that identity on the Dry River. On the other hand, welfare censuses show that the Yangman identity was still given as their own in the late 1960s by a number of (mainly elderly) people in Katherine (eight in all). Following their deaths (and even though several had children who were members of their families in which there had been multiple marriages and were therefore sets of part-siblings), the Yangman identity has not been reproduced in Katherine: it, like Dagoman identity, has become obsolete in town.[11]

As I got to know Bobby better (and also, in the early 1980s, in the course of the broad consultation task I had taken on in preparation for the Katherine Area Land Claim), I learned that many Jawoyn people emphatically considered him Jawoyn and that he had impeccable kin credentials to be so considered. His closest relatives lived at Bamyili and Beswick, and a niece (Bobby's sister's daughter), near Mataranka. These people claimed ties to country around Beswick, both in a broad sense and in the more specific sense that they thought of their father country as Bogolorrkmi, a name applied to an expanse of hills north of Beswick. These relatives claimed Bobby as their own and as "really full Jawoyn" even though they had not had close daily contact for many years; they saw him from time to time around Katherine.

When I returned to explore this further with Bobby, he confirmed his relatives' story. But, he said, he had gone as a young man—somewhat unusually for a Jawoyn person, although a few others who had worked for a station boss with business ties to Katherine town had also done so. Bobby had worked on Willeroo, where people of Wardaman, Mudburra, and other Victoria River identities predominated. There he had married a Wardaman woman. Wardaman people at Willeroo and, later, at Katherine, knew his origins, and that he was not one of them. But he had come to be a countryman in many ways, sharing their daily camp and work life. I don't know whether he or his camp mates started identifying him as Yangman in certain circumstances, but I do know this is how he was first pointed out to me, and he himself had apparently begun to regularly identify himself in this way, for some purposes at least. When I asked him whether he spoke Yangman, he laughed and said, "Nothing." When I showed him that he was identified as Yangman on various welfare censuses (quite likely as a result of what he had said at the time), he observed mildly, "Well, I been away from my country long time, I been married this country" (meaning, "western side" or "Wardaman side," as locals might say). And indeed, some of his numerous children have since furthered this process of shifting into specific western-side networks, some of them having married Walbiri spouses and having lived for long periods at western side communities, especially Lajamanu. Those children's sense of themselves as Jawoyn is highly attenuated (as far as I know, limited to a recognition of where their father came from in quite general terms), while their more current and precise identifications at this level derive from their mother's side and from their relations with in-laws.

The attribution of Bobby's new identity illustrates a close social calibration of difference. Wardaman, as the majority of people with whom he lived at Willeroo considered themselves and that place, recognized Yangman as significantly different, territorially and in other ways, from their own identity. Yangman had been a known minority identity at Willeroo in Bobby's stock-working days, and Yangman country was conceived as adjacent to but different from Wardaman. Records show there were from time to time a few people at Willeroo who claimed affiliation as Yangman. Thus, Bobby's identity was refashioned as one from south of Katherine rather than from the north, but still distinctively different from that of his immediate associates. There was a spatially relative and sensitive "logic" in his assignment to Yangman identity, basically from a "Wardaman-centric" perspective.

Given extensive kin networks and the broad regional knowledge that particularly older people have of interconnections, however, his original identity was not forgotten quickly but was variably reckoned at different points of conjuncture of an extended cognatic kin network. His niece at Elsey Station, in particular, was able to construct for me a broad picture of extended cognatic kin relations in which he figured. This ranged over people (alive and deceased) normally identified (through maternal and paternal affiliation) in terms of high-level identities as Jawoyn, Yangman, Mangarrayi, and Dagoman. It also included a large number of people of mixed descent from the Katherine area, Bobby's sister's descendants, whose association with wider country has been limited and whose identification with it is thus attenuated and diffuse. They think of themselves as people of Katherine.

Arndt's Findings: The Aboriginal Identity of the Town

By the time Arndt arrived in Katherine, the landscape had been dominated by settler sites for decades—by stations, mines, farms, and the town itself, its significance intensified during the enormous disruption of the war period and the relocation of Aborigines from near and far in compounds in the vicinity of the town. Aboriginal people were living in more constant company with certain others, and certainly more concentratedly at a few places, than before. Some, for instance, had intense ties to Manbulloo Station, as a place where they had lived, where they and their relatives had been born and had died, where they had had ceremony, fought, lived in close but unequal relationships with whites, and so on. Relations to places were continually being reformed, more or less transiently—for example, to the Donkey camp where many Aborigines lived for a few months or years during the war.

Katherine Aborigines speak of "mobs," time-bound aggregations (Sansom 1980, chapter 1). "Manbulloo mob" are those who live together at that station, "Gorge mob" those whose attachments to each other are at least partly constituted through their co-presence at earlier or present locations around Katherine Gorge, "High Level mob" those who camp or have camped together on that riverbank, and so on. The actual personnel of mobs so designated changes over time. It would be as much a misinterpretation to take designations like "Manbulloo mob" as referring to enduring groups of fixed and completely stable membership as it is to take "tribal-level" designations in that way (though the latter misinterpretation is common). The way in which they are constituted is similar, the level of their generality different. Given the inherently shifting processes of mob formation in time and space, use of such designations is as much evocative, or performatively and selectively constitutive of social identifications with respect to a present context, as it is referential. The identities themselves, constructions of relations as ones between persons and place, have an enduring dimension in that place quite literally becomes their ground. Places have a powerful role in these modes of social constitution.

From Nolgoyma, Arndt gained insight into Dagoman identity as associated with a continuous stretch of country, rather than only with the limited number of places at which Dagoman people had lived in recent decades. Arndt (n.d.) reports Nolgoyma's account of Dagoman country in the following terms (see map 6):

> The long axis stretch[es] from the Ferguson River and the lower King across the valley of the lower Edith mid Katherine [*sic*] river to the headwaters of the Roper River. It straddles the watershed between the Indian Ocean and the Gulf of Carpentaria. The key site of the northwest extremity was a place called Bamboo Creek junction on the Ferguson River where the supplies of bamboo spear shafts were obtained. This was quite definitively Tagoman property and their rights probably did extend somewhat beyond this point as Tindale indicates. Also Edith for axe heads. The key site at the southeast end of the territory was Leach Lagoon which drains into Roper Creek. This was the Turtle Dreaming place and the source of pipey (?) timber for didgeridoos.[12] . . . The waterholes at Oludune Durrinyan and Wongalla [Wangala] on the King River were also in Tagoman territory. . . . The SW limit of the territory was fixed by the right bank of the Katherine river from the Ferguson junction upstream at least as far as the Limestone Creek junction.

Arndt also gained insight into country as "continuous story" (Myers 1986:69), that is, into how principal stories were organized as the bases of social demarcation while also serving to formulate the country as continuous entity. A certain Dagoman family he knew, some of whom lived at CSIRO, were charged with the care of some Bush Fly Dreaming stones on

Limestone Creek (see map 6), which he recorded as Mar-go-ann. This name is clearly identifiable as the name "Wumardgawun," which Wardaman people have given me for this creek (if one recognizes that *wu-* is a Wardaman noun prefix found in many place names). Aboriginal men told him that this place figured in an enormously important mythic and ceremonial complex associated with subincision, the ritual cutting of the ventral surface of the penis, formerly practised by Wardaman and Dagoman alike. This story "came in" to Dagoman country from the southwest, through country identified by a variety of his informants as Wardaman. From older Wardaman and other men from this region he was able to gather considerable detail about the story and associated ritual. Many of the specific significances of places in the immediate Katherine area, especially along the river, were clearly part of this complex.[13]

What Arndt referred to as the northeastern Dagoman "boundary" was what his informants named as the end-place of mythic travels associated with the subincision complex. They (some Jawoyn men as well as Nolgoyma) further regarded this place, a creek junction near the original Overland Telegraph Station (the location Gumbitjbay on map 6), as a significant marker between Jawoyn and Dagoman:

> The creek now known as the Two Mile was called Kumbidgee,[14] which refers to the rare local patch of lancewood on the ridge that it drains. The deep water hole at the junction is the legendary home of the rock bat, known as Wallan, and an important Djauan [Jawoyn] legendary character. The junction is variously called Wallan-baa and Wallan-luk. The place name ending "luk" is definitely Djauan. This place was said by some to be the meeting place for the Tagoman and Djauan tribes, i.e. the boundary. A basalt column was erected to mark the boundary. The column [of which Arndt apparently intended to include photographs][15]. . . also serves to mark the northern terminus of subincision which Wardaman migrants brought into Tagoman territory. This stone column is located right alongside the old north-south road from Maranboy to Katherine at the point where it meets the Katherine river. Other informants claimed that the boundary was along this old road.

Arndt suggested that the stone marker "has been progressively shifted in a SW direction since European occupation began." He took the view that the original Dagoman-Jawoyn boundary was the Arnhem escarpment, or the rim of the Katherine Gorge in the sandstone uplands. This seems to be his own speculation, perhaps based on a notion that spectacular geological formations like the escarpment would naturally have been

Aboriginal boundaries. He offers no independent evidence to this effect. But he does offer reasoning concerning the social processes among Aborigines. He surmised that

> the boundary was shifted from the escarpment to the road so that the Djauan could have contact with European settlement. This move would also have been logical because the Maranboy terminus was in Djauan territory. The indications are that the Tagoman tribe did not resent this encroachment because they were attracted to the pastoral holding to the south and west which offered more to them than the O.T. station and shanty town that the Djauan gained. It seems however that the Djauans became the "town blacks" and the Tagoman became the "station blacks" of the district. In time the town was recorded as Djauan territory and later the district was also assumed to be Djauan. The Djauan encroachment was furthered by 3 progressive downstream shifts of the township itself. As the town moved the Djauan house servants police trackers etc. moved with it. The present position is 25 miles from the Arnhemland escarpment.

Arndt also suggested there was a second shift occurring in the conventional assignment of areas to Jawoyn and Dagoman identities by Aborigines. He observed that the railway line (which runs through town, just south of the Stuart Highway) was agreed to be the working boundary in his time, presumably because Dagoman then lived largely in town at CSIRO and/or at Manbulloo. During the war, many Aborigines—including Jawoyn and Dagoman—had been on the Katherine River on the farms, at Donkey camp, and near the old airstrip, precisely in the vicinity of the old Two Mile Creek and "Kumbidgee" (Gumbitjbay). The bombing of Katherine in February 1942 caught many of them in the vicinity of the airstrip, where the sole fatality was a man who was (then) recognized as Dagoman, "Dodger" in English. Some Jawoyn present at the bombing, who knew the country to the north, took off up the Katherine River after the bombing and went far upstream, into Gimbat Station and thence into Arnhem Land, for some months. By the time of Arndt's arrival in Katherine in the immediate postwar period, Jawoyn (and Mayali) were the only ones left in any numbers on the river to the north of the township. Dagoman were either at Manbulloo or on the river near the old army facilities. Those of Dagoman background had come to be the core of the CSIRO camp after a number of wartime shifts that Ivy Brumby (Dodger's daughter) described to me as part of her personal story as follows: "Army been pick'im up [from the Katherine River] and shift'im first Springvale; next on top to Seventeen Mile [in the Katherine Gorge area]; back to Donkey camp [closer to the township, on the river], then back to Dortluk [near

Beswick Station, about 70 km to the east of Katherine town]; from Dortluk back to Fordinay ["14A," a camp on Manbulloo Station]; then I been get married and go CS."[16]

Arndt had a sense of the prominent social position of Dagoman people among other Aborigines, in relation to the changing Katherine scene of the immediate postwar era. That (at least certain) senior Dagoman people may have enjoyed special prerogatives in the Katherine area is indicated in his report that, in the army camp settlement during the war, the "most central hut in the camp was occupied by Nipper [Nolgoyma] an old single man, whilst whole families of other tribes lived in inferior huts."

Arndt also suggests that the location of the CSIRO research station (within the five-mile stretch between town and Manbulloo) may account for the "stability of the labor force on this station, which is predominantly Tagoman. The complete absence of the so called "walkabout problem" encouraged the building of a small village of decent cottages which has become the most important, if not the only, Tagoman community."

The good, and unique, living situation the CSIRO camp offered must also be considered in accounting for the stability of its occupants. Yet the selection of Aboriginal people at CSIRO clearly reflected not just the objective advantages of that situation, but also that those regarded as local were able to assert their preferment. They became members of the workforce in a way nonlocals generally did not, with the exception of a few people who, sooner or later, married into the CSIRO community.[17]

Reflecting on their contemporary situation more generally, Arndt wrote that Dagoman were "sandwiched in a five mile wide section between the railway line and Manbulloo Station." This must be taken as a description of their residential distribution because, even today, there is a clear sense (mainly among some older Wardaman people) of Dagoman country as extending as far south as Scott Creek, and Wardaman associate a scatter of known sites with the Dagoman identity to that point.[18]

Arndt described the Dagoman as "attracted" to the stations to the south and west and so not resentful of Jawoyn encroachment on the town area. He writes of the Jawoyn as gaining a shanty town and the Overland Telegraph Station in the Kumbidgee area and seems to think of this as very little. That, however, is an outsider's judgment. Knott's Crossing was an important place for a considerable time, from the building of the Overland Telegraph station until World War II. In the early period, it was the only place where the Katherine River was fordable. The telegraph station site had been selected in November 1871. Station quarters were built in 1883, also serving as a post office from that year. A store and pub were opened on the site in 1883, Barney Murphy's Sportsman Hotel and Pioneer Cash Store. Tom Pearce rebuilt the pub in the 1890s and remained its licensee and manager until 1906. As an important point on the main north-south road, the Katherine crossing was very busy until, with the extension of the railway from Pine Creek to the Katherine River completed in 1917, the new town focus developed around Emungalan, at the railhead. Still, it was not until 1930 that the police station was moved from the old crossing to the new site of Katherine, after the railway bridge had been put across the river in 1926. A new crossing of the river for vehicular traffic was not built until the war period, at the old Springvale Crossing, the Low Level. In the 1930s, Fred and Mrs. Knott had a store with a "gallon" (liquor) license just upstream from the old (Knott's) crossing. During this period, when alcohol was still officially prohibited to them, Aborigines with a few shillings could buy small quantities of opium ash at Knott's store.

In short, over years, the area of Knott's crossing, with its telegraph and police stations, store, pub, and resulting concentrations of people, constituted a major focus for Aboriginal people as well as for others and could not be evaluated as just a run-down "shanty town." Proximity to it was probably important to Jawoyn people living on the peanut farms and otherwise seeking a foothold and subsistence around the town. The location (or relocation) of the basalt column boundary in this area positioned Jawoyn just on the northern periphery of the town, as outsiders or nonlocals. Whatever may have been their former northern-eastern range, this arrangement left Dagoman the acknowledged locals of the existing town area, as well as of the area farther downstream. And whatever its former significance, the importance of the basalt column, the Bat Dreaming, near the crossing may have been enhanced, perhaps even significantly constituted at that particular place, as a boundary marker of differential Aboriginal relationship to the area of the town.

In any event, the presence of that marker suggests that, in the prewar period at least, Dagoman were *not* prepared to concede the town area as Arndt suggested they were. After the war, however, with the establishment of CSIRO as an Aboriginal camp from 1947, local Aborigines who had been living on the Katherine River (at the Donkey camp, one of the army compound sites, and also farther downstream) were prepared to move to a more favorable situation, but still in their own country, as they saw it. The town focus had definitively shifted from the old crossing to the new town. Thus, Dagoman were effectively leaving what had become a backwater, an area now largely occupied by Aborigines of more distant territorial origins, but with whom some Dagoman people were now interacting closely.

Dagoman, as they then identified themselves, were the core of the Aboriginal people permitted by whites to live within (even if on the fringe of) the town site. While the local people moved into this new position, most Jawoyn (except those who came to be closely associated with CSIRO residents by marriage, and who also worked there) remained on the river to the north of the town and as far downstream as the rail crossing of the river. But by the same token, the close association of Dagoman with CSIRO, and the increasingly close association of Jawoyn with them and with the town, set in train the redefinition of the town area as shared between Dagoman and Jawoyn. That was the situation of Arndt's time; knowledge of the earlier situation, and indeed detailed knowledge of the town area in earlier mythic terms, had become attenuated, and thinly distributed. Arndt was able to recover the rich terms of the subincision story only from a few older people.

In the postwar years, any notion of demarcation between Dagoman and Jawoyn outside of town came to have much less meaning in current Aboriginal social terms than had been the case earlier. In particular, it had less meaning because a boundary outside town did not adequately symbolize the contemporary intense focus on the town of people's lives, patterns of residence, daily activity, and interaction. It must have been during this time that the railway line through town came to be thought of as a notional marker by Aborigines, still distinguishing Dagoman from Jawoyn but demarcating the town space as shared between them and preserving the original relative orientations, Jawoyn country to the north and Dagoman to the south.

How was this kind of transformation lived out by those affiliated to Dagoman identity? Judging from the accounts of those people with whom I have worked closely, I surmise that this transformation happened without their explicit recognition of shift in identity at this level in relation to the town area, and indeed, to themselves.

From Dagoman to Jawoyn in Katherine Town

My attempts to follow up leads about people through whose lives these transformations occurred always led back to Julie Williams.

Julie, recall, was Nolgoyma's granddaughter. Julie's mother, Nolgoyma's daughter Ngetngeta, lived into the late 1970s. I met her briefly, toward the end of her life, when she was in the care of the Sisters of Charity, unable to talk about the matters I am describing.

I had observed that Nolgoyma was often referred to by Wardaman and other people in the southerly town camps as *Yi*nolgoyma, with the general Wardaman-Dagoman-Yangman animate prefix. My curiosity was aroused by this, and I asked Julie how her grandfather had identified himself. As Jawoyn, she thought. She was more certain that he had spoken both Jawoyn and another language, which she variably called "Wardaman" or "Dagoman," fluently. (Jawoyn is very different from both Wardaman and Dagoman, which are closely related).[19] I also asked her whether he had ever told her what his country was. Julie could not remember having heard anything of this sort directly from her grandfather; but she volunteered that her mother had showed her some places just downstream from the first Gorge. One of these, Bemang-luk, is a Blanket Lizard Dreaming. Her mother had regarded this place, a jagged hill, as her own, through her father, and her Dreaming as blanket lizard. She had told Julie that Nolgoyma was of a clanlike identity called Jorrolam.

Julie, her daughters, Alice Mitchell and I, and a few others from the Gorge camp made a trip to visit the blanket lizard place, then continued to another one a few kilometers away, called Bilkbilkbam. The latter was a small but spectacular Arnhem-style plunge pool, with steep red sandstone sides, a long waterfall, and a beautiful small beach of fine sand surrounding the pool. We had a walk around the place, down below and on top, but not until after Julie and I had rushed to the pool with our fishing lines. Julie was not sure, but she thought Bilkbilkbam had been the country of a woman called Moyongla, long dead, but whose name, I noted, bears the tell-tale Dagoman place suffix *-la*.

On that trip Alice Mitchell, with her broad knowledge of people extending back to the peanut farm days of the 1930s, spoke of a number of men as Jorrolam: Peter Barrarndila and Yarlitja, who she said had been *gany-barrakbarrak*[20] (diver duck), linked to Barrakbarrak-luk in the lower Gorge; and Ngorolayn and Nolgoyma, who she said were two brothers, the latter Julie's mother's father.

Julie's "second" father, Fortymile (the one whose country was Leech Lagoon, identified by Nolgoyma to Arndt as the "key site" at the southeast end of Dagoman territory), worked for years on stations on the Edith and Daly Rivers as well as on the railway at Pine Creek—in places where Jawoyn and Mayali people had come to be strongly represented. Having grown up in Katherine and also having lived for periods of time in Pine

Creek, Julie as a young girl was promised in marriage to a Jawoyn man who originated from the Gimbat area (northeast of Pine Creek). He and other members of his family had made their way to Katherine, footwalking. Eventually, instead of her original "promise," Julie married his older half-brother, Peter; the two brothers agreed on this, "no fight," according to Julie. The brothers were actual first cousins of Soupy Marapunyah, the northern Jawoyn man who came to be prominent in the CSIRO camp, warmly remembered by Arndt and L. J. Phillips of CSIRO, as a "top man." Soupy married Julie's actual cross-cousin (daughter of Yibijuba, her mother Ngetngeta's brother), Amy. These, then, were Jawoyn men marrying women who were probably not then so recognized. As a result, though, both Amy and Julie have always been considered closely associated with (northern) Jawoyn. But marriage ties as formative of her own and wider familial identification with Jawoyn people go back farther, to her mother's and uncle's generation, when Julie's own marital destiny was provisionally established.

Besides Yibijuba, Julie had another uncle named Jackson, her mother's full (and older) brother. Julie remembers Jackson mainly from his later years, when he was around Pine Creek. Julie and others today do not know who may have been Jackson's first wife. But in later life, while living at Bonrook just outside Pine Creek (where Jawoyn were again present in numbers), he took as his partner Maggie, mother of the Jawoyn man, Peter, who was to marry Julie, Jackson's niece. By that time, Maggie's children by an earlier marriage (including Peter, Julie's future husband, whose father, Charlie, was of northern Jawoyn Wurrkbarbar clan) were already young adults. Jackson was Julie's mother's brother, in terms of Jawoyn notions of kinship, an uncle suitably positioned to give away his niece. Jackson's marriage to Peter's mother Maggie contributed to Jackson's giving this niece to his wife's son, Peter (see Hiatt 1967). (Had this not happened, Peter could have considered Jackson his "second father"; see diagram 1.)

After Fortymile died, Julie's mother married another Jawoyn man in Katherine, David Williams (Na-Bamjokjok). He was Girrimbitjba clan, a close paternal relative of Sarah Andrews and the "father" who figures in Julie's narratives in chapter 2. He originated from the Mainoru area, far to the east, and like many others had made his way to Katherine via Maranboy, where he had spent much time when young, drawn along with his relatives and countrymen into the camp life around the peanut farms and the bush and escarpment beyond it.

Nolgoyma died in 1956, when Julie would have been about thirteen or

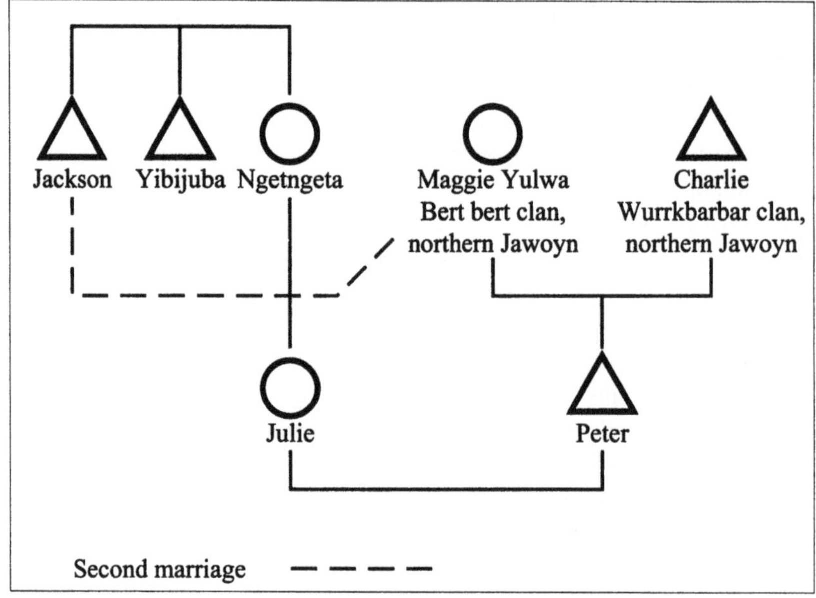

Diagram 1. "Jawoynizing" Marriage Influences

fourteen. Fortymile, too, apparently died in the late 1950s or early 1960s, of injuries he sustained while working on a property on the Edith River. How Fortymile identified himself, I do not know. In the meantime, at locations including Bonrook, Pine Creek, and even eventually at Katherine, Jackson and other members of his family came to be more and more closely identified with Jawoyn people. Julie's mother ended her days at the Sisters of Charity Home in Katherine, thoroughly "Jawoyn-ized" in the eyes of many Katherine people, even her remaining contemporaries; her last husband, David, ended his days in the Katherine Gorge camp among Jawoyn and Mayali people, on the river he had come to regard as home.

These shifts in personal identification would not, by themselves, have been sufficient to bring about the shift of identity of country around Katherine. But at the level of country, the populated centers were susceptible to attenuation of earlier identity and to redefinition in terms of what had become the town's predominant Aboriginal identity, that of Jawoyn people who were recent arrivals from "bush" locations and who continued to relate to country and people in terms of modes of identification established there.[21] As associations with persons of Jawoyn identity came to be more important to Nolgoyma's descendants (and a small number of other kin clusters) than personal and territorial identification in the Katherine area as *Dagoman*, the latter lost currency, to the point of obsolescence. The welfare census conducted in 1968–1970 shows only one man who was identified (presumably, by himself) as Dagoman.[22]

Julie's particular sense of local belonging, and of herself as part of a specific clustering of close kin in Katherine, is strong, though now merged with her sense of self-identification as Jawoyn. She also sustains a sense of connection through her father Fortymile to Leech Lagoon and through her mother and grandfather to Bemang-luk at the Katherine Gorge, both of these, again, fused with her sense of Jawoyn identity. Increasingly, too, with such changes, the sweep of country around Katherine has come to be thought of as Jawoyn, though in a somewhat diffuse way, involving considerable change and attenuation of people's sense of the significance of specific places, especially in many areas away from town that have been little frequented.

Today even Wardaman people, though some tend to be more aware of the earlier presence of Dagoman identity, sometimes say that Dagoman merely "came right up to Springvale," thus omitting the town area from this identification even though some of the place-names still recollected by older people within the town area (e.g., Yimunggalan or "Emungalan," Wurliwurlinyjang on the north bank, Garlirliwa in the southwest area of town) are clearly recognizable to Wardaman speakers as Dagoman, some of them as meaningful,[23] and as formally similar to names in their own language, rather than as Jawoyn names. Older people at Bunjarri I have asked over the years about Nolgoyma have given varying social descriptions of him. Most volunteered that he had lived at Manbulloo most of the time they knew him and that he died at 14A (the army camp on Manbulloo). One old woman (now deceased), herself a scion of a Dagoman family (among Arndt's workers at CSIRO), said on one occasion that he was "Dagoman-Jawoyn mix," but men present (who were Wardaman and Jaminjung) said, no, he was "full Jawoyn." Thus, retrospectively, Nolgoyma himself has been partially reidentified as Jawoyn even by local Katherine people who remember him.

Julie's understandings of her mother's specific links to Bemang-luk near the Gorge, and her father Fortymile's to Leech Lagoon, are islands of specific continuity in her self-conceptualization as a local person in a tide of continuing, though never total, change. Together with Arndt's information about Nolgoyma, they allow one to recognize in her, and in certain close relatives, people who were until several decades ago socially and territorially known as Dagoman (with specific ties to places within the Katherine area and to the town), and distinguished from others identified as Jawoyn.

What may not be obvious is the social logic of the reidentification of Dagoman descendants and the Katherine area as Jawoyn, rather than Wardaman; but it is similar to that operating in the case of Bobby, the individual who was originally Jawoyn but reidentified through his western-side associations as Yangman. Involved is the play of sustaining difference in a changing field of closer and more distant social relationship, in which territorial difference and relativity continue to be important. Some Wardaman and Dagoman people had lived together for years at Manbulloo, at a time when there was a clear notion of these two as socially and territorially distinct identities. It was not possible for the Wardaman, who still recognize strong links to country at Willeroo and farther south, to think of themselves as belonging to Manbulloo: they thought of Dagoman people there that way.[24] As the character of Dagoman presence in the Katherine area became more circumscribed; as the settler presence became overwhelmingly determinant of Aboriginal people's presence at a few particular places (Knott's Crossing, CSIRO, etc.) and not elsewhere; as close contact and intermarriage developed between Jawoyn and Dagoman earlier identified with the town area; and as Jawoyn people became more visible as the predominant Aboriginal grouping within the town itself following its relocation downstream from 1926, the scions of Dagoman families did not become identified as Wardaman, with whom they were closely linked socially but whom they knew to be territorially different, originating from farther south and west. Rather, many came to think of themselves as Jawoyn, their reidentification with the broad social identity of familiar people who were becoming ever more locally oriented and with some of whom they were by then thoroughly intermarried.

This shift of Aboriginal identities can be understood only in relation to the processes of white settlement. Aborigines deployed culturally specific modes of identity construction in a historical situation in which a central issue for them had become the nature of differentiated relationship to the town, as an aspect of sociality among Aboriginal people there and in terms familiar to them.

However, Aboriginal identification of the town area as Jawoyn, while general, is not universal. There are other viewpoints and kinds of awareness of the past, and it is revealing of changes in the nature of consciousness, and the kinds of variation to be found in complex social settings, to briefly consider these.

Aboriginal Viewpoints on the Town

Certain older Wardaman people, as I have mentioned, retain the strongest sense of the identity of the town and adjacent country as Dagoman. They retain concepts of particular places, and place-names, along the river that are recognizably similar to those given by Arndt. They identify certain people as Dagoman descendants, like Julie, who do not think of themselves in these terms, but who, like her, have sustained their sense of close connection to the town area, and sometimes to particular places in the vicinity of Katherine, in other terms.

There are varying perspectives among people recognized as Jawoyn. Perhaps a majority of those who maintain that the town area is Jawoyn see this as their own identity and that of their countrymen who have had long-term ties to the Katherine area (but among those they take as indicative are some people like Julie, whose story, as I have shown, is a complex one).

A few older Jawoyn people who worked on farms on the river south of town near Manbulloo do not conceptualize the situation in terms of a change of the kind I have sketched. Some of them assert that the area is and has been Jawoyn. They speak of Dreamings at particular places, identify some place-names, and obviously have a degree of practical familiarity with portions of the area. But the Dreamings and place-names they cite do not coincide, by and large, with those recorded in Arndt's notes or ones still known to some Wardaman people. Other Jawoyn people, especially those who retain strong personal senses of connection with the river north of the township and have spent little time to the south of it, will simply say they have "nothing to do" with this area or show some reluctance on the issue and may deny that it is Jawoyn or say they do not know.

Those Mayali people who also worked on farms south of the town have some practical knowledge of this area, some allegiances to particular places (ceremonial sites and so on); but together with their sense of the town as home, they also retain a strong sense of their own origin far to the north. Influenced, it seems, by their close association over decades with Jawoyn people, they may support claims that this is Jawoyn country.

Given the historically complex and variable situation, it is not surprising that many people are unclear about identification of country in the vicinity of the town. There is some lack of particularity and of shared conception among Aboriginal people, sometimes expressed as debate about where Jawoyn country "is" or "goes up to" with respect to the town. Particular personal and family histories are relevant to the information that individuals have to contribute to such debates. Chapter 2 suggests that the town, with its particular history, resists definition in holistic Aboriginal terms of high-level identities partly by offering impediments to the maintenance of places within it in Aboriginal mythological terms. Chapter 6 is further concerned with resistances and limitations to the definition of town spaces in Aboriginal terms.

In what seems qualitatively different from the range of varying viewpoints discussed so far, a few younger Aboriginal people have begun to order the situation in something much more like the terms of historical shift I have sketched here, thereby implicitly and explicitly countering the efforts of certain older Jawoyn people to recreate a framework of inherent relationship to this area through the citing of Dreaming stories, places, and personal experience. Those young people who do so most clearly are certain members of Wardaman families, with higher levels of education and training than average and employed in Katherine Aboriginal organizations. While they recognize their own familial ties to country much farther south, they also rankle under what they see as a lack of recognition of long-term Wardaman presence around the town. They are thus predisposed in a number of ways to historicize the situation, focusing more explicitly upon the issues as ones of change than older Aboriginal people tend to do. They refer to stories told them by older relatives about how the Jawoyn, in earlier years, were reluctant to come farther downstream than the High Level and how initiations of local Katherine boys were earlier held upstream from the High Level when this was not thought of as Jawoyn country. Most significant, they explicitly relate such stories to denial that the town is (solely) "Jawoyn."[25]

It is revealing to compare with these varying forms of relation to the situation, and especially with Julie's seamless sense of association with the town, a quite different form of experience: a personal story of radical dislocation in which socio-territorial identity has become torn loose from daily experience of its lived modes and of an attempt to rediscover personal connections.

Alan (I will call him) had been born to an Aboriginal mother and a white father in the days when "cohabitation" was prohibited. This white man (let us call him Fred) bred donkeys and also worked as a carter and drover around Katherine in the early years of the century. He was in fact the nephew of Tom Pearce, the highly respected publican at Katherine and sometime owner of Willeroo Station. As a carter, Fred went to many stations, including ones to the east as well as southwest of Katherine: Hodgson Downs, Victoria River Downs, Willeroo, Delamere, Wave Hill, and others. He had children by a number of Aboriginal women in different places. Alan's mother came to live in Katherine, at the Donkey camp on the river near Fred's camp. Nominally, his mother was a domestic and housekeeper.

Alan's mother had earlier had a daughter by an Aboriginal man from a station to the southwest of Katherine, her own apparent country of origin. From this sister, Alan has nieces who still live in Katherine camps. Though they are seen as Jawoyn by many, some older people still remember not only their mother as a westernsider, but also their father's actual place of origin, quite distant from Katherine and from any part of the area recognized as Jawoyn country. Thus, the family identification as "Jawoyn" has been built upon their long-term association with the town rather than upon familial links of longer term; in certain circumstances, this discrepancy is remarked upon.

Alan has spent some time trying to find out about his family.[26] He said to me of his mother, ". . . She never used to tell me about that, ah, about my, ah, language or anything. See, I never had much to do with my mother, I was taken away when I was three and a half years old, and I never seen my mother 'til I come back after the war, and I was twenty-seven years of age you see."

As a child, Alan was taken to Kahlin Compound, an institution for people of mixed descent in Darwin (Cummings 1990). Later, as a young man, he was sent to work at a remote station in central Australia. He had some hard and lonely times when he was left out in the bush to work on his own without companionship and other times when he was "sorta loaned out" to other stations to work and had to go because he was under eighteen. When the war broke out, he "put up" his age a bit and joined, "to break that sort of link" that had bound him to these institutions, but social stigma was difficult to escape for those "somewhere between white and black" (Palmer 1978). Ironically, his return to find family was rendered more difficult once he had joined the army and was perceived to be on the road to assimilation. When he returned from the War, he looked for his mother in Katherine: "I come back, and I went to that mission over there, there was a policeman there, that compound there [on the Katherine River], and I was in uniform, before I got in the civvies. And I visited my mother, and they tried to get me away, and I said, look, I said, I come to see my mother, I never see my mother, taken away and that, and he said to me, 'If you are not out of this place in five minutes, I'll have you up for cohabitating with the wards of the state,' then there was wards of the state."[27]

Alan's mother's Aboriginal name strongly suggests a southwestern identity.[28] Indications of her likely origin had been given to Alan by a number of Katherine-dwelling Aborigines from that area, who tried to steer him toward others with some knowledge of his mother and her family. But Alan had never developed close familiarity with the way in which local Katherine Aborigines understand and negotiate identities, using social category ("skin") terms, socio-territorial identities, and kin connections: "See, everytime I go I just name my whatsaname, see, they say, that's my Granny, that's my Mummy, that's sort of you know, I think, just through that skin clan, you see. . . . Like that see, that's why I'm really trying to place it, but Harry and that old Frank, that's my mob, you know, and old Willie's mob."

The latter three (for whom I have used pseudonyms) are locally recognized as belonging to quite different mobs, affiliated with distinct socio-territorial identities (none of them Jawoyn). Alan was also convinced that some of the Gorge people had recognized his mother, who lived at the Donkey camp north of the town, as Jawoyn: "Yeah, they been look after my family too, see my group . . . they used to always call me Jawoyn, like I had my skin all the time . . . and my blackfella name."

With his enforced experience of white institutions, Alan had a familiarity with the conjuncture of Aboriginal and white at a different level from many Aboriginal people who had always remained in Katherine. He had lived in Darwin, Alice, Pine Creek, Katherine; travelled more widely than most; had Aboriginal connections in all these places. But he had only a fragmentary picture of the local Katherine scene, its people, and their senses of social interconnection and relative discontinuity. His mother had lived and was buried in Katherine. He believes on the basis of what he knows that she must have been Jawoyn, and indeed the common identification of his nieces as such seems to point toward this identification. But he had no way of evaluating this, and other information pointed elsewhere, south and west to a complex social scene that probably could have yielded some of the answers to his questions had he been able to relate the social terms in which genealogical information is partly embedded to the specific, and more Westernized, terms of his quest. The ways in which Aboriginal people explained his family ties were always somewhat out of focus, parts of systems of making identities with which he had little practical familiarity and that therefore had no clear meaning to him. They always led him to people who, with the best intentions, never could reconstitute a comprehensible personal history for someone gone so far and so long.

Creating the Other as the Other

Fried (1975) has argued that all tribal organization should be understood as secondary, that is, produced under colonial conditions. However, in Australia in general and in the Katherine area in particular, such identities as are referred to in this way have continuity with the precolonial period, despite change in their relative prominence among the range of ways in which Aborigines make relationships with places and wider country. More relevant to Australian circumstances is the issue of how such identities are experienced and interpreted in increasingly diverse and intercultural arenas of social practice and how they may change in light of this.

We may return briefly to Arndt's quandary, developed early in the chapter, about how there could be living "members" of a "tribe" before him, yet the "tribe" had gone unnoticed by anthropologists of repute and had effectively "disappeared"—not only from the academic record, but also, his thought seems to have run, largely from the world as well.

There are two senses in which identities of this kind do not just disappear or go "extinct." The background to the first has been developed in this chapter; that to the second remains to be developed in the following chapter.

This chapter has shown that it is difficult to identify the nature of change, and continuity within change, unless one attributes a less concrete character to the kind of social entity Arndt was concerned with as "tribe" than he did. This difficulty parallels what was said about "clan" in the previous chapter: there it was shown that traces remain after the salience of the clan level of organization as ideological sedimentation and mode of formulating relations among people and country has partly or largely dissolved.

Terms like "Dagoman" are best understood as complex products of representation of several different dimensions of social experience (language, large-scale territoriality, and personal belonging at this level). At given historical moments, these dimensions are held to intersect in certain ways and (within ranges of variation) to have certain kinds of empirical reference. Changing sociohistorical experience can bring about shifts in the range and nature of empirical reference and in Aboriginal understandings of these levels of identity. Thus, there can be shifts in the nature of the intersection understood to be designated by each term.

The chapter has shown as a matter of social history that the sedimentation of a previously salient, particular intersection of this general type, Dagoman, dissolved, but not completely. Its traces came to be encompassed within other named person-country relationships which Aborigines represented to themselves and summarized in their diversity as "Jawoyn." The older Dagoman sedimentation of relations continues to be manifest in certain traces: the particular attachment of certain persons and families to the vicinity of the town over other locales and the degree of social distinctiveness they and others attribute to themselves as a localized cluster of kinspersons (which nevertheless continues to change in its social connections through new marriages, new movements, and so on). At some point, as may also happen with the dissolution of clan-level organization, one may no longer be able to detect such traces or to relate current forms of organization and representation to earlier, known kinds.

This brings us to a second sense in which high-level socio-territorial identities in general have not simply disappeared—but one that has depended upon a quite different taking up in an intercultural context of what is seen to be involved at this level, more in line with Arndt's notion of "tribe." This is a sense in which others' representations of Aboriginal social organization come to have a profound influence upon their lives, an influence in which some Aborigines come to participate in new ways.

Sider (1987:7) has written that colonizers are caught between "the necessity of creating the other as the other—the different, the alien—and incorporating the other within a single social and cultural system of domination." So-called tribal identities have long presented themselves as salient. However, anthropological as well as popular misapprehensions of this level have involved notions of sharp discontinuities, separate morphologies and bounded entities, rather than processes of identity formation within a socially and spatially interconnected world.

In the last two decades, in the context of benevolent, increasingly liberal management of Aboriginal affairs at higher government levels, Aboriginal relations to country have become of wide concern, and more laden with consequences for the position of Aborigines within the wider Australian polity, than before. In this context, so-called tribal identities have again presented themselves as among the most salient terms in which to create the Aboriginal other as the other (in this part of the Northern Territory and areas to the north, along with "clan"). In earlier terms of

Aboriginal sociality in which this level was one among others, interconnection rather than disconnection was essential to constructions of social difference cast and managed partly in these terms. But increasingly, these levels of Aboriginal social organization have come to be seen as perhaps providing forms with fixed boundaries, determinate membership—indigenous possibilities for the management of Aboriginal affairs. Further consequences flow from this. After the Katherine Area Land Claim, an incorporated body, the Jawoyn Association, was formed; Wardaman Association followed a few years later. To the north of the Katherine region, incorporated bodies have been formed to receive and handle mining royalties. With all such organizational structures come issues of managing social fields in rapidly changing circumstances, for new purposes. But new circumstances and purposes sometimes do not easily mesh with existing Aboriginal understandings of social practice and representation.

Reified understandings of Aboriginal organization also now enter into the way socio-territorial designations are used among Aboriginal people struggling to come to terms with their new circumstances. For instance, I referred above to the situation of some younger active participants in town Aboriginal affairs, whose attempts to systematize, understand, and act in terms of concepts of the distribution of socio-territorial identities is increasingly informed by recognition of social change. This combination of recognition and attempted systematization has burst the bounds of unproblematized notions of identification of the town area in socio-territorial terms. On the other hand, as a spotlight has come to be focused on the issue of who belongs to the town area, these younger people increasingly use high-level terms of identity more as Arndt did, as if they designate nonoverlapping and therefore manageable segmentations of the Aboriginal social field, and of country. But as we have seen, what such terms designate is always socio-historically complex. The signification of "Jawoyn" as used with respect to the town has changed. Among other things, it is now one form of identification through which Aboriginal people continuously attached to the Katherine area designate their sense of affiliation to it; it does not designate a neatly manageable segment of a social field divisible into component parts.

These kinds of (increasingly, even if partly, intercultural) adaptations of historical forms of organization to "creating the other as the other" and "incorporating the other within a single social and cultural system" reveal one mode of the recent era of benevolent recuperation to be imitative, or mimetic (Taussig 1993). Apparently Aboriginal forms of organization come to play a role in new ways; but this aspect of their survival cannot, in my view, be seen as one of pure continuity in Aboriginal culture. Although mimesis may appear most clearly as a postcolonial rather than colonial form of power, in its emphasis on cooperation rather than imposition in a combined moral and practical quest for coexistence, it has some roots in and commonalities with earlier, more clearly colonial forms of power. For, as I have tried to show in this chapter, change and continuity are not absolute. In the next chapter, I attempt to establish some perspectives on change in forms of governance of Aboriginal affairs. These perspectives provide a framework for the final two chapters, which consider complexities in the lives of Aborigines under these changing forms of governance.

Five

Imposition and Imitation: Changing Directions in Aboriginal Affairs

THIS CHAPTER, like the last, considers what can be meant by change and continuity. But it differs from the last in looking at the issue from the perspective of the external management of Aboriginal affairs, rather than beginning from an Aboriginal perspective. At the end of the last chapter, I suggested that it is important to do this because the survival of "tribal" identities cannot be understood as pure continuity of Aboriginal culture. In recent times, the "tribal" level and other forms of organization have been elicited from Aborigines, and given greater concreteness and fixity than they previously had, as part of a wider project of management of Aboriginal affairs. In this chapter, I attempt to place that project in sociohistorical perspective, especially in relation to the development of the Australian nation-state.

The principal, explicit policy change in Australian Aboriginal affairs over the past two to three decades is often summarized as a shift from an earlier, long-standing concept of "assimilation," in terms of which Aborigines were to come to live in a manner indistinguishable from other (which?) Australians, to a concept of "self-determination" (Sanders 1982). The aim of government policy, in the words (in 1972) of Labor Prime Minister Gough Whitlam, was to "restore to the Aboriginal people of Australia their lost power of self-determination in economic, social and political affairs," so that they may take up "as a distinctive and honoured component in the Australian society the position to which their rights as the first Australians entitled them." I think this shift can be understood as signaling government intention to move from a style of overt coercion, or imposition of non-Aboriginal modes of action, aspiration, and regulation upon Aboriginal people, to one that in many respects seeks to elicit from Aboriginal people what are taken to exist as their own modes of organization and to recast the management of Aboriginal affairs in what are seen to be indigenous terms. This is a style I call imitative or "mimetic" in the kind of complex mirroring relationship described by Taussig (1993:2): there is appeal to a "magical power of replication, the image affected by what it is an image of, wherein the representation shares in or takes power from the represented." Representations of Aboriginality as made most powerfully by others come to affect who and what Aborigines consider themselves to be. The imitative relation as lived out in Australia has rested on an assumption that Aboriginal cultural production continues to be autonomous from what previously sought to encompass or displace it. Further, the relation often requires from Aborigines demonstrations of the autonomy and long-standing nature of what is seen as their cultural production. This requirement is reminiscent of Roosens' (1989:153) claim, based on his work with the Huron Indians of Canada, that "culture struggle" is a recently developed mode of interaction between indigenous peoples and wealthy, liberal, democratic nation-states.

In this chapter, I examine in its imitative aspects what has been one of the major dimensions of recent Aboriginal affairs, especially since the late 1960s, galvanizing both government policy orientations and Aboriginal activism: land rights. I will focus most closely on the context of the implementation of land rights legislation in the Northern Territory in 1976 and then, more briefly, also consider the nature of the federal Native Title Act 1993, which has implications for Australia as a whole. One of the questions I will raise is how to understand that the issue of "land" has played such a large role in recent Aboriginal affairs. Under certain assumptions, the answer might be taken to be obvious and the issue simply as one of the preservation of continuity: land has always been the ground of Aboriginal being, and this relationship is finally given recognition. But in light of the concept of imitation as an aspect of recent relationship between Aborigines and the state, the focus on land comes to have a less obvious and natural character and therefore needs to be considered in other ways.

Examination of relationships between Aborigines and the state is linked to questions concerning changing forms of anthropological representation. To some extent, the Australian government has long relied on anthropological appraisals of Aboriginal life to inform policy directions. But these appraisals have varied over time, and in a general sense shifts in predominant views can be seen to have paralleled broad shifts in Aboriginal affairs policy. We need to be able to reckon with the following kind of paradox: in the 1930s, 1940s, and 1950s, A. P. Elkin, professor of anthropology at the University of Sydney, visited Aborigines in remote Australia who had little concept of the wider world and envisioned granting to them civic rights, as yet foreign to them, in ways that he imagined eventually would produce tax-paying, voting, overall-wearing workers productive in a harmonious, united Australia; more recently, anthropologists whose writings arguably constitute the present mainstream of Aboriginalist ethnography, visiting remote settlements forty years later, have emphasized (despite considerable evidence of change) the transcendence and persistence of meanings and dimensions of action originating in the distinctive, precolonial form of Aboriginal life. Is this a new (or renewed) form of anthropological traditionalism? And if so, how may one understand its relationship to the broad policy shift sketched above? Is a new traditionalism characteristic of anthropological accounts of Fourth World peoples, as Riches (1990) appears to suggest of Eskimology?

As we consider land rights as instantiation of an increasingly imitative rather than overtly coercive relationship between Aborigines and the nation-state, it will be important to differentiate the locations in which mimesis is seen as progressive and is administratively, legislatively, and judicially supported. We will consider evidence of Euro-Australian resistance at the local level of towns like Katherine to change emanating from the national center and seek to identify some general as well as distinctively Australian aspects of this struggle.

People and Land: Colonial and Postcolonial Australia

By looking outside Australia to the history of the British in India, we are able to gain some perspective on the question of continuity and discontinuity between more and less coercive forms of management of colonized peoples, the difference now often phrased as one between "colonialism" and "post-colonialism." Cohn (1996) has written about what might be called the "culture struggle" between Britain and India at different levels. His work shows clearly that prominent Britons, particularly many who played a role in the evolution of the administrative relationship between the two countries, saw India as a great civilization with a past worth preserving. Some, like Edmund Burke in his address to the Parliament of 1783 regarding the mismanagement of the East India Company and its future, in that context went so far as to declare that the populace of the "great empire" was neither "abject" nor "barbarous"; there were in it "princes once of great dignity, authority, and opulence" (Burke 1960:272). High regard, however, as this quote suggests, was often specialized in its reference to kinds of Indians. The collections of objects, the colonial cataloguing of things and peoples and territory, went on for decades under the assumption that the British could salvage and preserve a past that was now decadent. It was widely assumed that contemporary Indians were incapable of appreciating and preserving this past properly, that it would be lost without British management of it.

In this history, the tendency toward preservationism is seen to be compatible with a largely coercive administrative style. In fact, it is historically linked with the British effort to develop a manageable system of "indirect rule," one that relied on working through existing indigenous forms of authority, reorganized in fealty to the English Crown.

The colonial history of Australia differed profoundly in many basic respects. It was a settler colony, what quickly came to be its dominant population originating from Great Britain, and thus largely attuned to the thinking that informed colonial policy; thus the indigenous population was rapidly dispossessed and suppressed. After a long time and many disparate events, the management of Aboriginal affairs has come back to something that has in common with indirect rule the concept that indigenous formations may provide the most desirable basis for a relationship of their coexistence with the nation-state. It would seem that imitation as a mode of relationship is neither inherently colonial nor postcolonial and may be more or less coercive and feasible at different periods and under varying conditions. There would seem, though, to be strands of continuity between the preservationism that was part of the British appreciation of Indian culture and the increasingly imitative mode in which modern nation-states cast their relationships with indigenous peoples.

Following an early period in which explorers, upon encountering Aborigines, sometimes echoed the Rousseauian view of Captain James Cook that "they are happier than we," the longer-term history of settlement was dominated by sentiments that the natives of Australia were abject and that their way of life had little of permanence or worth—better that it be replaced by a way of life characterized by "industry" and productivity and opening up of the land. But there were always elements of both kinds of thinking, recognition and denial, present in the colonial context (as there were also in India, viz. Macaulay's denigration of the Sanskrit classics in reaction to earlier, he thought excessive, appreciation of them). Recently, the pendulum has swung in the direction of recognition. There was always, however, some colonial sense of duty, of care and recognition, recently brought more centrally into the current debate by the work of Australian historian Henry Reynolds (1987), who has argued that concessions made by the British government to Aborigines early in the nineteenth century might now be taken as having amounted to the granting of land rights. This brings us to some consideration of Australian colonial history and the shifts in relationships between Aborigines and the modernizing nation-state.

Bhabha (1990) has recently vitalized the investigation of how the field of meaning and symbols associated with national life is constructed. Deleuze and Guattari (1987:456) suggest that the basic constituents of a nation-state are a land and a people, where land is understood as a deterritorialized geographical area and people as a decoded population, a free flow of labor. Changing interrelationship between these as culturally constructed lies at the heart of meanings and symbols of Australian national life. Many of the recent pressures for recognition of Aboriginality have been generated within the social and discursive struggle for definition of nationality (and also *inter*nationality, that is, the imagining of the Australian nation as a mature subject in a wider field of national subjects), rather than within a purely internal field of relations. Part of the process of coming of age in a former colony of settlement, but now a modernizing nation, has been to conceptualize as a people those rendered marginal to the body politic through dispossession. The logic is one by which the Aboriginal, as a kind of political subject under construction (the searched-for "self" of "self-determination"), is produced and contested as a type of nationality, problematically related to the changing national subject itself. Just as the nation is territorially based, so the territorial attachment of such a subject is also envisaged in a shadowy manner even by those who deny it and contest its continuity with the past and its contemporary strength. Let us consider some aspects of the temporally disjunct formation of Australian and Aboriginal subjecthood at this broad level.

Only fairly recently have politicians toned down proclamations of a British Australia. At the time of federation of the Australian Commonwealth "under the Crown of the United Kingdom" by an act of 1900, Australia was seen as an outpost of Britain. The connection remained strong for a long time, though class, religious, and ethnic divisions (as between English and Irish) underlying this were manifested in an Australian strand of anti-English democratic egalitarianism, oppositional sentiment between Irish Catholicism and Anglo Protestantism, and not least, in an aggressive labor movement.

Against this (relatively homogeneous) background, Australia was renowned, if not infamous, for its "White Australia policy" (London 1970, Wilton and Bosworth 1984). This was not embodied in any single parliamentary act, but was a form of words capturing widespread negative attitudes toward the immigration into Australia of people seen as "colored." The Immigration Restriction Bill, the main law that gave effect to the White Australia policy, was introduced into the first Commonwealth Parliament. Rejecting the view that the bill was primarily seen and justified in its time as a form of economic protectionism, aiming to bar cheap labor, Ward (1977:34–35) points out that proponents of the bill were much more strongly moved by arguments concerning the innate inferiority of the colored, the need for Australia to protect itself against "contamination," and in some cases by concerns about the vast cultural differences separating the Chinese and other people to be excluded from the Australian majority, strategically and neologistically designated in this context as Anglo-Celts (Ward 1977:31). These racially explicit arguments were thinly disguised by the requirement that immigrants pass an English-language (amended to European-language) dictation test. Sydney historian George Arnold Wood's words of 1917 express a defensive sense of the regional location of what was then seen as the Australian people: "White Australia is not an opinion; it is the watchword or war cry of a tiny garrison which holds the long frontier of the white world in front of the multitudinous and expansive peoples of Asia" (Crawford 1975:310).

In the period before World War II, immigration restrictions applied to a large category of colored undesirables that included not only Asians, but Lebanese, those who might generally be designated Mediterraneans, and any others considered "non-White." In 1945, the Australian nation of seven million knew itself to be "very largely British," with qualities "only drawn from the British race" (Wilton and Bosworth 1984:1) and with a strong preference for filling up its empty spaces by Bringing Out a Briton, as the slogan of one post–World War II assisted migration campaign went. But finally heeding the injunction of Billy Hughes, prime minister during the World War I era to "populate or perish" and what were seen as the lessons of World War II, in 1945 Arthur Calwell, Australia's first minister of immigration, inaugurated much-more-sweeping programs that went well beyond Great Britain in the drive for immigrants. For the first time, large numbers of other, formerly nonpreferred continentals (including some of those, like southern Italians, who had been considered among the colored), were admitted. Another aspect of change was the growing perception that Australia was, in some sense at least, part of Asia: trade ties with Japan strengthened as those with Britain and European nations weakened. Australia had Asian allies in the Southeast Asia Treaty Organization (SEATO). In the context of the Asian region, continuation of the White Australia policy was an embarrassment. Yet despite the changes he helped bring about, Calwell remained an advocate of the policy, as did many other Australians. Immigration had been broadened as a tool of nation building, and Australia was increasingly conscious and proud of its immigration-driven diversity, but it was not ready to abandon the concept of a unitary nation-state in which the normal and preferred type of citizen was held, by government at least, to be the "Anglo-Celt," or similar to him.

Although Prime Minister Robert Menzies continued to proclaim a British Australia until his retirement in 1963, by that time an enormous influx of diverse peoples had been going on for nearly twenty years. As to principal sources of social and political influence upon Australia in the postwar, an increasing number of Australians would have agreed that Menzies, in his sixteen years in office, had gone on "using comfortable British symbols even if they were now concealing Americanised reality. Though a rhetorician of monarchy and Britishness, it was he who presided while the British connection disintegrated" (Horne 1980:2).

The scale and organization of postwar immigration has brought Australia to see itself as "multicultural," despite periodic surfacing of public sentiment and nostalgia for a homogeneous Australia (recently, in 1983–1984 and in 1996, manifested in the rise of a rhetoric of intolerance, principally in relation to Asians, who currently constitute about 5 percent of the Australian population, and Aborigines, who in terms of the liberalized Commonwealth definition of 1970 constitute less than 2 percent). Multiculturalism Australian-style has involved increasing consciousness of national diversity and conscious cultivation of tolerance for it. As governmental rhetoric and action, it is perhaps preeminently a set of practices relating to cultivating regard for others different from oneself, with some support of exemplary pluralist practice and the maintenance of "cultural" heritage. The polity is enriched, strengthened, and matured (Hage 1993) thereby, the diversity not demanding denial of singular nationhood.[1]

Becoming a People of Worth

Assimilationist policy with respect to Aborigines remained vaguely formulated for several decades while the principal carriage of Aboriginal affairs rested severally with the states and territories, rather than with the Commonwealth. It was finally most explicitly articulated in 1961, at a Native Welfare Conference of ministers, as involving the concept that "all aborigines and part-aborigines are expected eventually to attain the same manner of living as other Australians and to live as members of a single Australian community enjoying the same rights and privileges, accepting the same responsibilities, observing the same customs and influenced by the same beliefs, hopes and loyalties as other Australians" (cited in Bennett 1989:23). At the time, this seemed a progressive notion, given the disadvantages under which Aborigines obviously lived. But it proved to be just on the cusp of the subsequent period in which the Commonwealth, by national referendum, was granted powers to legislate in respect to Aborigines with a view to improving their situation. The Commonwealth further constituted itself as a modern nation capable of encompassing rather than marginalizing diversity by that assumption of powers. The referendum of 1967, again, was understood at that time as an extension of the much-vaunted, democratic egalitarian Australian "fair go" to Aborigines, rather than recognition of them as a distinctive segment of the population. In the media campaign around the referendum, for example, the *Sydney Morning Herald* of May 19, 1967, urged,

> Vote "Yes" for Aborigines, they want to be Australians too,
> Vote "Yes" to give them rights and freedoms just like me and you,
> Vote "Yes" for Aborigines, all parties say they think you should,
> Vote "Yes" and show the world the true Australian brotherhood.

Aborigines, considered British subjects since colonization, were only recognized as Australian citizens in the context of the large postwar immigrant in-take. The Federal Nationality and Citizenship Act 1948–1955 was introduced to regularize the situation of the thousands of postwar migrants to Australia. Incidentally, under Section 10, every Aboriginal born in Australia was recognized as a citizen of the Commonwealth.[2]

Episodes of the referendum period indicate experimentation with the notion of a rainbow coalition that might have brought together "colored" people, Aborigines with others, in protest against discriminatory treatment of them as citizens of the Australian state. Charles Perkins, a rising activist and in 1965 an organizer of Freedom Rides through New South Wales (modeled on those that had taken place in the American South), sought to dramatize the inequities of Australian immigration and the White Australia policy by kidnaping a young Fijian girl, Nancy Prasad, who with other family members was under a deportation order (Wilton and Bosworth 1984:31, Perkins 1975:92–97). Later, with the development of more specifically Aboriginal activism, Perkins became convinced that "we should have no coloured immigration into this country until such time as the Aborigines are satisfactorily placed in Australian society" (Perkins 1975:97). Nevertheless, at the earlier time, because the distinctions previously drawn suggested the inclusiveness of the category of "colored," actions like the kidnaping could be understood to be making a statement about racial discrimination, and could achieve some effect, by locating Aborigines within this wider category.

Consciousness of Aborigines as a culturally distinctive people whose claims upon the state might be largely made in the name of that collective identity was in keeping with changes occurring internationally in the postwar period. By a 1960 resolution of the General Assembly, the United Nations made a Declaration on the Granting of Independence to Colonial Countries and Peoples proclaiming the right of all people to determine their political status and pursue their economic, social, and cultural development (cited in Brennan 1991:45). Faith Bandler (1983:15), a woman of New Hebridean (Vanuatu) extraction who was active in the latter 1950s in founding an organization in Sydney called the Aboriginal-Australian Fellowship, confirms the influence of refugees from Hitler Germany in raising consciousness against the policy of assimilation as a form of annihilation. In June 1971 Prime Minister William McMahon created a department of the Environment, Aborigines and the Arts. The historian Donald Horne (1980:7) has commented of the previous, long ministry that "it would have been psychically impossible" for the Liberal party's prime minister, Robert Menzies (in office 1947–1963), to have established such an organization. On Australia Day 1972, Prime Minister McMahon, soon to be replaced by Whitlam and a Labor government, declared that Aborigines were entitled to four kinds of determinations and rights: to decide to what degree and at what rate they would identify with "one Australian society" and to both preserve and develop their own culture (see also Stanner 1979:300–301).

But the colonial dilemma of the prior Aboriginal encumbrance of the land through these changes has remained. In this, immigrants belong to the majoritarian nation as those who came later. This dilemma as an aspect of the national formation has not been openly or broadly addressed until recently.

Given its sociohistorical origins in both originary and colonial domains and in the dynamics of struggle within which those identities are constructed, the concept of Aboriginality, and indeed of indigeneity, necessarily involves a territorial dimension. Aboriginality, as a category of political subjecthood relative to the nation-state that has given it life, has been underlain by the painful drawing out, bit by bit, of the historical dilemma at the basis of Australia as a settler colony: the prior encumbrance of the land, the life-space of the nation-state. We turn next to various aspects of Australia's relationship to its territory, Deleuze and Guattari's (1987) second basic constituent of the nation-state.

The Land

Relevant both to the reconstruction of meanings and symbols associated with national life and the centrality of images and issues of Aboriginality among them is the unusual geophysical nature of the Australian continent, to which are related long-term constraints on patterns of settlement and settler population distributions.

In an influential history, Hancock (1930) argued that Australian history was in large part the progressive mastery of the land. He called his first chapter "The Invasion of Australia," the second "Transplanted British," and the eighth, "Filling the Vast Open Spaces." Connell (1974:33) points out that many subsequent historians, following Hancock's lead, discussed the inflow of British settlers, their spread across the land, and their struggle with the environment and mastery of it, as formative influences on Australian life. To the imaginative absorption with Australia's open spaces must be related the slight and belated attention paid to Australia's urbanism

(Stretton 1975), despite its historical predominance and social significance. Australia has always been one of the most highly urban polities in the world. From a high point of rural distribution of settler population in the early 1900s, by 1960 more than two-thirds of Australians lived in cities, and in the present, more than 80 percent live "in the six capital cities and the 'urban sprawl' attaching to each" (Ward 1977:370).

There have been strong attempts to implant in Australia an ideology of people "on the land" (Ward 1977:274), the power of which lies partly in positive moral valuation of primary production. The difficulty of settlement of any significant number of people on the land is shown in Australia's ever-declining rural population. The last state-level close-land settlement scheme was abandoned in 1970 (Horne 1980:104).

Despite ideological emphases on the "land," its settlement in Australia has never been complete, if by this we mean its thoroughgoing productive domestication. The interior is arid and semiarid. Following exploration, settlement was early attempted in many places where it did not succeed and from which withdrawal was necessary, either temporarily or permanently (for an illuminating account of the Northern Territory, see Donovan 1981; see also Davidson 1966).

Major Australian settlement was everywhere coastal (Roberts 1968). From the sea, tentative inland excursions were launched, many of them failing to result in such hoped-for outcomes as finding an inland sea or lengthy navigable waterway on which permanent inland settlements might be established. The interior is still very sparsely populated, even if large sections have been considerably degraded and presettlement biodiversity altered by sheep and cattle pastoralism and other attempts at industrial uses. Australia's largest inland city is the federal capital, Canberra, which has only 310,000 people. A completely planned city, Canberra was sited where it is to resolve conflict between the two metropolises of Sydney and Melbourne about which would be home to the national capital; it is not a spontaneous inland urban growth. For the Australian Bicentennial in 1988, the last section of a national highway which for the most part hugs the coast, was completed. There are few major interior highways; there is currently no rail connection linking the Northern Territory with South Australia, nor the remote north of Western Australia with its distant capital, Perth. In the Northern Territory, Asian developers are investigating the feasibility of reestablishing a north-south, Darwin to Adelaide, rail line (closed in 1975).

Onto the enormous openness of the interior continent settlers have always projected constructions of Outback and empty or sparsely populated expanse (see, e.g., White 1981, chapter 6, "Bohemians and the Bush"). Depending on the climate of expectation, these expanses have alternately been seen as inviting development, as wonderful pastureland and endless opportunity or as remote, inhospitable wilds, as if an Aboriginal population had not been present, or if it were considered at all, as if its presence did little to mitigate the wildness.

Given the objectively enormous, relatively empty interior of the continent, it has always been possible to think of remote areas as a space of traditional Aboriginal life. The continuing possibility of unchanged Aborigines living out there somewhere in a traditional manner is something that excites interest, occasionally fed by events, as for example, when a small group of nine Aborigines walked into a remote Western Desert settlement in 1984 (Myers 1988). (They had, in fact, been aware of the settlement for a long time and had had sporadic contact with relatives there.)

Persistent national imagining of Aborigines "out there," able to cope in the uncharted vastness, has been manifested in written and visual media. In the film *Walkabout*, two city children, left stranded in the desert by their civilization-wracked parents, are led back to settlement by an Aborigine who finds them and guides them. He is ultimately destroyed by the encounter and their lack of response to him. In a more lighthearted vein, the 1986 film *Crocodile Dundee* both relies upon and satirizes nativistic imagery of the Aborigine in the remote north and of the unsophisticated but democratic and truehearted white Aussie bushman.

In contrast to the imagery of open expanses, recent years have seen a heightening of consciousness concerning the historical role of people, principally the settler population, in altering the Australian environment (Horne 1980:75–79). This has accompanied and strengthened environmentalist action. In Australia, high on the contemporary environmentalist agenda are issues of woodchipping and reversing the massive deforestation that has occurred since colonization, the degradation of soil and coastal environments, social and environmental questions concerning uranium and other mining, the scourge of blue-green algae on inland waterways, and so on. There appears to be considerable governmental support for converting remote lands formerly held to have rural industrial potential to parkland. A contentious issue continues to be the evaluation of mining within areas now desirable for their "natural" condition.

In the conversion of expanses of country to parkland, Aboriginal people have been more widely recognized and represented as those whose role of stewardship in relation to the land, although the subject of some academic as well as public debate (see, e.g., Marcus 1988, Barsh 1990, Sackett 1991, Swain 1991, Rose 1992), was one of benign use and maintenance rather than transformation. But representations of Aborigines as originary stewards are also contested, along two lines. Some critics (often representatives of industrial interests) contend that the price of benign precolonial stewardship was lack of productivity that cannot be a model for the modern world. Others argue that contemporary Aboriginal relations to the land are so changed that they do not provide useful indications for contemporary management. But parks managers commission considerable research in the attempt—related to the concept of imitation discussed in this chapter—to discover the nature of earlier Aboriginal forms of land management. In these ways, traditional Aboriginal relations to the land are recognized and engaged in wider debates about contemporary land use, especially of remote areas whose industrial potential has been reassessed as largely residing in tourist and other visitor values and, in some areas, in mineral potential. "Touristic space" is that made available to visitors to experience the nation, and there is a current effort to entice Aborigines into that space, not exactly in a capacity as stewards of the land, but to exhibit themselves in fetishized form as interesting and even essential to what the nation is (Povinelli 1993:217–219, Hage 1993:128). The space of mining is rather different in the ways it is seen to engage Aborigines, with its possibilities of royalty monies, industrial transformation, and progressive imagery on the one hand, and culturally based resistance to mining on Aborigines' part on the other (see Kolig 1987).

Also part of the history of Australia's relation to its territory is the way in which land has been a medium in the evolution of governmental structures. Historically loose integration of Australia's political system is related to geophysical constraints, both within the continent and in the distance that separated Australia from the colonizing power, Britain (see Blainey 1982). Integration was tightened in the period following World War II, and the nation-state is now characterized by a high degree of political centralization, combined with continuing resistances of certain states and regions to this.

Perhaps the greatest resistance to political centralization has been manifested by those states with a large proportion of rural-dwelling population dependent on rural and extractive industries, notably Western Australia and Queensland. Perth is the most isolated capital city in the world, separated from the eastern population centers by an enormous expanse of desert. Western Australia, originally populated in the course of gold rushes, voted to join the Commonwealth only at the last minute, as a result of a renewed influx of voting "other siders" from the eastern colonies. As the Depression deepened in this century, Western Australians, more convinced than ever that they could not compete with established manufacturing in the eastern states nor resist the imposition of protective tariffs, agitated to secede from the federation and set up as an independent dominion within the Commonwealth, its voters favoring this option by a majority of nearly two to one (Ward 1977:205).

In Queensland in the last century, and in New South Wales during the Depression, there were rurally based movements for subdivision of certain regions as new states of the federation, based on resentment of political domination from Brisbane and Sydney respectively. Attitudinal independence of certain states and regions has not been matched by their actual and potential fiscal independence at those levels, however (Ward 1977:135, 156–157).

Northern Territorians, like settlers of other remote regions (Jull 1992), have long taken the view that with respect to some issues, they are political and fiscal hostages to the federal government. There is a Northern Territorian rhetoric of their superior knowledge of the "real" conditions of their region, versus the unreality of the thinking of federal bureaucrats (mentioned in chapter 2). Tension in this relationship of dependence has been mitigated by the establishment of Territorian self-government from 1978, but not yet amounting to statehood. A crucial aspect of the relation has been Northern Territorian reliance upon Commonwealth funding (at least since South Australia, the original mother colony, passed its burden to the Commonwealth in 1911). One of the implications of full statehood for the Northern Territory, which may soon be realized, is the necessity for expansion of a local revenue base (Gibbins 1987 discusses the implications of statehood for Aboriginal people). This underscores Territorian concern with the earning potential of the region's primary industry and rural industry and with land management and control that is manifest in the sensitivity of the issue of Northern Territorian versus federal control of national parks and of uranium mining.[3]

Given the liberal democratic nature of the Australian state and its highly urban population, governments have tended to reflect the electoral strength of the historically weaker secondary (manufacturing) and tertiary sectors of the economy, manned by the concentrated populations of the capital cities. On the other hand, a succession of (regionally, variably profitable) primary industries—formerly wool and agricultural products and now mining exports—have provided the bulk of national earnings. In the case of the Katherine region, pastoralism was, overall, historically unprofitable, made so by a whole series of physical, market, and other constraints. That situation was accompanied, despite ideological emphases upon the independence of the man on the land and the moral value of primary production, by producers' demands for government assistance, as well as by protest against government initiatives concerning wage structure and objection to what are seen as forms of unearned welfare. Enactment of a comprehensive land-rights package with major redistributive effects, discussed later in this chapter, was possible in the Northern Territory only because of its dependent status. Conviction to enact such a measure could not have been elicited politically from that regional population. A sense of the political relation between the Territory and the federal government as this has manifested itself in Aboriginal affairs has been summarized in this way: "If the Northern Territory is different it is different because of the extensive accommodations that are being made to Aboriginal power in the growth of political institutions. Historically the least successfully colonized political unit in Australia, it has also been the most affected by the pro-Aboriginal mandate among settlers of the south eastern industrial seaboard" (Rowse 1983:82).

By about 1970, conditions had been established for the recognition of Aborigines as a distinctive people with claims to regard. Aborigines were a potential nation, but without matching territory. Since the passage of the Aboriginal Land Rights (Northern Territory) Act 1976, nearly half of the Territory's land area has come under Aboriginal title, a situation that will probably remain unmatched elsewhere in Australia.

Land Rights and Imitation

Jones and Hill-Burnett (1982, but based on survey work of the mid-1970s) have argued that the demands of an oppressed population are poised between the "cultural" and "political" as competing bases for groupwide identity. They suggest (1982:240) that the history of interaction between Australian Aborigines and the nation-state has involved the reduction of a full scope of Aboriginal claims to the more limited demand to retain racial and cultural heritage. This suggestion is debatable, to the considerable extent that land and its resources have played a significant role and have a materiality of which the wider Australian populace is very conscious. The demand for land rights (and the granting of land) can be seen as a signifier of political claims by Aboriginal peoples, if not of a unified nationhood, and is not just a "cultural" claim as the latter term is commonly understood. Jones and Hill-Burnett may, however, be right if they are understood to say that there is some effort among supporters of claims to argue for them as restoring and preserving Aboriginal culture, to the extent that this may make them more acceptable in the wider political arena. (For a fuller account of Australian land-rights provisions than is given here and reference to other states and territories, see Bennett 1989:29–37 and a considerable body of recent material on the Native Title Act, discussed briefly below.)

Perhaps partly because it is neither simply "cultural" nor "political," but both material and "symbolic," cultural and profoundly political, the claim of land rights for Aboriginal people became a central issue around which Aboriginal demand and liberal protest from non-Aborigines on their behalf were able to crystallize. The raising of a much-publicized Aboriginal "tent embassy" on the lawns before Parliament House on Australia Day 1972 helped to unite these voices in putting forward claims among which land rights were central. Although drafted during the Whitlam Labor government, the Aboriginal Land Rights (Northern Territory) Act 1976 was passed during the subsequent Liberal–Country party ministry of Prime Minister Malcolm Fraser: recognition of land rights as a significant issue in a recuperative Aboriginal affairs strategy was bipartisan.

Drafting of the legislation was a response to recent denial of Aboriginal ownership of land in the Northern Territory, near the community of Yirrkala in far northeastern Arnhem Land (see Williams 1986). In light of proposed bauxite mining development near them and the excision of a mining lease for the purpose by the federal government, Aborigines of Yirrkala were plaintiffs in a case alleging their ownership of the area in question, which came before the Supreme Court of the Northern Territory in 1968. (Williams 1986 provides full discussion.) In his findings of 1971, presiding justice Blackburn deemed them to have demonstrated the systematicity of their ties to land, though not exactly on the bases the plaintiffs had originally stated. But he judged that they did not "own" the land: they had not demonstrated that theirs was a right of property at the common law. Among other things, he considered they could not definitively show the historical continuity of particular (clan-level) relationships to the area from colonization in 1788. He also found that the plaintiffs did not demonstrate the characteristics of proprietary relationship—the right to exclude others, the right to alienate—as he alleged this was understood at common law.

As a result of the plaintiffs' failure to gain recognition of their ownership of the land in this widely publicized case (and given the rise of claims for land rights in the Victoria River region, see Hardy 1968), it appeared to many supporters of Aboriginal rights that only by the passage of specific, beneficial statutes could Aborigines be empowered to gain some recognized form of title to what they regarded as their lands. A royal commission was established in 1972 to inquire into the means by which this might be brought about. The queen's counsel who had acted for the Yirrkala Aborigines, Woodward, was appointed to head the commission. It was given wide-ranging powers and could have made recommendations for Australia as a whole, undoubtedly an extremely difficult exercise, given the different conditions of land tenure and the diversity of Aboriginal people's conditions; its final reports of 1973 and 1974 laid the basis for the subsequent drafting of the Aboriginal Land Rights (Northern Territory) Act 1976 which, as its title suggests, has operated since then in the Northern Territory only.

A major political factor in this situation, referred to above, has been precisely the territorial status of the Northern Territory and the fact that in it, Aborigines constitute about 22.4 percent of the total population of about 175,000, a much higher proportion than anywhere in any other Australian state or territory. Under the Land Rights Act, claim can be made by Aborigines only to vacant Crown land, in which no other person besides the Crown holds an estate or interest. There were in the Northern Territory large areas of vacant Crown land. In these pragmatic political terms, it was more feasible to legislate for Aboriginal land rights in the Northern Territory (or impose them, as many white Territorians have seen it), than it would have been to establish a land-rights regime with such significant redistributive effects anywhere else in Australia.

Another issue, however, is the form of demonstration of Aboriginal relationship to land that was required under the legislation. Some argued that only traditional Aboriginal relationships to country should be a basis for claim, those demonstrated to be of long standing and assumed by Aboriginal people from their forebears; others argued, as did Justice Woodward in his original recommendations, that many Aborigines had been "deprived of the rights and interests which they would otherwise have inherited from their ancestors" and needed land granted to them to live, though their relation to it might be other than "traditional." The latter basis was termed a "needs" claim, one that might begin a process of recuperation following upon what Woodward called the "breaking of the spiritual link with his own land which gives each Aboriginal his sense of identity and which lies at the heart of his spiritual beliefs" (cited in Neate 1989:9; see Merlan 1994 for the contrast in political negotiation of the land-claims process between notions of "entitlement" and "need").[4]

Ultimately, the legislation was written in a way that was intended to reproduce or imitate the basis of traditional Aboriginal socio-territorial relationships—to which the history of anthropological inquiry into and representation of Aboriginal relationships to land may be said to have had some material relation, even if not a simple one. Let us consider the form that requirements of proof took and relate this to questions of anthropological representation and those of change in Aboriginal life that have been the subject matter of this book.

Under the Land Rights Act, to be found to be "traditional owners" in respect to claimed land, Aboriginal claimants must go through a hearings process before a land commissioner and must be found to be: "a local descent group of Aboriginals who: (a) have common spiritual affiliations to a site on the land, being affiliations that place the group under a primary spiritual responsibility for that site and for the land; and (b) are entitled by Aboriginal tradition to forage as of right over that land."

Demonstration is required of relevant ownership through proof of the existence of a "group" that is in some sense local and constituted by descent. Commonality of affiliations to land on the part of the group's members is to be shown, and primacy of spiritual responsibility on the part of the group or its members. The requirement of entitlement to "forage as of right" has a more material ring than some of the other provisions but is to be found in conjunction with them.

At the time, anthropological advisers to Woodward assumed that such a formulation was relatively clear-cut. Anthropologists expected that proof would largely take the form of demonstration of clan (or clanlike) organization as the basis of relationship (see Neate 1989). When many claims turned out to diverge from the simplicity of this notion, anthropologists criticized the Land Rights Act for having foisted upon the claims process an outdated, Radcliffe-Brownian view of the Aboriginal world as composed of socially and spatially bounded and autonomous units like clans. To some extent cutting across the conservatism of the act's formulation and anthropologists' expectations has been the land commissioners' conception of their task, as lawyers, to hear Aboriginal evidence as the "facts" of each case and decide whether those facts meet the statutory requirements, leaving the possibility of how they may be said to do so more open than many anthropologists had expected. In fact, the range of accepted claims has been expanded well beyond the limits of a clan model, but the extent to which change as anthropologists might feel it appropriate to recognize change is still, in my view, highly constrained. The act is clearly constrained, too, by bounding "rules of the game": according to an established "sunset" clause, new land claims cannot be lodged after June 1997.

In the years following the negotiation and passage of the act, anthropologists vigorously refocused on the nature of Aboriginal socio-territorial organization, to the extent that questions of territoriality and relationship to land became the signature of much Aboriginalist work of the 1980s (cf. Strathern 1990 on regional ethnographies). Perhaps the most masterful and lasting work of those years, Myers' *Pintupi Country, Pintupi Self* (1986), grappled with the problem of the excessively concrete and structural character of the body of writings on Aboriginal social organization. The ethnographic present of his book should be located, in the main, in 1973–1979. Myers writes of Western Desert people (Pintupi), largely living on remote area settlements. Writing against notions of action as strongly determined by social "forms," Myers revises those kinds of analysis partly by locating agency at the level of the cultural subject whose choices exist in the persistent tension between "autonomy," the potential and drive for individuation in action (which he found to be strong among Pintupi), and "relatedness," binding persons to others. He develops the concept of a regional system (apprehensible in Aborigines' notions of "countrymen") wherein individuals act on multiple bases, in terms of available cultural constructs, in forming aggregations. Moving away from strong determinism, Myers characterizes the achievement of social coordination ("polity") as problematic and the "Dreaming" (*tjukurrpa*) as a master objectification, grounded in country, compelling precisely in that it is seen to be outside everyday sociality, "not our idea," as Pintupi say. Through the concept of Dreaming, Aborigines project for themselves images of persistence amidst social action that is in fact intensely negotiated, its course never unproblematically given.

In another work of the period, not as explicitly focused on issues of emplacement but also, though in a different vein from Myers, addressed to conceptual problems in earlier structural accounts of Aboriginal social organization, Sansom (1980) wrote of a kind of social scene around the capital of the Northern Territory, Darwin, that has been given little attention by anthropologists: urban fringe-camping (but see Collman 1988). He develops a phenomenologically and transactionally inspired view of the essential character of modes of action, focusing upon a concept of an Aboriginal social economy of the "word," the time- and person-bound objectification of shared experience that shapes the present and projects it as the only known form of futurity among these "people without property." This, like Myers' book, is an insightful rendering of the ways in which Aboriginal modes of action are fluid and negotiable within a given range of cultural values and constructs—and of the experientially rather than structurally shaped character of social action as typical of this setting and perhaps of others where Aborigines continue to associate intensively in small, face-to-face groupings (Sansom 1982).

These works and others, then, were addressing themselves to theoretical problems in social description as these had become particularly obvious in Aboriginalist anthropology—the rigidity and unproductivity of concepts of social structure in relation to anthropologists' experience and attempts to supersede those characteristics through exploration of concepts of agency, emotion, and the finding of appropriate levels at which to relate concepts of person and politics. They were also, Myers' book especially, written against the background of the land-rights era as part of what gave immediacy to the focus on territoriality and relationships to place. These and other works provided treatments of Aboriginal social action more sophisticated in concept than previous ones and applicable to the present to the extent that they explored modes of human action in relation to Aboriginal constructs like *tjukurrpa*, cultural formulations of relatedness, and others.

But alongside this, relevant to my discussion here is the extent to which the works researched during the period emphasize persistence, on the whole suggesting the relative superficiality of outside influence upon Aboriginal modes of action. The tenor of Myers' (1986:11–12) argument in this respect is condensed in his claim that the "substance" of hunting and gathering social organization, if not its form, lies beneath the apparent squalor of contemporary Pintupi communities. What this might mean cannot be reduced to an issue of truth or falsity. Whereas there are undoubtedly, dimensions of continuity in the cultural forms Myers describes, there are also very likely aspects that might be seen as discontinuities and problematizations (see Myers, chapter 9), but these receive lesser attention and are certainly not the book's focus. The economy of values that informs the rhetorical structure of the account privileges continuity. Sansom's work may also be seen to do so, for instance in his claim to focus upon how "social continuity vests in cultural forms" (Sansom 1981:258), his interest in Aboriginal modalities of exchange as belonging "to the hunter-gatherer forebears of the fringe dwellers of today," their lives as representing an "alternative reality," cultural continuity "in a world of material change."

If these are indications of (revised?) ethnographic traditionalism, how do they relate to the wider context that has been sketched here? Intellectually these works clearly made advances in relating ethnography and social theory. More ably than had ever been done before, each author demonstrates the ways in which Aboriginal social practices are lived in space. As well, these books and others (e.g., Rose 1992) hint at the ways in which colonizing practices overrode and transformed the profoundly spatial character of the Aboriginal social order, seeking to reduce it to an unproductive emptiness in the case of the Desert Pintupi, a sometimes recalcitrant productive force in the case of Aborigines in pastoral areas and a series of hard-won and barely permissible urban margins in the case of Darwin fringe dwellers. Each work ultimately suggests that the Aboriginal people described are still in some sense on the border of association with the wider society, their interactions with whites perhaps problematizing their forms of social action but without fundamentally altering them. Nevertheless, these works bring the relations of Aborigines with others into sharp enough focus so that we want to ask how new meanings are produced for space and time as Aborigines come to live in new ways in space and time.

Constraints that affect academic anthropologists partly emanate from valuation of cultural difference and diversity (also shared by many members of the wider public) and partly from recognition of the sensitivity of the relation of indigenous people to the wider polity that holds expectations about what they are and the worth of traditionality and distinctiveness in Aborigines' locations within it. Because what is widely understood as worthy in what is "Aboriginal" is assumed to involve certain distinctive and traditional forms of social relations—in respect to place, dependence on the countryside for survival, intimacy with it, reproduction of personhood in relation to it, and so on—to speak of change in those relations can be seen to deny Aboriginal identity and worth and to weaken any political position that Aborigines might achieve on the basis of deploying these representations. Yet to pass over the question of change is to abdicate the effort to understand contemporary complexity and to accept an economy of values of cultural authenticity. Given constraints on the effort to represent change, let us see how the land claims process elicits authentic, traditional imagery, but in Taussig's sense: representations of Aborigines by others affect what they are allowed to be and become. This is the sense in which I argued that "tribes" cannot be understood as pure cultural continuity.

In my experience, land claims are not presented or argued at the level of sophistication of the recent ethnographies discussed above but at a level much closer to the concreteness of Arndt's views of social structures. A good deal of reification goes on in the presentation of claims, not only on behalf of the claimants to make a clear and tenable case, but also by parties opposing claims, sometimes to argue the inadequacy of Aboriginal relationships to country in these "traditional" terms. Let us consider the example of the Katherine Area Land Claim in this regard.

Although land claims are not organized as adversarial proceedings, the Katherine Land Claim (like many other claims, particularly where great material and cultural interests are seen to be involved) was highly contentious. Both the Northern Territory government and the Katherine Town Council took advice and hired counsel to "test" the Aboriginal evidence. The Northern Territory's counsel were experienced, having participated in another land claim in western Arnhem Land involving socially connected people (the Alligator Rivers Stage II claim, heard in 1980–1981). From this, Northern Territory counsel were familiar with Arnhem concepts of clan organization. In that claim, for much of the area, clans were presented as the most likely relevant "owning" groups, in keeping with the widespread assumption among anthropologists that this level was presupposed by the act's formulation. Intensive cross-examination by counsel for the Northern Territory in that case had revealed great weaknesses in claimants' evidence as members of clan groups for much of the area, and about 95 percent of the area had not been recommended for grant to the claimants. The tenor of people's relationships to country in the Katherine area and the currency of attachments to country as mediated by notions of clan-level organization was comparable to the Alligator Rivers situation.

As a result, counsel for the Northern Territory approached the evidence in the Katherine Area Land Claim with the clan group model of traditional ownership in mind. Northern Territory Counsel said in his open-

Photo 3. Female witnesses during the Katherine Land Claim. *Left to right, facing camera:* Sarah Flora, Ivy Brumby, Phyllis Winyjorrotj, Fanny Birlamjam, Margaret Katherine *(foreground)* (Courtesy Robert Blowes).

ing remarks, "We will be contending that the traditional model of land owning group [*sic*], namely the clan—that which finds its classification midway between the tribe and the family—is, traditionally has been, and still should be regarded as the land owning group" (KALCT 1982:92). However, the anthropologists' report in the Katherine case (Merlan and Rumsey 1982) had not put the clan forward as currently the most relevant level at which the claimants conceptualized their relations to country. Most older people were like Fanny Birlamjam, the nature of whose relationship to her clan country was discussed in chapter 3, in her sense of uncertainty about it. Many were more uncertain than she, a particularly knowledgeable person, about the actual locations of places they associated with particular clans, and a great number of potential claimants, especially younger people, simply did not evince a sense of relationship to country as mediated by clan-level concepts. Further, that there were only fragmentary traces of earlier clan-level organization in the immediate Katherine Gorge area was undoubtedly the nub of contention. What I assume to have been earlier salience of *mowurrwurr* as one level at which relationships to places were organized had been dissipated by the refocusing and narrowing of Aboriginal people's experience of country around the possibilities and requirements of the changing settler regime. In that context, the

Photo 4. Julie Williams *(left)* and Phyllis Winyjorrotj at Dorriya Gudaluk cave near Barunga during Katherine Land Claim.

notion of attachment of people as Jawoyn to "Jawoyn country" clearly had much greater relevance as the terms in which even the oldest adults tended to express their relationship to places, particularly to the area around Katherine where many had lived most or all of their lives. The matter of the relative salience of the higher- and lower-level grouping was of course one of degree. And knowledge and experience of country on the part of the claimants was variable among them, and a matter of degree.

If the hearing had proceeded as the inquiry into clan-level organization the Northern Territory heralded, its lack of currency would have been a crucial issue. As things turned out, much of the area was granted on the basis that the wider group met the act's requirements. However, that this as the most salient level at which relationships to country were articulated represented a considerable change at least of degree did not escape presiding justice Kearney, who also wrote in his report that clearly, the "claimants' forebears were among those Aboriginals who bore the full brunt of the non-Aboriginal settlement of the Top End in the late nineteenth century, and the later dislocations of World War II in the north" (Aboriginal Land Commissioner 1988:20).

Aboriginal people were questioned about whether their current relationships to country matched certain forms of representation of them that were argued to be relevant ones and that clearly, earlier at least, had been one significant construct in terms of which relations to country were organized (and elsewhere, may still be to a greater extent). At the time, as discussion of Myers and other current ethnography has indicated, the way in which such constructs as "clan" were to be understood was undergoing theoretical revision, partly stimulated by the wider context of Aboriginal land rights. But it was difficult for such revision to find its way meaningfully into land rights processes. In those, issues in theoretical understanding of "Aboriginal culture" were swamped, in my view, by the paucity of anthropological terms available to interpret the character of contemporary Aboriginal socio-cultural formations in a way that would not be completely disenfranchising and could make views of continuity and change

Photo 5. Sandy Barraway showing porcupine painting on didgeridoo to land commissioner's party during Katherine Land Claim.

intelligible without limiting these to the choice between notions of "a shattered Eden" and "inflexible tradition" (Errington and Gewertz 1995). Pragmatic and conceptual constraints of the land-claims context left no space for serious efforts to interpret the outcomes of long-term intercultural process. With respect to the Katherine scene, constructs like "clan," as well as "tribe," were now partial, undergoing change. That is not to say they were entirely meaningless or outmoded: they were present to consciousness for some Aboriginal people. As I have described in chapters 3 and 4, they were present as traces and forms of influence on contemporary Aboriginal subjectivities and action. They were part of the way the past was shaping the present, and the future. But they were inappropriately understood as structural and fixed in character, just as they were inappropriately understood in that manner by Arndt and just as Myers and Sansom have argued against that kind of understanding.

Separating conceptual revision from practical process in which, nominally, the same social construct figured, amounts to its elicitation in the land claim as the "shadow of science" (Taussig 1993:2). The land claim is an intercultural social arrangement that has the power to ensure the concept's realization in new material terms.

The Jawoyn Association was incorporated in 1984 in anticipation of the claim's outcome, its membership initially composed of the set of claimants. Subsequently, all of the issues involved in this kind of concretizing of what was formerly one element in a field of grounded identity constructs formerly lived out in a quite different context has given rise to debate within the organization about "membership." I have summarized some of the conceptual issues (Merlan 1995) as ones emerging among members around differing perceptions of belonging ("Who belongs?"), especially when this is now connected to the distribution or the prospect of material benefits (park lease-back monies and so on). Questions of belonging must often be seen as a matter of degree and intensity rather than as absolute. There is also a performative dimension involved in maintaining such an identity, especially under contemporary conditions: some would-be members live elsewhere or maintain limited contact with the Katherine area and its Aboriginal people; in other cases, like that of "Alan" described in chapter 4, discrepancies in family connections that had been allowed to remain covert now take on a new importance. Such forms of institutionalization bring forward elements from the past in new ways. They are a joint product, not pure "cultural continuity." They arise from great pre-existing power differences, gradual shift in the balance of which is testimony to the power of the mimetic faculty as part of a social technology of management.

I hope in this section to have given some indication of the complexity of the circuits into which "anthropological representations" enter, of their temporal layering, and of the degree of commonality they have with wider public thinking, as well as ways in which they continually diverge from it.

The Native Title Era

Following a historic High Court decision in *Mabo vs. Queensland [No. 2]* in 1992, Australia passed the Native Title Act (1993). The main finding of the High Court was that Murray Islanders of the Torres Strait have native title to the lands they claimed as theirs. The decision behind this specific case was portentous, for it both recognized the general concept of native title at the common law and left open the possibility that it may have survived colonization elsewhere in Australia (except where "valid extinguishment," a contentious concept, is considered to have supervened). A Native Title Tribunal was established under the 1993 act and has sought, among other things, to register cases, have them researched, and develop processes of mediation, rather than refer cases immediately to the federal court for time-consuming and costly legal resolution (see Bartlett 1993, Brennan 1995). Subsequently, a major and (in 1997) still unresolved issue, presently contested with respect to the Wik peoples of Cape York Peninsula, has become whether pastoral lease as formulated in the Australian context does or does not extinguish native title.

The Mabo decision and the act recognize native title as a potentially continuous entitlement, stemming from prior occupation. The act marks two considerable shifts from the previous situation. First, it assimilates native title to the existing class of property rights at common law in the sense that such title is said to be justiciable, or can be dealt with, at the common law. In short—countering the sense of the 1971 Yirrkala decision—native title is seen to involve property rights, not just a nonequivalent indigenous system of tenure. Second, it is much less expansive about what native title may consist in, as compared with the Northern Territory legislation's specification of requirements of "traditional ownership." The Native Title Act says only that the common law "recognises a form of native title that reflects the entitlements of the indigenous inhabitants of Australia, in accordance with their laws and customs, to their traditional lands" (Preamble). In principle this, like the Land Rights Act, foreshadows a mimetic relationship. Representations of what native title is seen to be, in ways that necessarily have a considerable past-orientation, may have some power in shaping the intercultural institutions of the future. The power of representations and their mirroring effects are important aspects of what we can mean by postcoloniality, Fourth World–style.

However, interpretations of native title are emerging that would allow some freedom from constraining, traditionalizing strictures. Although many interpretations of native title are realist in taking title (as the act itself says) to reflect "entitlements of the indigenous inhabitants," Noel Pearson, lawyer and participant in ongoing native-title issues, has described title as a "recognition concept." Commenting that native title is neither a "common law title but is instead a title recognised by the common law" nor an Aboriginal law title because "patently Aboriginal law will recognise title where the common law will not," he defines native title as "the space between the two systems, where there is recognition . . . the recognition space between the common law and the Aboriginal law" (Pearson 1997:154). This seems to me to appropriately recognize native title as an intercultural product, not simply as something that "survives" from precolonial times.

Change and Continuity in the Local Intercultural Domain

A statement by former prime minister Gough Whitlam is still often quoted for its clear and trenchant formulation of the centrality of Aboriginal issues to nationhood, in a way not previously familiar in the public domain. In a policy speech of 1972, he said,

> More than any foreign aid programme, more than any international obligation which we meet or forfeit, more than any part we may play in any treaty or agreement or alliance, Australia's treatment of her Aboriginal people will be the thing upon which the rest of the world will judge Australia. Not just now, but in the greater perspective of history, and further, the Aborigines are a responsibility we cannot escape, cannot share, cannot shuffle off; the world will not let us forget that. (Whitlam 1985:466)

Whitlam also said that "The Aborigines are our true link with our region," thus explicitly conceptualizing Aboriginality as an autochthonous extension of the national self.

At about the same time, in 1973, white townspeople of Katherine learned that federal land-rights legislation was being drafted. They also heard rumors of plans for purchase of two cattle stations on behalf of Aborigines. A contributor to the Katherine newspaper asked, "Who decided that recognition of land rights was the basic concept in solving the aboriginal problem? . . . Surely before we start giving out prime pastoral land for 'past injustices' we should draw upon the experiences of other countries of the world with similar situations" (*Katherine Times*, August 25–31, 1971).

Earlier parts of this chapter provided background for understanding the extent to which local and regional views of changing relations of Aborigines at the local level might differ from those promulgated at the national center. From the 1970s, several groups were formed in Katherine to protest changes in the social and political situation of Aborigines; these groups garnered a considerable measure of local support. First calling itself Equal Rights for Whites, an organization was formed in March 1973, largely by people of rural and pastoralist background. It shortly changed its name to the slightly less incendiary Equal Rights for Territorians. A Land Rights Action Group was formed in 1977 by some of the same people, just after passage of the Land Rights Act. The latter group determined to investigate the act's constitutionality, on the basis that it operated only in the Territory and was therefore discriminatory to its (non-Aboriginal) residents compared to those who lived in the various states. A year later, this group had taken the democratic-sounding name One Nation One Law, and in a final metamorphosis into the Committee for Community Ownership of the Katherine Gorge National Park was active throughout the years of the Katherine Land Claim, especially 1982–1983 when hearings were held at Katherine and Barunga.

While a detailed account of these organizations cannot be given here, especially notable in their public self-presentation was the sense of deprivation expressed in relation to Aborigines in this period. Aborigines were seen as doing nothing, yet getting "everything for free"—this, despite the objectively poor conditions in which many Aborigines lived, especially around towns where they were highly visible, and that would have been intolerable to those complaining of their privilege. One of the most upsetting elements to critical whites around Katherine, besides the proximity of Aborigines in those conditions, was their apparent lack of abjectness and apology about it.

From about 1973, a principal focus of these organizations' activity was land rights. From seeing white Territorians as discriminated against and Aborigines as unfairly privileged, about the time of the Katherine Land

Claim the One Nation One Law group particularly focused their objection on claims over national parks like Katherine Gorge. These, they argued, should belong to "all Australians" and also should not be jointly managed by Aborigines with the "Canberra-controlled National Parks and Wildlife Service," a point on which they got support from the Northern Territory government.

The group organized a march in protest of the claim in October 1982 and others in following years. Although group members thought that the claimants were bogus and did not have the right or the requisite knowledge to make the claim, a committee spokeswoman did not say that, but simply that "enough was enough": "Aboriginals have over 28% of the Territory with a further 18% still claimed. . . . For a quarter of the Territory's population . . . they have been given enough" (*Katherine Advertiser*, September 30, 1982).[5] The local newspaper printed a cartoon, about which speculation in the town was that it had been drawn by a ranger at Katherine Gorge, showing a building under construction and one simian-looking Aborigine saying to another, "Let's let them finish before we claim it."

In October 1987, Northern Territory Chief Minister Steve Hatton came to Katherine to speak to Jawoyn claimants. He wanted to urge on the federal government the exclusion of Katherine Gorge National Park from any grant of land, but said the balance of the claim would be unopposed. He also wanted joint Jawoyn and Northern Territory Conservation Commission management. By this time, there was fairly wide acceptance that the claim would be successful, at least in part. Once again, he took a familiar line, distancing himself from any suggestion of direct criticism of Aborigines: "This is not a fight with the Jawoyn people. . . . This is a fight against an imposed legislative regime . . . which sets the Territory up as a salve to the imagined national conscience and as a playground for every social engineer in Australia" (*Katherine Times*, October 22, 1987).

In 1988, the success of the claimants with regard to the Gorge (and some other areas of the claim) was announced. The title handover did not actually occur until September 10, 1989; but well before then, in February 1989, Mike Reed, member of the Legislative Assembly for the (redrawn) electoral area including Katherine, headed his newspaper column "Gorge Worry Ends." He announced that agreement had been reached for the park to be leased to the Northern Territory Conservation Commission for ninety-nine years, at an annual rental of $100,000, plus 50 percent park revenue from concessions. Showing the strength and consistency of Northern Territory government position in opposition to federal or fed-

Photo 6. Nitmiluk National Park Handover Ceremony, September 1989.

erally supported bodies, particularly Aboriginal organizations, he said: "That the agreement was reached without full involvement of the Northern Land Council and the fact that the Land Council is not included on the board of management is a significant milestone."

On August 18, 1989, about eighteen years after the first alarms concerning Aboriginal land rights appeared in the local newspaper, there appeared an article entitled "Jawoyns Consider Business." It spoke of a multiparty business luncheon being planned for a few days hence, explaining: "Recognition of ownership of the Katherine Gorge will be given to the Jawoyn people in an official ceremony at the Gorge which is expected to attract about 4000 people."

On August 30, 1989, in a related article, a local businessman prominent in the growing tourism industry said of new management structures at the Katherine Gorge National Park (by then called Nitmiluk, after the Aboriginal name of the place closest to the park's main ranger station), "Once all the [changes] have been implemented, it will give the vast majority of visitors to the area the chance of interacting with the local Aboriginal people to ensure a greater understanding of their lifestyle and culture. . . . It will be an opportunity to show how well the two cultures can work together."

By a quite different but intersecting circuit of representations to that described in the preceding section, an imagery of intercultural relationship based on cultural difference had grown up, with some of its strongest roots in the concept of economic development of the town and region as a distinctive part of the nation.

Conclusions

In this chapter I have considered perspectives on the management of Aboriginal affairs within the changing nation-state and their implications for understandings of change and continuity. This understanding has involved consideration of the formulation of Aboriginal and "other" identities in reference to changing concepts of Australian nationhood, changes in recognition of their relative groundedness in the national territory, and differences at local and regional levels as distinct from a national one in conceptualizing and acting with reference to notions of Aboriginality.

At the level of explicit government policy, change has involved a move from the concept of "assimilation" to one of Aboriginal "self-determination"; but, I have argued, this change has involved generation of new conceptions of Aboriginal selfhood in relation to the nation, partly through a developing social technology of mimesis. In this, existing representations of Aboriginality are engaged to produce images partaking of continuity with the past but also yielding definitively new intercultural products and representations. These will go forward to diversify conceptions and practical realities. "Land" has constituted a prime material-symbolic medium in which imitative processes have been developed.

In recent writing, Sahlins (1993) has argued that the hooking in of formerly peripheral peoples to a world system of material and representational flows has enabled them to adapt these flows to reproduction of what remain their own cultures. Some Australian Aboriginalist ethnographers, more concerned with the reproduction of material and symbolic inequalities in Australia, have developed concepts of Aboriginal resistance—for example, the notion of "oppositional culture" (Cowlishaw 1988)—as the most salient form of that which is distinctively Aboriginal. What these seemingly opposed views share is their vision of indigenous cultural production as autonomous, whether drawing resources from or in oppositional relation to a domain of nonindigenous otherness. In this chapter I have tried to develop an argument that the contemporary Australian scene, and indeed I would say the wider indigenous scene, cannot be fundamentally understood in this way, despite the ideological attractions of the two approaches I have sketched. That scene is not one of autonomy, but of still unequal, intercultural production.

six

Struggles in Town Space

CHAPTER 1 presented a sectoral picture of Katherine, relating the distribution of the various Aboriginal camps to the orientations of their residents to hinterlands and particular regional "mobs" of countrymen. This chapter is concerned with further exploration of these and other aspects of socio-spatiality with respect to the town area. Although Aborigines' use of town spaces is, to an extent, shaped by wider social and territorial orientation in Aboriginal terms, the town is a complex space also strongly shaped by the co-presence of Aborigines with others. The town area is not neutral in relation to Aboriginal presence. As I showed in chapter 2 through the rainbow story, it has proven difficult for certain kinds of specificities of Aboriginal definition of places to be sustained within the town.

Contesting Spaces

The definition of town spaces as Aboriginal mostly goes on in a very different way, not closely related to country as storied. There is contestation over how spaces in and around town are defined, over the nature of Aboriginal presence in town and uses of town spaces. There is a continuing tendency for Aboriginal uses of space, and Aborigines themselves, to be associated with the margins and interstitial spaces of town rather than central ones. But to say this begs the question of how marginality and centrality are constituted through human interaction, and the material in this chapter is intended to clarify this question with respect to Katherine.

Henri Lefebvre (1991) argued that the capacity to shape space is also a capacity to shape the processes of social reproduction. From the angles of vision that I develop in this chapter, I think it will be clear that there has always been strong, though historically changing, restriction upon Aborigines' capacities to shape town spaces, or at least to imprint accepted social meanings upon them. Within the town, curtailment occurs daily through external censorship, as well as some self-imposed constraints, upon Aborigines' customary and preferred modes of interaction. It also occurs through their general exclusion from domains of action that whites consider central to what the town is, combined with devaluation of Aboriginal forms of action, and thus spatially, continued relegation of Aborigines to its margins. This marginality results in continuation of a differentiated and highly unequal usage of town spaces as between most Aborigines (I refer particularly to people of the town camps) and most non-Aborigines.

The latter part of this chapter is devoted to extended discussion of what is undoubtedly one of the most fraught issues in Northern Territory towns like Katherine—for many years now, in the press and elsewhere, labeled "public drunkenness," considered a problem, and strongly associated by whites with Aboriginal presence in town. This, as local whites see it, is a propensity of (some) Aborigines to refuse to take responsibility for their behavior or to internalize control over drinking and obviously drunken deportment. One of the elements that whites find exasperating is evident in the qualification "public"—visible drunkenness on the streets and in other spaces deemed public. This irritation is intensified by the open pursuit of alcohol by Aborigines who drink: their gathering on the main street in the morning; waiting for the hotel bars to open; taxiing and walking to alcohol outlets; and carrying back cartons of beer, flagons of wine, and other liquor to camp or other drinking spots.

Though some readers might wonder at the emphasis I give this topic, my intention is not to focus upon or reproduce negative stereotypes. However, I think the issue has been absolutely central to the contestation over town spaces, particularly since the early 1960s, when Aborigines were accorded the right to drink under the Social Welfare Ordinance. Repeated debate among townspeople over how to view the situation has produced more and less drastic suggestions about what to do. It has often been said in these debates that there is a higher proportion of Aboriginal than white teetotalers and that drinking is not just an Aboriginal problem.[1] But while all of this is so, I would claim that there is an objective sense in which the "grog" issue strongly affects, if not dominates, the lives of many Aborigines in town. The consequences of alcohol abuse by some are constantly present in the lives of others; and they are so because of the massive restructuring and, in many respects, emptying of daily life that the history of interaction of Aborigines with others has entailed. Further, as I argue in this chapter, the use of alcohol fosters abridgement of some socio-spatial conventions in the conduct of relationships among Aborigines, and this is seen as problematic by some of them. Anyone familiar with the Northern Territory scene will recognize that around the alcohol issue has grown up a stark and salient sense of difference as one between Aborigines and others. Those familiar with indigenous life in Canada, the United States, and elsewhere may find similarities with situations they know.

Different ways of dealing with the issue have been suggested and adopted, formally and informally, in the Northern Territory. Some of these suggestions, from Aborigines and others, have spatial dimensions and thus belong to the discussion of socio-spatiality in this chapter. These solutions contrast to a considerable extent with the imitative kind of social technology of management of Aboriginal affairs discussed in chapter 5.

White and Black in Town Space

Over many decades, Aboriginal people have valued their relationship to Katherine town. They have sought to sustain and modify it partly through their concepts of relationship to it at the level of broad socio-territorial distinctions made in Aboriginal terms. Each Aboriginal person who has been around town has a history of relationships to particular campsites, work sites, and other locations, lived out in part with reference to current social identifications of town areas and Aboriginal people at the high level of named identities and in terms of kinship clustering, regional association, intensive daily interaction, and other dimensions of community.

Aborigines' concepts of relationship to the town in socio-territorial terms, however, seem not to have been widely known to the town's non-Aboriginal residents at any period (there has been rising consciousness of this since the Katherine Area Land Claim and the growth of the Jawoyn

Association). On the other hand, townspeople have been intensely aware of Aboriginal presence in the town, especially with the increase in Aboriginal numbers since the 1960s. The growing and changing town has always offered real resistance to Aboriginal people's presence within it, largely on the grounds that their behavior and manner of life are unacceptable to the wider (largely white) community—if not all Aborigines and always, then at least some of them and enough of the time to make their presence seem problematic. The modes of Euro-Australian resistance to Aboriginal presence have varied over time and have become increasingly informal rather than officially specified.

Declaration of prohibited areas was an early moment of the formalization of Aborigines' marginality with respect to the town. In 1926, shortly after the Katherine River had been spanned and the town center had shifted away from Emungalan (the railhead) back to the south bank, a prohibited area was declared from the river, one and a half miles along the railway line and a mile wide (gazettal No. 162 of 1924). A prohibited area at Emungalan had been gazetted in 1925 under the Aboriginals Ordinance No. 9 of 1918. According to it, a protector of aborigines had powers of removal of Aborigines ("including any female half-caste, or any half-caste male child under the age of 18 years") from one district to another or from any "municipality, town, township, public house, or wine and spirit store" to wherever he directed; to remove any "Aboriginal or half-caste loitering" in a township; and to declare any place within a town district to be a camping ground for Aborigines.

The provisions of the ordinance reveal some of the ostensible bases for administrative concern about Aborigines within towns. One of these was the issue of supply of alcohol and other prohibited substances by whites to Aborigines and the sexual and other exchanges that sometimes went along with this supply. There is ample archival as well as oral historical evidence concerning the supply of alcohol. For example, there was an inquiry in 1938 arising from an allegation made by several Aborigines who were questioned about their obtaining drink. They said that they had been supplied methylated spirits by Mrs. Kitty Bernhard, the publican at the Sportsman's Arms Hotel. Police Sargeant Robert Wood declined to take the matter farther, saying that Mrs. Bernhard would hire good legal assistance to assert that all the Aborigines who had affirmed this had something against her or wished the hotel in different hands; and so the matter was dropped. Henry Scott told stories of men he referred to as "death adders" who, during the Depression years, camped on the riverbank, drinking and dealing regularly with Aborigines. Spaces along the river and railway line were close to the township but were not the immediate living space of respectable townspeople. Relevant to this is that, periodically, flooding may occur along the river, so that some riverbank locations are not suitable for building. The riverbank and railway were zones of proximity between Aborigines and whites who engaged in licit and illicit exchanges; Aborigines could station themselves there—hence their designation as prohibited in a period when officials and most townspeople wanted to keep Aborigines out of town.

With respect to prohibition of spaces, the war was an interregnum, in the sense that for all its apparent liberality, the military regime operated on the basis of strict official definitions of space. Aboriginal compounds were designated, and relations between soldiers and Aborigines were supposed to be regulated. (Both found numerous ways of flouting the regulations, nevertheless.)

In the postwar reconstruction, F. H. Moy, director of Native Affairs in Darwin, noted that the original gazettes of prohibited areas at Katherine were not to hand, and he took steps to create new areas. Demilitarization and the reorganization of the town led to the redeclaration of prohibited areas in a way intended to conform better with the current layout of the town. The new area proposed for Katherine, drawn up by Police Sergeant James Joseph Mannion, went from Knott's Crossing to the Low Level (see map 3). In other words, it included the entire developed town to that date. By the time the old Emungalan prohibited area was repealed in May 1950, it too had already been replaced by a new gazettal, No. 41 of October 1948 (Commonwealth Archives, F1 48/98).

By 1947, Katherine's population had risen again to 371 as people returned who had been transported south after the Japanese bombing of 1942. Given the long-standing institution of attempted administrative control of Aboriginal presence in towns and the significant evidence of white and black collaboration in flouting the laws relating to supply of liquor and other matters, permission was required for Aborigines to come into town for even what were seen as harmless entertainments, because such visits breached the norm of the reservation of town space for whites and because it was thought necessary to "protect" Aborigines from what were seen as the ruinous influences of the town. Katherine welfare officer Ron Ryan issued permission for local and settlement natives (including those from Tandangal, Beswick, and Roper River) to attend Jack Neal's movie show in Katherine (at first held on Wednesday and Saturday nights, later, on Saturdays only). Alcohol supply provoked continuing administrative concern. In the postwar period, too, Aborigines around Katherine were obtaining alcohol. People like Alice Mitchell, and some whites too, have told me that on weekends rural employers of Aborigines regularly gave workers a bottle of wine, and sometimes metho (which Jawoyn people called *mukul* [green ant] after its pungent taste and which they and others who lived on the river north of the town also sometimes managed to pilfer from the hospital supply).

In 1952 Bill Dumigan was convicted of providing drink to Aborigines. He was one of the employers of Julie Williams' parents, the father of a family of six, who lived near the house of one of the railway workers just on the north bank of the river. Ron Ryan (in a letter of May 7, 1953) described this as a "popular gathering place for aborigines" and the living area of ten white families as well. Dumigan was sent to Fanny Bay, a Darwin jail. Convictions for illegal consumption of liquor were numerous in this period, and by 1957, well before Aborigines could legally drink, Ryan reported that there were significant problems with alcohol in the CSIRO camp. Peanut farmer Nigel Bruce, central to the lives of Aborigines around the town for years, was also convicted of supplying alcohol to them (though Henry Scott insisted to me that Bruce was framed by police).

Police Sergeant Mannion, who had been involved in drawing up the new proposed prohibited areas boundaries in Katherine, felt that they should be more than nominal. On April 26, 1953, he arrested twenty-two "natives" for "being within the prohibited area of Katherine," hauling them all away in a truck. These Aborigines were bailed by Patrol Officer Ryan and appeared in Katherine Court next day before F. W. Dowling, J.P. On behalf of the first five men to appear in court, including Julie Williams' father Fortymile, Ryan submitted a plea of "not guilty" to the charge of "being in a Prohibited Area without protector's permission contrary to Sec. 11 (2) of Aboriginals Ordinance 1918–52" [*sic*] (Commonwealth Archives, F1 52/615). After hearing from Sergeant Mannion, however, the justice ruled there was a case to answer. Knowing that the evidence against all of them would be the same, Ryan agreed to a guilty plea for the five; the remaining seventeen were convicted and fined the same amount, 5 shillings with 10 shillings costs.

This case received some southern notice and gained sympathy for the Aborigines. In May, a letter of protest was received in Darwin from H. R. French, town clerk of West Geelong (near Melbourne), saying that "we should give the greatest possible consideration to our Australian natives" and putting the view that the arrest was unconscionable. This protest has to be seen in light of an already established, frequently hostile (and still-continuing) dialogue between people who adopt positions as northerners and southerners, urbanites and rural dwellers, on Aboriginal affairs, in which the urban and southern assert moral suasion from afar concerning people nationally imagined as the most traditional Aborigines, and the remote-area rural dwellers complain that southerners know nothing of the realities of everyday northern life.

Katherine officials agreed that, given the existing ordinance, the Aborigines apprehended by Mannion were technically committing an offense at the time of their arrest. However, I found that camp-dwelling Aborigines had different, and perhaps surprisingly limited, awareness of prohibited areas provisions and of the associated nighttime curfew. I asked the surviving relatives of the three men arrested in 1953 whose identities I knew what they knew or thought about the episode. Some of these people had been adults at the time, some children. Julie Williams would have been only eleven or twelve. She had spent a lot of time at that age on Katherine's rural margins, and I asked her with regard to this arrest and other matters about her sense of being within the town.

FM: When you were little girl, all the Aboriginal people around town, they been let you come night time la [to] town?
JW: Yeah.
FM: You could walk around, any time?
JW: Walk around, go la [to] picture.
FM: You used to go to the picture.
JW: Yeah, like still had picture [there is no theater today], Jack Neal used to run it.
FM: Jack Neal, yeah, you used to come picture, you used to siddown white people and black together, or . . .
JW: Yeah.
FM: Siddown different place?
JW: No, the white men la [at] back and we were up front.
FM: Right.
JW: See.
FM: And after that, any day of the week, they let youfella come la [to] town, walk around.
JW: Yeah.
FM: No trouble?

JW: No trouble.
FM: They didn't have curfew [we had discussed this word] or anything?
JW: No.
FM: And did you know any time they been arrest people playing cards or something?
JW: No.
FM: Like your father?
JW: No, nothing.

On the other hand, I found that a number of people of part-Aboriginal descent, who were designated "half-caste," "part-caste," or "colored" in the period of the prohibited areas episode (see chapter 1, n. 1) and if adult would have had to obtain an exemption ("dog tag") to drink, showed a lively awareness of the restrictions of curfew that applied to Aborigines and of the sensitivities of their own position.

In the 1930s, a part-Aboriginal family surnamed McGinness lived on the north bank. The father of a large family, Jack McGinness was a builder who worked for the railways. He was also an acclaimed sportsman, who used to travel up to Darwin on the railway to football matches and often returned in triumph, on the railway again. Henry Scott, commenting on social status in Katherine's earlier days, observed that, in general, "the railway people were the number one . . . soon as the railway lines came in the railways took over and they were the heads." And then, specifically recalling Jack McGinness, he added, "I remember the bloke that run this town, ah, Jack McGinness, he was a colored man, but a terrific guy, well educated, and he was more or less the mayor of the town, they called him."[2]

One of Jack's daughters, Cathy Mills, returned some years ago to live in Katherine. She is a person well aware of the kinds of restrictions that Aborigines and "coloreds" lived under. Some long-term white residents tend to say that "everybody" got along in the old days and nostalgically contrast this amity with the contemporary racialized atmosphere in the town. But regarding this halcyon depiction of the postwar era Cathy remarked, "They would not have gotten up town to be aware that all the blacks were off the streets at six." And though it is true that some white and "colored" children used to play together, not all of them did, or were allowed to. People who talk about how good it was in the old days, she added in her quiet way, don't always stop to consider that it was unfair.

Tom Kelly worked for the railways for more than twenty years in

Katherine. Born of an Irish father who was a stockman out Wave Hill way (see map 1) and an Aboriginal mother from there, he like many others of mixed descent was taken to a home in Pine Creek in the late 1920s and early 1930s. He observed that in the 1940s, while he was working on transport around Katherine, "Mannion was here and fairly strict. Natives were only allowed in town to go shopping, or to go to the pictures Saturday and Wednesday. Mannion would stop and ask people where they were from; he didn't like riff-raff around town."

The temporal precision of such observations, and the terms in which they are made, reflect a quite different consciousness from Julie's and different sensitivity concerning the levels and nature of administrative control in Katherine's earlier days.

Present Divided Uses of Town Space

Despite formal liberalization, including revocation in the 1950s of the legislation authorizing prohibited areas, the use of town space in Katherine still broadly distinguishes many people in Katherine as Aborigines and non-Aborigines. One aspect of this is the extent to which Aborigines *walk* around Katherine, not only in its principal business district along the main street, but also on trajectories that take them through it and link with destinations, some of them used exclusively by Aborigines, in bushland on the town's edges (see map 3). Some of these are drinking venues and meeting places over the disused railway line toward the Warlpiri (Transient) camp (location 4, map 2), along stretches of the river, and in grassland on the eastern margin of the main section of town along Lockheed Road. Aborigines from different camps, and thus, broadly, of differing social identities and backgrounds, make differentiated use of areas of bushland and riverbank (but sometimes with some overlap of personnel). Warlpiri tend to frequent the railway line near their camp, Kalano people the riverbank under and near the High Level bridge. Rockhole and Bunjarri people often sit in Ryan Park, just at the Stuart and Victoria Highway intersection (around location 7, map 3), when they are waiting for each other or for a lift back to their camps.

Many Aborigines who live in places at medium distance from the town center (Kalano, Katherine East) and have limited access to vehicles can often be seen walking into and around town. Pedestrian traffic over the High Level bridge is almost exclusively made up of Aborigines (along with a few generally younger and less affluent hitchhikers), as is the main pedestrian traffic along the sidewalk that has been put in along the Stuart Highway between Katherine East and the central part of town (see map 3).

Many of the pedestrians who walk along Riverbank Drive are Aborigines, and the groups of people who walk and sit along the river's course in town—under the High Level bridge, near the Aboriginal hostel, and near the blocks of Housing Commission flats—are largely Aboriginal. Whites who use these sidewalks are mainly early-morning joggers; schoolchildren riding bikes to school; or exercising, late-afternoon "power walkers." Their use of these spaces tends not to overlap much, temporally, with uses by Aborigines.

A variety of townspeople go along the river, but in the town area the riverbank is used primarily by Aboriginal drinking parties: whites tend to go farther afield for their outings, to out-of-town locations both downstream and upstream from town. As potential recreation area, the riverbank within the town is neither inherently desirable nor undesirable; it is the historical and present pattern of usage, and the fact of the establishment of the Aboriginal town camp just across the High Level bridge, that has made the riverbank area near the central business district undesirable to whites. There are now proposals to reclaim the riverbank area along which the town stretches and to establish picnic areas and walking trails along it. In the early 1980s, the earlier High Level (Silver City) camp, easily visible from the main highway, was removed (to Kalano, just upstream), and the Katherine Community Center, with the mayoral office, established just across the High Level bridge.

The Low Level crossing is used by both Aborigines and whites, among the latter many tourists who come to swim in the shallow river pools and observe the flying foxes hanging in the trees along the bank. Significantly, there is no Aboriginal camp in the vicinity, so that the area remains desirable to white townspeople. In such places of joint use by non-Aborigines and Aborigines, there is a large measure of spatial separation. If Aborigines see whites ensconced, they will go much farther up- or downstream. Frequently they seek out more secluded spots from the beginning, knowing where whites tend to go. Whites will also tend to separate themselves from Aborigines. The hot spring, near which the old CSIRO camp was situated, now has on the bank above it a motel and tourist park and so, especially during the tourist season, is largely frequented by non-Aborigines. In Julie Williams' childhood, it was part of an area intensively used by Aboriginal residents of the CSIRO camp. Along riverbanks and floodplains in other places in the town area, where Aboriginal use predominates, are massive amounts of debris generated by groups of drinkers—beer cans, the plastic inner bags of wine casks, food wrappers, plastic bags, bottles—often left spread around like the circular crater of a bomb blast. This becomes the main indicator of Aboriginal presence to white townspeople (despite the fact that Kalano residents also go to the river near their camp to fish).

Although young people of any color sometimes sit at the picnic tables in the grassy median strips on the main street of town (reflecting the quite different tendencies of young as opposed to older people to spend time there), it is Aborigines who actually sit on the grass on the median, at Ryan Park on the north end of town near the public toilet block, and on the grass along the levee. This use is a manifestation of a strong difference between Aborigines and whites in the extent to which, respectively, they spend their rather differently organized living time outdoors as opposed to indoors and of a strong difference in socio-physical orientation to ground level as opposed to levels of the sitting and standing person accustomed to being within built environments. Many Aborigines feel comfortable sitting on the ground, do so regularly in camp life (some camps have few or no chairs, though people may sit on up-turned flour drums), do not find it inherently demeaning or threatening, and station themselves in these locations in the middle of town to sit and watch what is going on, taking special notice of the movements of familiar Aboriginal people (cf. Sansom 1980, chapter 8). When I was first in Katherine, I saw Aboriginal adults sitting on the sidewalk in front of Katherine Stores on pension day, waiting for rides home; but that practice seems to have declined, though it has not entirely ceased. However, it is still true that, because most Aborigines do not have access to private vehicles and therefore must use community buses, both individual Aborigines and family groups often have to wait for transport home once they have finished their business in town.

Aboriginal young people sit on the ledges of store fronts during the day to rest, observe the scene, and perhaps wait for other people; Aborigines of all ages—mainly men—sit on the ledges along the north side of the Crossways Hotel. Very commonly, groups of a few Aborigines are to be seen on the grass median in front of Kirby's, the second pub on the main street, just across from the Post Office (location 4, map 3). A recent report related high Warlpiri use of the grass median in the main street to the lack of facilities at the Transient camp, where Warlpiri are numerically predominant. The grass on the medians—watered in the early morning—is well tended and lush; there are drinking fountains, and the shops and facilities of town are to hand. Some respite (the shade of an occasional tree, availability of water) from the intense heat and sun that characterize much of the year, combined with the lack of facilities at certain Aboriginal locations and proximity to the business area including liquor outlets, are all factors influencing high levels of Aboriginal use of the median strips.

Only Aborigines and, occasionally, tourists waiting for the imminent arrival of a bus are to be found sitting in patches of shade along the footpaths of Giles Street, the town's second main street, which intersects Katherine Terrace (near location 4, map 3), perhaps resting and having a cold drink, then continuing on. And it is almost exclusively Aborigines who sit at the cement bench in the shade of a huge tamarind near the old courthouse on Giles Street, occasionally with a white man or two in their midst. Aborigines also gather, eat, and drink on the grassy area near the old school, which now houses the library and Open College (location 1, map 3). It is one of the few open, grassy areas in town, but still somewhat set apart. And Aborigines can often be seen sitting on the riverbank near the Aboriginal hostel (location 3, map 2), playing cards in numbers. Not allowed to drink at the hostel, they often go down the levee into the riverbed, carrying the now-familiar rectangular, green bag-in-a-box wine casks, tautly suspended in white plastic bags—ironically referred to (in my experience, mainly by whites) as "green suitcases," in a phrase combining ironic comment on Aborigines' perceived disregard for material possessions and the avidity of drinkers for grog. Sometimes, at night, groups of Aborigines are on the street in the vicinity of Kirby's and Crossways, where weekly discos have been held for the past several years.

In the town area, there is no place where Aborigines can acceptably (to whites) gather in numbers and socialize as they might in the town camps or outside of town. Groups of Aborigines who have done their shopping, often consisting predominantly of women and children (see Merlan 1991b), are tolerated, though frequently characterized by whites as producing mess and litter if they sit for periods of time and unwrap take-away foods. The greater unacceptability of some other groupings is related to the fact that they often drink considerable quantities of alcohol and play cards in large "schools." Although serious card playing almost always occurs in camp locations, drinkers may settle themselves in town within long-range view and, less commonly, earshot of non-Aborigines. Both these activities, strongly censored by white townspeople, are also considered by Aborigines as unacceptable, or at least shame producing, in spaces in which they can make no pretense to social command. Few who live in the town camps ever frequent sit-down restaurants, although they will buy at take-away shops and other less formal fast food and drink outlets. But then they must have somewhere to go, eat, and sit in the town center, and there is no place really given over to Aboriginal patterns of time-in-town. Often, Aborigines do not intend simply to eat, but to find a place to spend a longer time. There are only temporary little islands of Aboriginal sociality on the median strips or in the grassy areas. A grassy area outside Kalano offices is often the locale of long-term gatherings where people wait for pension checks, health visits, and so on. But Kalano is quite far from the main town area, approximately two kilometers over the High Level bridge (but much closer on foot, as all Kalano residents know). In the view of many white residents, even parks are not meant for this kind of communal sociality, quite apart from the "mess" that many associate with Aboriginal presence. Considering all of these constraints on their presence in town that Aboriginal people are constantly aware of, their own home camp space has greater social centrality of another kind than the town area could ever have for them, in the sense of affording them a feeling of belonging and control. Exceptional areas are the sports ovals, where Aborigines gather to play and to watch baseball and football. Spectators are particularly interested in teams with high levels of Aboriginal participation, including the teams that come in from Barunga, and go to see and support their relations.

The question of indoor space in town is fraught for Aborigines, too. Most Aboriginal organizations find themselves having to discourage people from sitting down and spending time in their offices and from making phone calls and using the facilities. Any such friendly environment might quickly be overrun with people looking for comfortable places to be in town. One of the few kinds of indoor places where Aboriginal people may spend time and socialize (and of course spend money) is the pub. Many Aborigines drink outdoors (for example, along the riverbank), in groups, and such drinking parties are often characterized by behavior and noise that would not be tolerated in central town areas.

Aborigines' movements are constrained by the lack or limitation of transport available to many, combined with social demands upon them to take account of not just their own requirements but also those of their companions. Many experience difficulties in accomplishing routine maintenance and subsistence tasks (such as cashing checks or filling out forms) that require interaction with bureaucracies and agencies whose functions and modes of operation are still somewhat foreign, and often off-putting. Some Aborigines adopt the strategy of limiting the purposes to which they intend to devote any given trip to town from their camp. Having experienced impediments to the achievement of what they seek to accomplish in town, many Aborigines do not think in terms of an "efficiency" model of allocating limited time to the completion of any given task. Experience has taught them that purposes of trips into town may eventually be fulfilled if one is persistent but that there may be many obstacles in the way of their completion; and there may be plenty of other, unforeseen things that one winds up doing during that day, or those hours, in town. This leads to the recognition, too, that Aborigines do not simply frequent town to accomplish specific ends that are given in the range of town services, shops, and so forth. Many of the things they wish to do are better described as mediated by an internal social dimension: the wish to check out what other Aboriginal people are doing, to wait for a relative to receive and cash a check because some of it will be redistributed, to accompany someone who has some such purpose, and so on. In the sometimes dense Aboriginal social scene of the town area, where one sees many familiar people walking, sitting, and driving around, many side trips, interactions, unplanned diversions, and conversations fill up the course of a day in which one's principal aims were, say, to take one's grandchild to the Kalano clinic, to visit an elderly relative at the hospital or Red Cross home, or maybe to do a bit of food shopping. The intensive sociality possible in town, combined with the difficulties of accomplishing one's central aims that involve certain bureaucracies and institutions, and the inevitability of getting drawn into a range of different interactions in which others are trying to put their own partly overlapping and partly divergent plans into effect leads, I think, to a sense of overload and frustration that Aborigines sometimes indicate they experience during trips to town. It is particularly noticeable in people who feel they are being "humbugged" for money, particularly on days when pensions are being paid out (see Merlan 1991b for discussion of uses of money by Aborigines).

In short, patterns of distinctive use of town space by Aborigines and whites are associated with continuing differential access to private vehicles, differences in the nature of destinations that Aborigines and whites tend to frequent, and activities they tend to engage in during the day. There are thus still many places where there is likely to be relatively little overlap between Aborigines and non-Aborigines in space and time—along the riverbank in town, along footpaths especially at certain times of day, and in most of the businesses with on-site services. This somewhat disjunct use of space represents a change from the situation of not so very long ago, when prohibited areas ordinances were still in effect, partly in that Aborigines' preoccupations in town are very different from what they used to be when Aborigines were, officially at least, around the town as managed labor. There are some kinds of spaces, however, that Aborigines and only Aborigines regularly frequent, and through the intensity of their presence and the forms of usage, many of these come to be seen by white townspeople as marginal or interstitial with respect to the town, despite the fact that some of these spaces (like the riverbank near the town center) are not inherently undesirable. Today, though there are no official or legislative bars to Aboriginal and non-Aboriginal co-presence in town, there is still very notable separation, reinforced by different dispositions and the discomfiture that some Aborigines experience as a result of their recognition that they are seen as not conforming to dominant notions of organization, behavior, standards of dress and cleanliness, and activity.

From the perspective of many whites, the ways in which Aborigines use town space are evidence of basic flaws, which are attributed to their social lives in general and regarded as characteristic of them: lack of ambition, dependence on state and taxpayer economic support, and social inconsequentiality—were it not for government intervention.

Grog and Socio-spatiality

"Better langa [in the] bush," Aboriginal residents of Katherine town and the town camps now sometimes say; "too much grog la [in] town." They are talking about what some feel is the difference between the lack of fulfillment in town, the constant need of money to sustain oneself, and the easy availability of grog and the inroads it makes on people's lives—and the possibilities of rural life away from town: hunting, fishing, and quiet, orderly camps revolving around a satisfying, unhurried productive routine not driven by requirements for money, but oriented to basic subsistence. Though not for everyone all of the time, there is nonetheless a strong association of grog with town, and the possibility of living without it, with spatial remove from town.

Aborigines were allowed legal access to alcohol by the Social Welfare Ordinance of 1964. Drunkenness was decriminalized in the Northern Territory in 1974. In 1982, the Northern Territory government—after months of considering what to do about a problem formulated as one of "public drunkenness" and clearly targeting Aborigines—instituted what is known as the "Two-Kilometer Law," which makes public drinking within two kilometers of an establishment with a liquor license illegal. Given not only late legalization of access to alcohol but also very different concepts of socio-spatial and personal organization from those presumed by the surrounding white community, Aborigines' use of alcohol has continued to be a problem.

We should not expect everyone who says "better langa bush" to pull up stakes and set up a remote camp somewhere or even to return to an out-of-town community to which he or she has some connection. The town is now a focus for Aboriginal people of the region, especially those of the town camps, and some of the reasons for this are evident: it is a center of resources and supplies, of a range of services—medical, educational, social security, and general consumer outlets—and of social intensity. It would require great desire and effort, forward planning and support, for those who are now there more or less permanently to live away from town. But "better langa bush" expresses a perception that, despite what it has to offer, certain aspects of the town lifestyle are oppressive. It is a notification that Aboriginal people sometimes see a sharp disparity between the way things are and the way they wish they could be.

A worrying aspect of such a remark, however, is that it seems to signal acceptance on the part of those who say it (and whites sometimes say something similar, that Aborigines are better off or should go bush) that the town scene is inherently full of problems, especially because of the ready access to grog, and that the only *real* solution to that would, indeed, be for Aboriginal people affected by it to move away and live in the bush. That is worrying because the last few decades have led to ever-greater concentrations of Aboriginal people in Katherine from its hinterlands and from elsewhere.[3] Given the accelerated growth of the town over the last few years, decentralization seems unlikely. Many Aboriginal people who have been in town since the 1960s and 1970s are very likely to stay, although the conditions under which they are there may continue to change. For them to finally accept a view of town as a place where community is difficult would be unfortunate; for community to be significantly based upon the use of alcohol, disastrous for those who live in this way; and for Aboriginal people to think of the bush as the only way to gain respite from trouble and "humbug" and for whites to think along these lines, equally a defeat insofar as it accepts an inevitability in the problem-fraught life in town and seems to concede there is no way of doing anything about it.

Sometimes, Aborigines even deride getting away from town as a way of dealing with the "grog problem." Once, for example, I was sitting and listening to some men at Kalano talking about how they ought to get away to the bush, to hunt and fish and leave the town round of pub, grog, cab back to camp with takeaway grog, camp fights, and so on. They taunted one of their number with the threat of taking him right out bush and leaving him there, away from the grog. "No matter, I bring 'im up gota taxi" [bring it with a taxi], he replied, meaning he would transport grog to the bush—going out of town would not interrupt his drinking. In saying this, he exhibited a style of graveyard humor in which people make the most of their excesses and try to attract others to join in, displayed ingenuous truthfulness about what he would do under the circumstances he was being threatened with, and showed independence by presupposing his command of the resources of a taxi, so nobody could stop him.

As this taunt shows, an explicit element in Aboriginal people's ideas about stopping drinking, "leaving the grog," is spatial remove: it is often seen as a matter of "getting out from the grog," changing one's location as *the* element that may be effective in one's effort to not drink. This is combined with a certain resignation about the possibility of directly influencing another's behavior, or exerting authority over another in this matter: "can't stop 'im, they like to drink," is a prevalent sentiment, which concedes self-direction.[4] This is despite the full recognition of the social concomitants of alcohol abuse: the way in which drinkers generate ambivalence, and demonstrate their own, testing the limits of Aboriginal relatedness by prodding others to react to them in their drunken condition; flaunting abusive, self-assertive behavior; often shouting and bellowing; getting physically close to people in a quite extraordinary way; at various stages of drunkenness becoming maudlin and self-pitying, but sometimes rapidly giving themselves over to rage at real or imagined slights and devaluations, the alleged "rubbishing" of themselves by those whose patience they test. When these things go on in town, they attract unfavorable attention from white townspeople, whose politest formulation of the situation is as one of "public (Aboriginal) drunkenness."

Les Macfarlane, formerly a prominent member (for Elsey) of the Legislative Assembly and pastoralist, like many townspeople was in favor of police action against drunkenness in public places. Asked whether the considerable public activity in town concerning this was primarily directed at Aborigines, he replied in what he prided himself upon as his forthright manner, "It is aimed at blackfellows, sure it is. They are the main offenders." To Mac, there was no question of discrimination. He wanted to make sure "the hard core drinkers have no where in Town to misbehave" (*Katherine Informer*, April 22, 1982).

In March 1980 a number of large trees were felled on what was then the "donkey block" (empty lot) opposite the Crossways Hotel in the middle of town. The destruction of the trees angered many townspeople. One letter to the paper claimed there was "increasing awareness of the importance of preserving shade trees in the town" (*Katherine Times*, March 27, 1980). An editorial in the Darwin paper on the subject tried to provide an enlightened viewpoint, saying that though such action was "apparently connected with the 'declared war on the town's dead-beat drinkers,' " it would not achieve its "purpose of mutilating the 'haunt of the rougher element' of society" but would only prove "counterproductive to other more thoughtful attempts to come to grips with the problem of public drunkenness" (*Northern Territory News*, March 18, 1980). The mayor of Katherine denied accusations that the trees had been cut by the town council. (Stronger local rumor at the time, in any case, was that they had been cut by private business interests.) The mayor also said it was "misleading" to say there was in the town "blatant rejection of people who part of [*sic*] sit under the shade of these trees." None of these comments specifically mentioned, but all presupposed, that Aborigines had been targeted by the tree cutting and that the problem was not *simply* one of their sitting under the trees, but also drinking and making noise and mess.

Sansom (1980) has emphasized the sharing of experience as the Aboriginal mode for the social identification of persons with others, insisting upon its centrality in the cultural construction of "kinship" rather than upon kinship as a given and stable cultural code, as it had often been depicted from Radcliffe-Brown onward. Social practice in the town camps fosters loyalty among close consociates, diffuse attitudes of compliance with others rather than an orientation toward taking immediate and direct action; concern with personal prestige and reputation in the general absence of structured possibilities for direct exercise of authority; and sensitivity to withdrawal and withholding as means of dealing with demand (Peterson 1993) and creating social distance in a context of fairly high interpersonal accessibility. There is strong collectivism of Aboriginal personal identity, the development of self in relation to others whom one defines as family and close countrymen. A sense of well-being is experienced among one's familiars, of oneself as known and valued within a collectivity (though particular personal renown is achieved in also cultivating connections with others elsewhere that one may turn to).

Daily living in the town camps shapes and reinforces identities oriented toward collectivities whose constitution and reproduction are fluid and constantly subject to contextual shaping (Myers 1986). One senses in the flow of social action among Katherine Aboriginal people not so much an emphasis upon building up internal mechanisms of renunciation, of disciplining and denying a "self" conceived as autonomous and ideally stable through time, but rather on constant monitoring in social action of the self-responding-to-others in a way consistent with recognition of the importance of collectivity, of being identified with a "mob," and on keeping the demands of others upon oneself at manageable levels that still allow one a sense of personal wants, goals, and room for individual renown.

Because of the strength of this collective orientation of Aboriginal personal identity, Katherine Aborigines' understandings of the personal and family identity of those who drink are not supplanted by definitions of them as drinkers, drunks, alcoholics, or diseased people (cf. Brady 1992). There is however a perception that drinking often involves high levels of behavioral fixation and dysfunction. Such dysfunction may disqualify them from being considered socially capable at any given time without erasing a sense of their personal entitlements and status. With respect to the alcohol issue, the renunciatory mode of Western self-discipline has limited efficacy, and the commonsense Western view of the "self" as individual and freestanding, limited application. Such a concept perhaps finds its greatest resonance in Aboriginal concepts of self-direction, being "boss" for oneself—but within a lived context of dense relatedness (Myers 1986, Brady n.d.).

The literature on Aboriginal drinking considers, among other questions, whether Aborigines are "alcoholics" in the sense of compulsive drinkers who develop total dependency. In arguments against this, a pattern has often been noted. Many Aborigines appear to be "binge drinkers"—people who can consume heavily for a time as part of a pattern of collective drinking (say, while on stand-down from seasonal work), then leave off for a considerable period, many without observable physical withdrawal effects (O'Connor 1984; see Brady n.d.). Certainly the physical and psychological effects of long-term drinking are significant (see Hunter 1993:118–124), but the on-and-off pattern is nonetheless notable.

I have observed this pattern among Aborigines in Katherine. One egregious "town drunk" lived for weeks "on the grog." He drank heavily and fought with his drunken, scarred wife in the street, both apparently often neglectful of the immediate needs of their two small daughters (whom they nevertheless kept with them much of the time). But when picked up by his "boss" for work at a remote cattle station, he and his family would put in several months of responsible station work. He was described by his employer as a "gem," "good as gold" when at the station. Within days of his return to town, he would inevitably get involved in the drunken round and become brutalized and abusive. I witnessed this pattern for about a dozen years. During all of this time he continued to be identified as a senior person of a family with particular territorial entitlements to the southwest of town. In other words, he occupied a status strongly defined in terms of his seniority within a kindred linked to particular "country" within a region of such "countries." This status endured despite some unfavorable running assessment of his current capacities and social worth as grog-impaired (cf. Sansom 1980:73). Finally, somehow, he decided to quit. He became involved with the alcohol rehabilitation program that operates at the Rockhole camp. Though this is only about twelve kilometers outside town, even this distance seemed to be a key element in his being able to reorient himself to other activities. Interviewed during a study of voluntary quitting (Brady 1995b:71), he said,

> Well, next time I been drink again, well, I bin feel no good, you know? Bit weak longa knee, and eye—couldn't see far away. . . . And doctor been come out and asked me I reckon, where the best place you want to go. And I been thinking, better go back to rehab [rehabilitation], you know? And this the last one now [i.e., the last relapse]. And so I come out over here [to Rockhole]. All them fellas and we used to come out and meeting there every morning, all day right up to 10 o'clock, then have a rest, you know? And all the time we been doing that, what been made me give it away grog, we used to you know, we used to come out, go hunting, gettim whatsaname white paint and red paint and too busy painting!

Such people often emphasize the importance not only of spatial remove, but of the related factor of getting away from one's drinking "mob," whose compulsive urging is hard to resist.

Commonly, a link is made between the Aboriginal history of social oppression and problem drinking as a resigned, despondent, defiant or resistant response (Wilson 1982, Atkinson 1989). Sackett (1988:76) argues that "through drink Aborigines express their antipathy to the idea and practice of others administering their lives." It is also frequently observed that not only were Aborigines oppressed, but that under those conditions of oppression they adopted the intemperate models of drinking behavior of whites around them (see MacAndrew and Edgerton 1969 for discussion of the significance of Western models of drinking behavior upon colonized non-Western peoples). In a positively phrased interpretation along this same dimension, Sansom (1980) has proposed that Darwin fringe-camp Aborigines associate their freedom to drink with the belated recognition by whites of their "citizenship" (with the passage of the Social Welfare Ordinance of 1964 in the Northern Territory) and thus their right to self-direction after a long period of oppression. Brady (1992:702) has recently commented further on this dimension of the meaning of drinking for Aborigines, suggesting that it may be possible to understand it (in part) as a "a signifier of equality with whites." Martin (1993:196), however, argues that to represent drinking practices as "solely the product of alienation" would be to deny the agency of Aboriginal social actors, for whom drinking and drunken behavior have taken on meanings and dynamics, becoming integrated into distinctive cultural repertoires of social action, now partly reproduced in this mode.

Certain other anthropological interpretations emphasize drinking as a modality of social interrelation and exchange, suggesting that drinking can be seen as continuous with these specific dimensions of Aboriginal sociality. Collman (1988), for example, interprets the "gift of spirit" in Alice Springs town camps as a particular moment in a broad social system of exchange. One strong motive for individuals to participate is the enhancement of personal prestige, another, the opportunity to experience (feelings of) personal power. The gift of alcohol involves the creation of generalized (and in fact often unrealizeable) debt and credit relations within an uneven Alice Springs town camp economy of regular welfare dollars and sporadic work payouts that work against development of an ethic of accumulation. This kind of interpretation may, I think, be legitimately criticized as an instance of "problem deflation" (Room 1984) for the extent to which it locates drinking within a cultural "social order and regulation" framework.

Sansom's (1980) discussion of drinking in a Darwin fringe camp is important in exploring links among issues of authority, social control, and Aboriginal definitions of urban space. For these people from Darwin's hinterlands, the urban camping scene is one of relatively free grogging. They can "live langa [on the] grog," without having to unduly compromise mob drinking style to whitefella impositions as other Aborigines may have to at missions and cattle stations. But there are dangers in the urban scene to which they respond by living in such a way as to attempt to secure main and satellite urban campsites to Aboriginal use through patterns of continuous daily occupation. Those who regularly occupy these Darwin sites accept a measure of responsibility for visitors from the hinterlands that Sansom portrays as largely realized through the controlled drinking styles of those he dubs "Masterful Men." Such men, who tend to be generally prominent in camp life, partly define themselves as such through their monitoring of the kinds of drink consumed by themselves and others, the tempo of consumption (particularly pacing their own), and their relationships of purchasing and indebtedness within the camp and in its residents' relations with businesses, police, and others. Sansom's depiction suggests a more positive and consistent notion of grogging than I think would be appropriate for the (perhaps significantly, smaller) town camp-and-margins scene of Katherine. There, though I think there are many links between status (as briefly exemplified above)[5] and social prominence, I do not believe there are direct correlations between these and the implementation of authoritative and self-monitoring drinking styles such as Sansom describes.

Other anthropologists (notably, on the Australian scene, Brady 1992 following Lemert 1951) have suggested that discussion of alcohol should not focus on some concept of "cause" but on ethnographically specific practices and processes of use and abuse. This suggestion may be amplified by returning to the significance and generality of Aborigines' perceptions that alcohol may be best controlled through spatial ordering. But a focus on this issue also needs to be combined with recognition of the extent to which such ordering has been problematized for Aborigines by long-term and continuing constriction of their capacities to define space.

I have observed that many Aborigines readily think of the possibility for quitting as dependent on the spatial strategy of remove, "getting out from the grog." The possibility for self-direction and disentanglement from blandishments of other people is seen to depend on movement, personal control on spatial reordering.

Another form of spatial solution to the grog problem that Aboriginal people have attempted, with assistance, in a number of Katherine communities (and elsewhere) is to define an area as "dry," a place to which it is illegal to bring grog.[6] Sometimes the entire community space is so defined; sometimes, an intermediate measure is adopted whereby a drinking area—beyond which grog is not to be brought—is defined (formally or informally) some distance away from the main residential camp. Analogous relations are often quickly established between the drinking area and the main camp as may exist (in general conceptual terms, if not in actuality) between town and bush camp: the former becomes associated with free grogging and is a place sober drivers attempt to bypass without stopping; the latter with restriction, a place where one should not bring grog but may, preferably quietly, come back and "sleep it off."

Despite dry area declarations, nondrinking residents in certain Katherine camps have not been successful in keeping the grog out because some residents, notably but not solely younger men, have not been motivated to do so. For years it has been common for residents to return to camp perimeters with take-away grog, and drunks and grog inevitably come into the camp. When surveyed about the results of dry areas legislation and asked why the dry area hadn't stopped the drunks, respondents in one camp suggested that their governing council is not "strong" enough—in other words, that there is a local failure of authority.

Certain Katherine camps have never been posted as dry areas. There is a general feeling that any attempt to ban grog, especially from Maiali Brumby just across the High Level bridge from town, would be ineffectual. Many people at Maiali Brumby consider proximity to town a critical element in their choice of living area partly because of the close and continuous access to alcohol that it allows. Nevertheless, there have been repeated suggestions, both by Aboriginal organizations and by town authorities, that more delimited areas need to be defined for "social drinking," where alcohol is permitted but in a pleasant environment where sociability, eating, and perhaps entertainment are encouraged.

Both these ways of addressing "grog" problems—distancing oneself from places associated with it or declaring spaces grog-free—rely strongly on a notion of social order having a spatial basis. Such concepts are variably supported and contested by non-Aboriginal persons and interests. For their part, some Northern Territory authorities and non-Aboriginal townspeople have long seen one of the effects of dry areas legislation in rural areas as the "export" of Aboriginal drinking to town (see d'Abbs 1990 in relation to Alice Springs).

Such an ideal social topology, a spatial ordering of social difference, can always be rendered problematic by action that calls the identity into question in some way. Among themselves Aboriginal people contest the definition of spaces as "dry" or "wet." Very simple action can begin to render the identity of "dry" or grog-free areas problematic. All that needs to happen is for drinkers to bring grog there or be drunk there. This violation raises an immediate practical problem for other people: they either eject the drinkers and attempt to maintain the identity of the space, or they allow the definition of the space to be compromised. Many people find it difficult to deal summarily with drinkers whom they know well and with whom they have long-standing, complex social ties. Consequently, many non-drinking Aboriginal people suffer the drinkers. Sometimes, all that can be done is to temporize with drinkers and tolerate them within suggested limits ("long as you quiet, no more humbug")—even though neither the drinkers nor anyone else thinks they will observe those limits. And the sense of responsibility of nondrinkers is tested because given the possible dangers and disorders of relatives' drinking in town in large and sometimes more mixed schools of drinkers than may gather at any particular camp, the relatives often see it as safer to keep the drinkers nearby, despite ensuing unpleasantness.

Strongly spatial Aboriginal modes of social ordering are thus relevant to the question of alcohol. At the widest level, sometimes the town is seen as a zone where grog is allowed. Visitors may view the town as a whole in terms of a grog binge, during which they rest periodically at relatives' camps. "Bush" living outside town appears as the alternative. The identification of areas outside the town as "dry," even if they are not very remote, allows some people to succeed in identifying themselves as belonging to that space and its declared purpose, to banish thoughts of the daily grog pursuit, and to turn to other things. It is in these terms that we must understand the enigma of the town grog-eater who becomes a model worker in the bush.

"Oppression" and "alienation" are not irrelevant to the problems of Aboriginal use and abuse of alcohol. But these terms have to be understood, as Martin (1993) also says, not in any simple and direct causal relation with the phenomena of alcohol use, but as arising from radical dislocation of the conditions for social action, in which distinctive Aboriginal social modalities were conventional, unquestionable, and regularly reproduced. Use and abuse of alcohol by Aborigines is a tenacious taking up of a medium of sociality, stimulation, and response that promotes the dissociation of Aborigines (Stanner 1958:99) from the surrounding environment while intensifying and simplifying sociality among themselves in the short term. It distorts the terms of earlier Aboriginal sociality, in particular, by creating the conditions for vivacious contestation, especially in the town context, of modes of socio-spatial ordering.

Most Aborigines of Katherine will say that feelings of "shame" (Myers 1986:120–125) deter them from thrusting themselves upon people whom they do not know and with whom they have no significant existing connection. This is strongly felt about unknown Aborigines and all the more so about whites. Recognized absence of connection among Aborigines also implies the converse: that "different" people have no claims they can legitimately make on one's things and one's social effort, such social bounding largely articulated in terms of the concept of shame. This kind of sentiment is illustrated by the words of a Kalano resident: "When I get my *layi, mayi* [meat, food], grog, I can't go la [to] anybody house, I just have'im here, I can't walk around anywhere, all about [they are] different."

The man quoted is a long-term resident of Katherine, and the context of this remark was that a house at Kalano fifty meters or so from his had just been newly occupied by arrivals to town from Roper River, people whom he did not know. Significantly, he associates lack of social connection with the need for self-regulated spatial restriction: one cannot "go" to people who are felt to be "different"; one must stay within the confines of one's own area. In the camp, this amounts to a house and yard and the houses and yards of one's close consociates, kinsmen, and countrymen, not anybody's house and yard.[7]

Quite different from his remark is the spirit of the graffiti prominently written upon the wall of a Kalano house where I am a regular visitor and adoptive family member: "Hello all the Grog People from Anywhere." This is an open-armed invitation to "grog people" without regard to origin or existing connection. People, in fact, do not usually drink with just anyone.[8] In Katherine camps, one's drinking partners tend to be "close" and known people. However, drinking partners (whoever they may be) may *become* close associates on the basis of the common pursuit and consumption of grog. Thus, the graffiti's poignant celebration of the relaxation of restriction that grog facilitates, notably, the emergence of a maverick or heterodox principle, an Aboriginal concept of "ubiquity." The sentiment contrasts strongly with expressions of "shame," which are otherwise a crucial element of Aboriginal practices of socio-spatial ordering and interpersonal dynamics.

Several years ago, Kalano Association formed a night patrol, on the model of developments in central Australia. The night patrol concept is meant to bring personalism and community relationship, in an Aboriginal style, into management of a "problem" that many whites and Aborigines alike see as certainly beyond the traditional forms of Aboriginal social behavior, and, some would say, are also beyond its resources. A degree or version of the notion of mimesis, discussed in chapter 5, is relevant here. Patterns of caring behavior and personal knowledge, imputed to Aborigines and explicitly identified as Aboriginal, are seen for that reason as appropriate to this difficult issue. This assumption, however, contrasts to some extent with the attitude frequently expressed by nondrinking Aboriginal people in camp life—that drinkers "like" to drink, cannot be influenced, and are best left alone.

Anglo-Australian and other European notions of personhood accord acclaim to the person who can remain the same, carrying that which is intimately identified with him wherever he goes (as in Goffman's 1959:34 concept of "personal front") and to the person who can find his or her feet in a strange and unfamiliar situation. Given such conceptions of personal independence of context and external influence, many white townspeople of Katherine would agree with old-timer and farmer Wally Christie in his sympathetic-sounding assessment of the "problem": "The poor buggers, you know, I'm very sorry for them in ways, but it's up to them to put a stop to it, like to steady themselves down." Personal integration and control come naturally as a recommendation, in a way that they do not to many Aboriginal people. For them, drinking is part of a complex issue of the displacement, literally and figuratively, of the conditions for the reproduction of familiar forms of social action under substantially changed conditions, which include the very accessibility of alcohol. That in the everyday conduct of this struggle, some Aborigines actively use alcohol as a medium of sociality and stimulation indicates that characterizations of alcohol abuse as explicable in terms of Aboriginal subjection, and as a manifestation of resistance, are incomplete and simplistic. Although its use apparently promotes sociality, it does so in a way that, as examples above have indicated, tends to modify existing norms of socio-spatiality in the regulation of interaction among Aborigines. This modification heightens the sense of opposition and of contestation over the definition of spaces, as one between "Aborigines" and others, around the issue of drinking.

Conclusions

There is some relation between present patterns of Aborigines' use of town spaces and the modes of identity formation involved in high-level socio-territoriality and the differentiation of places in Aboriginal terms. Uses of space are not "free" or unconstrained; they are informed by constant consciousness of where Aboriginal people are, over shorter and longer term, in relation to town space. This consciousness involves socio-spatial understandings about where Aboriginal people come from and the related issue of their current town location and patterns of sociality with other Aborigines. But despite these ways in which the town exists in Aboriginal terms, spaces within it are strongly shaped, their definition sometimes dominated, for Aborigines by struggle between themselves and other townspeople. This chapter has characterized some of the limitations on Aborigines' capacity to shape spaces in the town.

Empathy and personal experience of the scale of the alcohol issue in Aborigines' lives has led me to depict its implications for socio-spatial struggle in the town at some length. The last chapter dealt with issues in recent Aboriginal affairs, especially land rights, around which have developed what I called a mimetic social technology, whereby representations of what Aborigines are, are redeployed with benevolent intent in a way that affects what they may become. It is noteworthy that alcohol use is not understood by anyone to lend itself easily to imitative or any other kind of management. It is an aspect of the contemporary Aboriginal scene that is not widely seen as "cultural," though certain dimensions of attempted management of the issue, such as spatial remove and definition of some spaces as "dry," are seen as promisingly compatible with aspects of Aboriginal social practice. Many non-Aboriginal Northern Territorians form uncompromisingly negative views from highly visible aspects of alcohol use among Aboriginal people. Both the use itself, and others' reactions, reinforce stereotypic patterns of intercultural representation, interaction, and spatial separation in the town.

Seven

Do Places Appear? Further Struggle in Space

CHAPTER 2 explored loss of a place formerly differentiated in Aboriginal terms from its surroundings, through the evanescence of the rainbow's cave. This chapter is concerned with another aspect of change and continuity with respect to places in the recent period. It tells, as far I was able to follow events over a number of years, of the emergence of a place near one of the Katherine camps. The way in which the place came to be known was simple: as a finding in daily camp life. But from simple beginnings, the place came to play a role in complex current events having to do with changes in the participation of Aborigines in the town, region, and nation.

The episode points to issues of several kinds. First, under what conditions may mythically storied places appear around the town? Does sociohistorical process tend only in the direction of disappearance of places having the duality of temporary camp and enduring country (Myers 1986:57–59) through which places are made Dreaming story?

Second, the episode is relevant beyond the Katherine scene because of what it has to tell us about the way in which local cultural creativity becomes enmeshed in new and complex circuits of representation and action. This new circuitry gradually transforms local conditions. The episode is illustrative of problems concerning the extent to which indigenous "cultural" materials may persist in having a degree of independence and fluidity, rather than being pinioned under complex demands that arise as part of the changing character of Aboriginal affairs within the nation. All the complications described emerge, somewhat paradoxically, in the context of recent liberalization of thinking and action concerning "Fourth World peoples" within First World nation-states. They would not emerge, or be possible, were the political cultures of these nation-states simply repressive ones.

Third, the problem of the intersection of local creativity with wider forces brings us once again to the question of specifically anthropological representations as among them and to issues that have been recently discussed as ones of social constructionism (Anderson 1983, Keesing 1989, Guss 1995), invention (Hobsbawm and Ranger 1983; Hanson 1989; Jackson 1989; 1995a, 1995b; Linnekin 1991), and the issue of scholarly authority in research on these matters (Briggs 1996). Because of the typically long-term nature of anthropological fieldwork, the researcher comes to know situations in detail at particular moments, and thus is often able to see change in them over time. In the episode at issue, Aboriginal people recognized the novelty of the place in one way, but in another did not accept the notion of novelty. Where does the anthropologist stand who reports and analyzes such a situation? Does she, as Briggs (1996:462) has acutely posed as a problem, unconscionably remove constraints on the circulation of cultural representations and thereby limit any effective local control over the circulation of discourse? Would this be irresponsibility on the part of the anthropologist, and does it identify anthropological representation with postmodern concepts of the free play of signifiers?

Culture and the Politics of Invention

A great deal of current public debate in Australia ranges around the concept of "Aboriginal culture." Will this be seen as static or as dynamic? And if the latter, to what extent? Current social justice perspectives seek recognition of indigenous "rights" to culture (Dodson 1995, cf. Merlan 1995). Although there has been increased effort to create mechanisms for the protection and preservation of places of demonstrable significance to

Aboriginal people (e.g., the Aboriginal and Torres Strait Islander Heritage Protection Act 1984, under review in 1995), contestation over places has emerged most strongly over the notion of "sacred sites." Several sacred sites disputes of recent years in Australia have become nationally notorious (e.g., Noonkanbah in Western Australia: Hawke and Gallagher 1989, Kolig 1987, Vincent 1983; a dam near Alice Springs: Wootten 1992; Coronation Hill in the Northern Territory: RAC 1991, Brunton 1991, Merlan 1991a; and most recently, dispute over the significance to Aboriginal people of Hindmarsh Island in South Australia: Saunders 1994, Mead 1995, Mathews 1996, Brunton 1996).[1] In all of these, a central issue has been whether significance attributed to places claimed to be sacred sites is of long standing (even if not, as a current form of rhetoric has it, "40,000 years old") or has been subject to recent social construction or "invention." It is seen as problematic if aspects of significance appear to have been generated from the investigative or proposed development processes themselves. Investigation of the Aboriginal significance of a place or area, in fact, is usually undertaken in the light of development or other similar proposals. But it is generally understood to have the object of merely establishing or assessing already existing significance without affecting it or perceptions of it. The sense of the problem is captured in the complaint, often heard in Australia from business interests and other members of the public, that a place was not an Aboriginal site of significance until somebody proposed to lodge a land claim over it and mine it, build on it, or undertake some other development activity there.[2]

These questions about the static or dynamic nature of significance arise at a particular moment in anthropology. Increasingly, and correlated with the decline of structuralist approaches in anthropology (chapter 3), "place" is no longer acceptably conceptualized as passive, abstract, or homogeneous arena or backdrop on which things happen or within which social structures are merely contained. It must be understood processually and experientially, as a dynamic dimension of social process (Lefebvre 1991, Casey 1993, Harvey 1985, Gregory and Urry 1985, Gottdiener 1985). Anthropologists have made use of phenomenological writings for the perspectives they offer on the body as medium of emplacement and on the "phenomenal body"—one imbued with relationship to place, and that incorporates cultural patterns into its actions—as the potentiality and intermediary of a certain world (Bourdieu 1977, Merleau-Ponty 1994:106–147). In these terms anthropologists have been developing ethnographic approaches to how places may be meaningful and how they may show up (in the words of Munn 1992:116) *as* something of determinate significance in the relations to them of actor and action.

In light of this, and of other aspects of contemporary context (chapter 5), what may be appropriate anthropological positions on the investigation of issues relating to place and the possibility of new places? Do we demand evidence of the long-term nature of meaningfulness of places, aligning ourselves with a "heritage" perspective that focuses upon significance as already fixed and *in* places, and regard everything else as illegitimate? Clearly not, for that denies the possibility of contemporary agency and of interpretations of "culture" that move away from notions of it as "object" and toward understandings of modalities of social action and the ways in which these relate to each other. On the other hand, do we accept a fluid constructionist view that whatever indigenous or any other people say about a place ipso facto constitutes its present significance? A cynical version of this view has gained popular ground in Australia as an understanding of Aboriginal "sacred sites issues," that Aborigines can be made to say just about anything at all about places and that their objections to proposals concerning places are made up to suit particular situations. In reducing understandings of contemporary action to ones featuring pure opportunism and denying genuineness of Aboriginal concern and legitimacy of interest, this view is clearly unacceptable. One must, however, recognize the importance and responsibility, in the current context, of establishing the social character of meaningfulness.

In my experience in the Katherine region and elsewhere in the Northern Territory and Western Australia, Aboriginal people continually "produce" places, assessing and reassessing their significance in terms of current conditions and relationships. A few of these places are new. That is, Aborigines sometimes identify as places locales where the concept of distinct, socialized place had not existed or only been indeterminate before, appear to modify their notions of the significance of places, or both.[3]

Below is an account of one instance of such production, which I saw, in certain of its aspects at least, as involving *recent* production.[4] Despite recency, there is, I believe, no reasonable way of seeing the processes involved as straightforward ones of opportunistic constructionism. Nevertheless, I also want to argue that the character of meanings, and the way in which they are produced in this particular instance, provides insight into changing relations of Aboriginal people with places, in two ways. First, the way in which meanings are produced changes as Aborigines' lives are lived under different conditions of being in places from those that characterized earlier forms of Aboriginal social life (and inform such discussions about country as that of Myers 1986). Second, and linked to this, the production of meaning changes as a result of the significances that Aborigines now attribute to places emerging into, and being part of, an intercultural social context (of socially specific and changing character). In this context, kinds of meanings are possible, are attributed social value, and often have material implications in the constantly changing sociopolitical field.

Recognition of these two dimensions requires us to move beyond inadequate polarities between continuity or discontinuity, authenticity or opportunism, and motivated construction versus "authentic" cultural expression as the sole terms of understanding new places. It forces us to attempt to understand contemporary social processes as perhaps involving all of these, not as polarities but all potentially at play in the shaping of action.

Permanence, Change, and the Properties of Places

Munn (1970) and Myers (1986), in particular, have convincingly shown the commonality of cultural patterning of human movement and ancestral or Dreaming movement. Places are "the topographic remnants of the centered fields of ancient actors," "stretching out from a reference point to vague peripheries" (Munn 1996:454). Metamorphosis of ancestral bodies or parts of bodies into landscape (and ancestral bodies into landscapes of connected places that are given regional coherence in this imaginative mode, see Tamisari 1995) is frequently the kind of event that Aborigines consider to repose in places. The productive quality of human relationship with country is often imagined as a metamorphosis of body into place (Munn 1970). Further, the transformations of ancestors' bodies into places do not simply involve "their bodies in some generalized sense, but [are] situated in particular stances or states such as lying down, sitting, dancing, standing and looking at something, or scattered into fragments from a fight—all forms conveying some momentary action or participation in events at a given location" (Munn 1996:454).

The identity of a particular ancestral figure may not necessarily or easily be read off from the sensible properties of places (although they may apparently offer stimuli to the objectification of meaning). In many cases, the character of the Dreaming event is complex and opaque, relative to those sensible properties. Though the meanings of place may be suggestively linked to them, they cannot be simply read off from them. Overtly, traditional Aboriginal mythopoeia works from Dreaming event to physical form, not the other way round. For example, that Chambers Pillar in Aranda country is the phallic body of a knob-tailed gecko ancestor (Morton 1985, frontispiece) is not, in Aboriginal conception, to be read off from the shape of the country. Gecko inheres in this place as its truth, and this is crucial knowledge to be transmitted concerning it. The place looks the way it does because gecko inheres in it. Around this direction of coding, from Dreaming event to the visible world, lurks the ever-present possibility and ambiguity of physical form as a dimension informing the production of meanings.

Thus, a place must be learned. Continuing "production" of it is strongly mediated by existing human concepts of its meaningfulness, which are partly maintained and generated in terms of mythological schemata, which are not consciously systematized by Aborigines, but which have systematicity and may be analyzed. An example of such a scheme is the deflection of ancestral traveling figures from places on the basis that they are already occupied, replete with someone or something with which encounter must be prohibited (such as a sacred object, a mother-in-law, or the like; see Munn 1996 on "negative spaces"). Particular knowledge sustained by such a schema, and in turn sustaining it, might be the specific identity and sacral object forms of the creative agent. To the uninvolved, learning this kind of "deep" significance of places might seem puzzlingly meaningless and engender a "So what?" reaction.

For a place to be recognized as such, meanings must have been socially constructed at some time or combination of times by and in the presence of actors in relation to locales that become repositories of meanings through the social objectification of that intersection in a more or less definite, shared manner. There is always the possibility of varying or even competing interpretations. With codification of the intersection as an enduring basis of future relations of others to places, there comes acceptance and reinforcement of a particular set of meanings over time, repeatedly evoked at other "present" moments. The specific circumstances of such future intersections may result in modification in how meaning is understood and transmitted.

Aborigines are often heard to say about places that their meanings are forever and sometimes in invidious comparison, that whitefella meanings are transitory (see the quotes in Rose 1992:56). The apparent permanence of certain kinds of Aboriginal meanings of place, their "forever" quality, enthralls not only Aborigines' imagination, but also that of non-Aboriginal Australia. Myers (1986) has shown the extent to which specific meanings are actually produced and contested in interaction, in culturally distinctive modes. To put all of these elements together reveals what Strathern (1992b:40) calls a "naturalism" as cultural construct: Aborigines maintain that the meanings of places do not change; anthropologists can show that meanings are produced and shaped. As an activity of social inquiry, anthropology is not satisfied with the naturalism of the permanence of places but also seeks understanding of how Aboriginal feelings for permanence are reproduced even as the meanings of places are both socially sustained and altered. To do this is to go beneath the surface of Aborigines' as well as others' readily available understandings of social process, which they may explicitly formulate only in terms of the naturalism of permanence rather than investigating how they sustain this through change.

Myers' account shows that fixity of particular meaning cannot be assumed to be a necessary and objective property of the relation between people and places, despite Aborigines' claims of enduring significance. He shows to be problematic the assumption that the ontology of Dreaming correlates with objective fixity of particular meanings. I have mentioned that this assumption, nevertheless, appears as a working presumption of Aboriginal people and also of the wider Australian public, to the extent that they are prepared to regard the significance of a place as authentic. In showing how Pintupi social practice works to sustain that presumption, Myers reveals something profoundly different about this Aboriginal order of human relationships with places compared to Western ones, and different therefore from what most outsiders might expect. Myers describes the Dreaming as having for Pintupi a phenomenologically external, authoritative, emotively powerful character. To this notion of places as "Law," they subordinate consciousness of their practices as involving negotiability and practical unevennesses in the construction and transmission of meaning. Myers thus shows objective continuity in the meanings of particular places to be problematic not necessarily because of externally induced change, but as a result of the ordinary social processes through which such meanings are constructed and transmitted. But, we may ask, how much may the meanings of places differ and vary over time? And at another level, what of continuity in the practices through which such social construction is accomplished—are these subject to transformation?

My answer to the last question is Yes, of course. Changes in what Aborigines say about places are not only to be understood as loss of previously shared knowledge, though this is undoubtedly an aspect of what is going on for many. And certain semiotic tendencies—such as some transparency in the relation between a place's physical aspects and the attribution of meaning to it, illustrated below—have always been aspects of the processes of meaning-formation. But there are changes in degree and in kind in places like Katherine. In the context of changed relationship to country, Aboriginal people are not only more commonly proceeding from physical form to meaning, but are also relativizing Dreaming significances of place to other, known significances. Many of the latter do not relate to Dreaming but arise out of the recent, shared past of black-white interactions, work relations, and the usurpation of country that Aborigines see as having been "blackfella country."

Aboriginal claims concerning these kinds of significance come into arenas of public debate in which a mythic dimension of place is often accorded priority by powerful interests and agents, to the extent that it can be seen as of long standing. If suspected to be of recent origin, on the other hand, the mythic significance is seen as inauthentic. Those who have studied accounts of traditional Aboriginal relationships to country often wonder about the contemporary constraints on the wellsprings of mythic creativity. Some constraints are produced in the very yearning of the non-Aboriginal public for the maintenance of Aboriginal culture, as part of the search for unquestioned naturalisms (see chapter 8). However, the historical facts of settlement and the long-term intercultural nature of the resulting scene seem to me to disallow the notion of "culture" as completely independent, for instance, as completely Aboriginal. Such a notion dissolves in analysis of forms of action and representation, their authorship, intersection, and the sense in which they may be said to embody greater or lesser continuity with other actions and representations. But to say this is to say no more than we already think about the concept of culture in general: we should never delude ourselves that it is anything other than an abstraction that allows us ways of talking about complexity.

Catfish

Not far southwest of Katherine town is a place that has become known to many Aborigines and some whites as Catfish Dreaming. Right next to the camp called the Rockhole (after the enlargement of the nearby

Katherine River), the focal feature of Catfish Dreaming is a stone formation about a meter in length, fairly flat and elongate, which lies directly on the ground on a flat, reddish, sandy plain near the river. Its resemblance to a fish of some kind—perhaps, without too much stretch of the imagination, a flat-tailed catfish—is striking.

Use of a native-language term as a way of establishing the object's identity—as Catfish and also, as things developed, as Jawoyn—began, to my knowledge, in the following way. Alice Mitchell, with whom I visited the place in the early 1980s on first hearing of it (she was one of the people who assisted in its declaration as a site in 1984), referred to the object as *lorr*, that is, invested it with a Jawoyn name.[5] The use of a native-language term was a powerful performative assertion of recognition and identity. Alice also began referring to this place as Lorr-luk, where *-luk* is the Jawoyn locative suffix. This appellation creatively indexed not only the stone, but the surrounding area in terms of it.

As I have briefly recounted in chapter 1, Aborigines had lived at locations in this area before World War II, working on farms along the river and at Manbulloo Station. Given this, there had been ceremonial use of areas in the vicinity of the Rockhole and movement of small encampments of Aboriginal people up and down the river between Manbulloo and town. Associations of different kinds and time depths existed around the Rockhole location. Aboriginal association with the area was less intense after the war, which had resulted in great dislocations, until the establishment of Rockhole as a nondrinking camp in the 1970s following the closure of CSIRO.

Gradually, the establishment of the camp created a change in conditions. Features in the immediate vicinity of the camp began to be found and seen as things of importance, and new feeling for this place as camp and home, with a density of human associations, to form in relation to them. During this period, the unusual object was noticed and appeared *as* something, as Catfish.

At a meeting in June 1995 (held concerning the relevance of Catfish Dreaming to Aboriginal identity of Katherine town area, in a context of discussion of town camp development), one middle-aged woman, a long-term resident of the Rockhole area, succinctly told a story about the "discovery" of catfish a few years before: "Hannah brother been hunting around here and come around and find this thing and come back tell us, that one got accident." (Hannah's brother was hunting around here, came and found this thing, and came back and told us, the one who was killed.")[6] Other people had similar stories to add. Such accounts formulate a time at which the object was not known even to local Rockhole residents. It was distinctly "found" in the sense of first coming to the attention of a person, and the finding reported to others. This sequence of affairs does not diminish the importance for Aboriginal people of the thing's having been there before. Looked at in this way, the story is one of the object's coming to people's attention. Such a view complicates any definition of the situation as one of novelty, or "invention" of the place's significance—a definition I am sure many of these people would reject.

Aboriginal people evoke a combination of familial and other associations, mostly stemming from the postwar period, as relevant to the place's contemporary importance. One man at the 1995 meeting said, "We had camp on this side of river. Ring place [ceremonial ground] was on this side river, O's [his wife's] father been organize, and bla Andrew['s] grandfather [referring to a senior Mayali man]. This country belong to Jawoyn [the usual identity attributed to his wife's family], they been get all the Jawoyn, and Mayali and Ngalkbon; and used to come from Manbulloo."

Catfish first was noticed as an interesting particular feature in the landscape. It could be enduringly identified in a way that could signal, and be an aspect of, Aborigines' (now intense) relationship to this place and also could influence future human relations with it. But when it was found, its possible role was inchoate and indeterminate.

Shared knowledge and concept of what the object was emerged gradually rather than immediately and rippled out from a small core set of people to others. The identification of the object as Catfish was clearly very much based on the sensible properties of the stone, in a way that resonates with Lévi-Strauss' (1966) notion of the "science of the concrete." This involves "constant attention to properties of the world, with an interest that is . . . alert to possible distinctions which can be introduced between them." Lévi-Strauss (1966:3) would have this attention to the sensible serve an attitude toward the world as an "object of thought." I prefer to see this attention to the sensible here as a degree of continuity in the habitus (Bourdieu 1977), of Aborigines' interactions with places, of producing meanings that may be turned into more- and less-lasting bases of significance for human action, and some continuity in particular ways in which it is invested with meaning.

Even so, the relation of this place to others remained for a time indeterminate and unspecified. But events in the 1980s turned a spotlight on this area and raised an issue of its having wider connections.

The Katherine Area Land Claim was prepared and heard in the early 1980s. With Katherine Gorge the main issue, a small claim area called number 3, adjacent to the Rockhole camp, was of little moment. However Aboriginal relations to it might have been characterized, it was clear that the claimant group would have to be somewhat differently constituted from any claimancy to the large areas north and northeast. My research had by then yielded considerable, scattered, oral historical evidence of Aboriginal representations of the Rockhole as within an area earlier conceived as Dagoman (independent of Arndt's material, which I had not yet seen).[7] For purposes of managing what promised to be a contentious and difficult claim, area 3 was set aside for future action. The bases of attachment with the Rockhole area, and the Catfish Dreaming, were diverse.[8] People's connections with the area, and their remembering of the past in it, had been refreshed since the solid establishment of the Rockhole camp.

In the midst of discussions in 1995 generally relating to the town's socio-territorial identity and possibilities for town camp development, Julie Williams interjected, "Bla my grandfa this place, where Rhoda been have 'im, my *jabuj*." (This place belonged to my grandfather, the one Rhoda was married to.)[9] Here Julie was expressing her sense of continuing relationship to places around Katherine, as is her wont, in terms of family connections to them. Her words were scarcely taken up, quite possibly because her statements were not organized around issues of identity at the higher socio-territorial level in terms of which this issue had come to be strongly defined following the land claim and the growth of Aboriginal organizations.

The outcome of the Katherine Area Land Claim has been significant for the way in which the Rockhole area has subsequently played a part in the politics of Katherine Aboriginal organizations. In the wake of the largely successful Katherine Land Claim (in which the Gorge was granted to the claimants, along with other areas northeast of town), the newly formed Jawoyn Association remained dormant for some time after its establishment in 1984. It was galvanized into action by the dispute over mining at Coronation Hill, northeast of Katherine, from around 1987 onward (see RAC 1991, Merlan 1991a). After that, the association became a focal manager of affairs of that large group of people who were original claimants to the Katherine area portions. A subset of them have subsequently gained title (in 1995) to Gimbat Station even farther north, within which Coronation Hill is located. The Jawoyn Association has become involved in most major issues that concern the Katherine Aboriginal population, including many sites issues around the town. Its establishment gave support to long-standing conceptions, already present in Arndt's time, of the town area as Jawoyn.

In 1984, Catfish Dreaming was declared a site by the Aboriginal Sacred Sites Protection Authority,[10] based on information from senior people affiliated with three different socio-territorial groupings—Jawoyn, Wardaman, and Mayali. The area was not formally attributed to only one or another of these identities. There was recognition that some people of all of them had attachments to the area.

As far as I was aware then, there was no notion of the Catfish as having any "storied" or mythic connection to other places. But gradually, views about such linkage grew around the question of the "tribal" identity of the Rockhole area—particularly, whether it was "Jawoyn," or not—in a way that was intensified by another site-related development issue.

In 1985, a dispute emerged about the development of a gravel quarry a few kilometers from the Rockhole. Objection to the development was recorded by the Aboriginal Sacred Sites Protection Authority working with Katherine Aboriginal informants, on the grounds that a Kangaroo Dreaming had moved through the area and on toward the Roper River. I was not involved in this issue but was aware of stories of this kind having previously existed concerning the proposed development area. I had not specifically investigated how the kangaroo travels were conceptualized. The quarry matter came to participate in all the indeterminacies around issues of the town's socio-territorial identity in Aboriginal terms.

Debate over the socio-territorial identity of the Rockhole area was sharpened by a further development from the Katherine Area Land Claim. In the early 1990s, the Jawoyn Association entered into what has become known as the "Mt. Todd agreement" with Zapopan, a mining company. With exploration, Zapopan had determined there was a prospective gold deposit at Mt. Todd, a site previously mined. Having failed in the land claim to gain the area (well to the north of Katherine; see map 1) within which the Mt. Todd mine is situated, Jawoyn Association lodged a repeat land claim over it.[11] Rather than struggle with the uncertainties of a repeat land claim and other possible complications, a negotiated deal to which the Jawoyn Association and the Northern Territory Government were party cleared the way for Zapopan to mine, in return for certain benefits to the Jawoyn Association. One of these was the agreed handover of title to area 3, Catfish Dreaming.[12]

The Jawoyn Association wanted the area handed over to them. Some

Wardaman people felt that they should be recognized as title holders, even if jointly with others, in recognition of their relations with the area. (The Wardaman Association had recently been established in Katherine.) Mayali people were least demonstrative, but they reminded everyone of their connections to the Rockhole and the town.

In the end, title to area 3 was handed over to Jawoyn Association representatives at a ceremony in Sutherland Shire Council chambers, Sydney, in 1994.[13] Some members of the Wardaman Association were annoyed at not being invited to the handover. On the town scene, at the level of relations among Aboriginal organizations and actors in them, the Jawoyn Association was resented by some for usurping a leading, if not exclusionary, role in the attempted negotiation by Katherine Combined Aboriginal Organizations for new Aboriginal living areas, or town camp areas, within and near the town.

In the lead-up to the grant of area 3 to the Jawoyn Association, two women prominent in Wardaman Association affairs organized a women's ceremony and held it at Catfish Dreaming. They claimed this could be done on the basis of a link to a Catfish Dreaming place at Wave Hill (see map 1) to the south and west, in Mudburra country. Some other Aborigines in Katherine commented adversely on this, including some Wardaman people who said they had never heard of this association.

Some statements were made by Aboriginal people from Roper River, well to the east of Katherine, that Catfish was to be seen in relation to their own Catfish tradition many miles away, at Lake Allen near the Gulf of Carpentaria. This suggestion appeared to be based on the presumed identity of Dreaming—Catfish in both places.[14] This suggestion was heard around Katherine as the voice of senior Roper River people supporting the Jawoyn Association—and, more broadly, adding weight to the defense of Catfish as a place of significance to Aborigines.

Eventually, some senior people (mainly western siders who were skeptical of connections of the Rockhole with Wave Hill), within local camp contacts and intermittent attendance at Aboriginal organizations, began to explicitly doubt the identity of the place by questioning the identification of the object as Catfish. One woman, for instance, observed on a number of occasions that it looked more like a combfish; "a catfish is flat, not like that stone." A man contributed to this, "It looks more like a shark."

Both seemed to be implicitly accepting the possibility of identifying the object in terms of resemblance, what it looks like. But as in the Lévi-Straussian "science of the concrete," they were paying attention to sensible properties to make differences, in this case expressing alternative possibilities concerning the stone's identity that they considered more in keeping with its physical properties. Neither made a definitive, alternative identification, but both spoke with a clear understanding of the kinds of claims they could be seen by others to be denying with these remarks.

These events point to these people's sense of a problem of the authenticity of this particular identification, given their own traditionalism, or a strongly felt sense of the importance of remaining within the bounds of accepted and shared understandings that they saw as incontrovertible against the upstart claims of others. Some spoke bitterly about people "making things up," without there being any clear way of focusing this criticism under the circumstances.

This discussion brings us back to the issue of transparency in the relation between physical form and the understood significance of places. The episode is one in which the physical character of the place had a simple referential function, merely suggesting some specific entity as Dreaming. There was no elaborate Dreaming story. In this area, the regionality of Dreaming stories had been severely disrupted over long-term events involving the growth of the town. There were few securely established concepts of connections of places in the Rockhole area with others over the wider region. In their questioning of the stone's identity, the people quoted were showing how easily such identity can be contested where there has been significant disruption of regionwide senses of "country as story" to which subsequent renewals and changes in meaning of objects must be related. Where this exists, Dreaming must be linked to, and distinguished from, the existence and "truth" of other places. In the terms of its finding, Catfish was simply there; there was no immediate issue of its connections to other places. Since the war, in particular, stock working and other patterns of Aboriginal presence and absence over the countryside had been largely discontinued. The concepts of connections of Catfish Dreaming to other far-flung places (e.g., Roper River) originated in the rounds of Aboriginal organizational politics, beyond the regular and most meaningful contacts of most Katherine camp residents, and were not supported by their local knowledge. In the Rockhole area, the mythic significance of this place was now strongly relativized to Aboriginal people's sense of their historical occupancy of the area. There was less sense of Dreaming presences than there is, for example, at nearby Manbulloo—another instance of the growth of unevennesses in the landscape in a relatively small compass.

But the object and place had significance, especially for Rockhole people. Although Catfish had, in my understanding of Aboriginal people's relationship to it, little numinous quality (see Kolig 1981, 1995), it was the kind of familiar and even beloved object that makes of place a home—the object crystallization of a kind of relationship much smaller in scope, and more intimate, than it was permitted to have in the circuits of representation into which others drew it.

Anthropology, Aborigines, and Invention

I asked what attitudes anthropologists might take toward current issues involving the meaningfulness of places, and "new" places, in the light of changing anthropological points of view on place. I suggested that it is inappropriate to assume rampant constructionism as a fundamental approach or to demand evidence of complete fixity of meaning, for both would be at odds with fundamental anthropological understandings of social process. I argued, however, that it is important that anthropologists take a critical approach to the meaningfulness of place, and that such an approach must involve problematizing certain current processes in human relations with places that we are in a position to observe over the long term. Anthropologists have sometimes allowed themselves to be identified with defending the historically continuous nature of specific Aboriginal conceptions of particular places. My own view is that we need to attempt to clarify the processes in which meaning is produced, changed, and transmitted, even while recognizing the pressures and constraints under which such work is often carried out. Clarification must involve the effort to understand transformation at different levels, two of which may be usefully distinguished here.

One is particular, having to do with whether the application of specific meanings in relation to particular places appears to be characterized by continuity or discontinuity. The second level is more general, having to do with continuity and discontinuity in the broader set of concepts or practices through which we understand the production of place to be carried on. Once we separate these two dimensions, we see that no particular history of place production that I have given is simple or susceptible of absolute characterization as either continuous or discontinuous. We also see, in the example I have given, that there has been considerable shift in the conditions under which the production of place can occur, and become routinized, among Aboriginal people of Katherine.

All the evidence I have concerning Catfish points to this object having been unknown to Katherine Aborigines, at least in recent times. Its particular Dreaming association must be said, in this sense, to be new. But this newness does not preclude Aboriginal people's envisioning the process by which it became known as one characterized by continuity: as one woman described it, Hannah's brother found this thing and came and told us about it. The thing was already there, with its own presence and meaning. From this perspective, the only problem is to define that presence and meaning.

The attitude in terms of which the finding of something, and the recognition of it as other than a human discovery might, to some skeptics, be falsifiable, its authenticity as Aboriginal practice questionable. But assessment of this requires that we first have made appropriate distinctions among kinds and levels of social process and context. How Catfish came to be found is relevant: Hannah's brother came across Catfish in the course of an everyday, ordinary expedition from the Rockhole camp to the surrounding riverine country. The predisposition to read the countryside as meaningful in a certain way, to see it as full of meanings that make a difference to humans but are outside human manipulation, stimulated in-camp interest in the object. There is an element of continuity in the specific nature of this kind of relationship with places. That Catfish was close to a place of recently renewed human association made it particularly interesting: it is constantly nearby, a continuing presence.

Aboriginal association with this area had been attenuated for some decades before Rockhole was established. Many people, like the young man who found the stone, were newcomers to the Rockhole area at the time the camp was established. Given this discontinuity, the stone's meaningfulness was understood in basic terms of its having a Dreaming identity. The specific identity was motivated by its resemblance to a living creature. I have suggested that the principle of transparency between sign and object assumes greater scope in a case like this than it did in the past, when there was more continuous and fuller relationship of people with places. Under those conditions there was greater elaboration of country as storied. I allow for the possibility that meaningfulness of Aboriginal places, and of particular objects in the landscape, may regularly have involved the dimension of resemblance in some ways. But with Catfish, resemblance was apparently all that people had to work with. For several years after its identification became established, there was little concern, as far as I know, about the relation of this to other places—whether, for example, it was part of a Dreaming track or the like. Such questions no doubt were regularly part of Aboriginal attention to most, if not all, places in days when the mode of life involved regular, close, bodily movement through the landscape. In this case, however, the stimulus to define the meaningfulness of Catfish regionally and relationally arose in the context of recent Aboriginal affairs: land rights, sites matters, and the definition of living areas around the town. Had it not been for these, it seems to me that wider connections for Catfish might not have become an explicit issue.

Once the place had begun to be established through small and everyday acts of imagination and communication, "it" as inchoate social entity was made to bear much greater burdens of significance in relation to contemporary issues than it possibly could, given its origins. Attempts were made to make the place speak to the struggles of Aboriginal people with others—among them, townspeople, and business interests—for socio-spatial definition and legitimation. But the place had had its beginnings within a smaller compass. It had not achieved such a broad basis of significance as would have been required for it to serve in these ways. While I hope to have clarified the nature of Catfish as a place in Aboriginal terms I also intend to have clarified the extent of change in those terms, and the complexity of intersection of terms in relation to this place that make it impossible to see the process as the simple preservation of tradition.

Anthropological forms of representation clearly play a complicated role in cases like this: they usually play a more limited role in site declaration (where emphasis is often upon the nature of places in Aboriginal terms), but another kind of role in the fuller, more analytic sort of account of the situation I have given here. How incompatible are these two roles in the sort of highly politicized climate I have described? Also, has the account of Catfish brought any clarity to the question I earlier posed—whether analysis of this (or, for that matter, of changes in the socio-territorial identity of the town) unconscionably removes constraints on cultural representations? I return to these important issues in the concluding chapter.

Culture Struggle: "All Mixed"?

The local relevance of Catfish largely took the form of a question whether the place is Jawoyn or of other social identity. This has been connected to issues arising from the Katherine Area Land Claim and the subsequent Mt. Todd mining arrangements. It is also coming to be linked to the emerging question of the persistence of native title around the town and how any claim to this might proceed. As the Catfish story showed, local understandings bear relationships to wider agendas but may become reinterpreted in them. As the scope of Catfish issues widened, certain local perspectives—such as those of some Rockhole residents—tended to become residual, called upon as mere support for one or another position in a field of possibilities that they had little ability to affect directly. The widening of perspectives in these ways is relevant to how Aboriginal culture and heritage are coming to be understood, a topic I mentioned earlier in the chapter.

In recent decades, it has become conventional to talk about the importance of maintaining Aboriginal culture—for its own intrinsic worth, for its heritage values to the national and international community, and as part of processes of support and recuperation among Aboriginal people themselves. Ideas of cultural maintenance, in other words, inherently involve an objectivizing moment (Bourdieu 1977), in which some aspects of present and past life are crystallized as "cultural." Many ideas come to local communities through the expanded contacts and networks of contemporary Aboriginal affairs, sometimes intersecting with locally held concepts, and sometimes not. Emphasis on culture and its maintenance, naturally, has intensified concern with how culture is to be understood and conserved. This, in turn, stimulates many processes of the mimetic sort, in which representations of Aboriginal practices—including how practices are to be understood as "Aboriginal culture"—come to play a material role in the shaping of Aborigines' lives. Aboriginal people, of course, participate in these processes in various ways.

A young Aboriginal woman and mother at the Rockhole recently made some pessimistic-sounding remarks about issues of cultural "loss" and maintenance to me, forms of thinking about culture as a negative quantum that have gathered strength with the emphasis on culture. She did so partly in complaining about everyday activities in the camp. She said though it was very important for children to "learn culture," such learning was not going on in camp: "These people here don't move, only siddown and play cards. They [boys and men] always thinking about women. No kids know their culture, they just grow up and start drinkin', Bye! and off to pub."

She identified "mixing" of Aboriginal people of different origins, increasingly common in the Katherine camps, as a problem for cultural maintenance: "But trouble is, they all from different sides, like one from Jawoyn, and other from Wardaman. Nobody have wife or husband from same place, so nobody learning." She sees herself as having experienced something like this problem, having been raised by two old women from "Wardaman side," but "I'm really supposed to follow Jawoyn side, like my mother and grandmother." She spoke of certain upper-generation links of her family to certain other Katherine families, evoking what I have come to understand as some of the crucial Dagoman identities in those upper levels. She also spoke of a (white) employee at Kalano who was trying to encourage pride and interest in culture by encouraging her and others "to learn and go around, pick up ideas that way, learn some language." But she said that was hard unless people were prepared to "move" (be active). Thinking in terms of the encouragement she was given to "keep the culture," she asked herself what she and others could do in their situation of "mixing" and the whirl of town life. She thought maybe "we have like X from [an Arnhem coastal settlement], and old Y, and they should get together, get a white board and teach the kids. Maybe we could have all mixed. It's important for them to learn culture. But all they wait for is to play cards or watch TV."

Like some of the Katherine Area Land Claim witnesses I quoted in chapter 3, underlying what she says is the mimetic idea of assimilating "Aboriginal culture" to practices of schooling. Her idea involves the use of representations and practices of "white culture" to foster the practice of Aboriginal culture, objectified and rendered teachable.

There are, in other words, old people who know the (high?) culture—that which can perhaps be most easily formalized and made explicit—and even though they are from different places, they could pass it on. But, she mused, perhaps the younger ones don't want to learn that.

Her thinking seems to suggest the possibility of a less-locally-bound Aboriginal culture that can be taught by old people from different places to young people who are "all mixed." Contemporary emphases on cultural revival as a positive element of Aboriginal self-identification have, particularly in southeastern Australia, involved increasingly explicit borrowing, teaching and diffusion of "culture" in the reified and generalized sense she envisions (Creamer 1988; see also Myers 1988, who illustrates the attempt to show off Aboriginal culture in an international environment). Her attitudes illustrate a rising awareness, similar to that of many anthropologists and other outsiders, of difference between selected aspects of the traditional "culture" and today's social practices. The idea of culture she concretizes and has come to value most as such (though not as preferred practice in her everyday life) is past oriented. Those attached to culture in this sense may feel powerless to recapture what is "theirs," though some make an effort.

What are now to some extent shared (Western and Aboriginal) objectifications of "culture" as language, art, dance—the vivid, the material, the special event as opposed to the everyday flow of social action, while themselves important, nevertheless support a "high" view of culture as divorced from everyday social practice and experience.

Eight

Conclusions

In this book I have attempted to give ethnographic substance to notions of change and continuity through the Katherine material. Having described the Katherine Aboriginal scene in terms of sociohistorical and socio-spatial differentiation among its camps and people (chapter 1), I examined ways in which a place, originally differentiated in Aboriginal terms of country as storied, has became submerged within the town context. But I also gave an experience-near account of ways in which town spaces continue to be differentiated in other terms arising from Aboriginal people's particular sociohistorical experiences of the town, involving elements of continuity and change (chapter 2). Chapter 3, dealing with the character of some Aborigines' relationships to country away from town, showed that in the cases examined, relationships to remote places, especially those cast in Aboriginal terms of identity at the clan level, have dissolved to a significant extent and become past oriented. Despite this, senses of consubstantiality and identity with places continue to vitally inform the subjectivities of people for whom those modes were part of their lived experience. Traces and reorganizations of those earlier forms of relationship are manifested in new ways in the current orientations of those who have lived differently. Chapter 4, in dealing with change in Aboriginal identity of the town area and people affiliated with it, attempted to identify continuities and changes in Aboriginal life in the town context and to explore what is involved in change and continuity in socio-territorial identification of country and people. I distanced myself from approaches that treat indigenous terms of identity in too substantial a manner, arguing that a satisfactory account of them and of the changes on the Katherine scene must involve a more representationally oriented approach to the concepts and relations involved. Chapter 5 dealt with changing modes of definition of the Australian nation-state, showing ways in which this background must inform the Katherine ethnography. A significant aspect of change at this level has been the transition in government policy from the concept of assimilation to one of self-determination. This shift has been characterized by abandonment of policy overtly demanding of Aborigines that they become like other Australians and by moves toward recognition of them as a distinctive people and, in qualified ways, as people of the land. These trends are closely paralleled in other First World nation-states, as part of the formation of a world concept of "indigeneity." I argued for the relevance of the notion of imitation, or mimesis, as a principal template for the intercultural reorganization at this level. Chapter 6 dealt with the contestation between Aborigines and other townspeople over definition of spaces in and around the town. Previously, Aborigines were formally excluded from the town in many ways, but in practical terms were marginalized rather than completely excluded. A shift toward qualified inclusion has involved continuing socio-spatial marginalization, jointly produced but in a situation of continuing power differences between Aborigines and others. This shift shows how increasing willingness to appropriate Aborigines within the national imaginary is met with local resistance, although this, too, has changed in character. Chapter 7 returned to the theme of places as differentiating in Aboriginal terms and the constraints and burdens placed upon cultural creativity in the contemporary context, partly despite and partly because of its liberalization. The episode described in Chapter 7 provided a focus for exploration of some issues of continuing concern in Australian and international heritage politics and in sites and development disputes.

My effort to write an ethnography that explores change and continuity from these socio-spatial perspectives is motivated by a feeling that much of the ethnography of Fourth World peoples is too radically divided between idealizing accounts of indigenous cultures as worthy or autonomous on the one hand and of domination and encapsulation of indigenous cultures on the other. Both kinds of accounts suppress or bypass close consideration of continuity and change as instantiated in contemporary sociocultural formations.

Convinced of the importance of attempting to characterize the Fourth World scene in intercultural terms, in parts of this book I have adopted the notion of mimesis as a way of formulating the strikingly greater salience of imitative behavior and the material power in the lives of indigenous people of others' representations of them in recent relations between those now called Aborigines and the nation-state. In the conclusions that follow, I attempt to draw out how I understand the significance of this imitative dimension as a way of viewing Fourth World–First World relationships in intercultural terms. In various parts of the book I have also indicated that I think it important to consider the nature and authority of anthropological practices and representations as a dimension in these relationships. I will return to the question I posed in chapter 7 but left unanswered there: What is the position of the anthropologist in using the discipline's fieldwork methods and critical styles of thinking to clarify the intercultural character of the indigenous scene? The question is important, for such anthropological practices lead to recognition of change—in particular, in ways that might be seen as surprising or even disadvantageous to the subjects of one's writing (I refer especially to my discussions of the changing socio-territorial identity of the town) and of novelty and invention in relation to places.

Mimesis, Social Technology, and Anthropological Representation

Asad (1979:624) has said that the main problem with colonial anthropology was not any definitive operation in the ideological service of imperialism, "but its ideological conception of social structure and of culture." One aspect of this "ideological conception" has been traditionalism. By this I mean the reproduction of idealized representations of native societies as they allegedly are, in the terms of how they supposedly were (Rosaldo 1989:69). This conception yields categorical terms of representation that to some extent suppress or by-pass history and the theorization of change and continuity. While perhaps historically pervasive in anthropology's representations of its conventional "others," traditionalism has been noticeably so in relation to Fourth World peoples (cf. Riches 1990).

What Habermas (1987) has claimed to be a new temporality of presentness characteristic of modernity is related to the construction of forms dividing the modern from premodern and to a now unsavory aspect of the specifically anthropological legacy that, especially in the nineteenth and early twentieth centuries, assisted in the "creation of a creature on the periphery of civilisation, 'the primitive', unchanging, immutable, thoroughly unmodern" (Miller 1994:59). The specific forms of this creation have changed considerably since then, but there are continuities.

While the phrase "Fourth World" is clumsy, it is not arbitrary, for it allows us to keep in mind the relevance of these people's location within expansionist, affluent, modernizing, industrial and capitalist, liberal and democratic national-political entities, with their forms of imagination and historical trajectories. In these contexts, a form of problem, a distinction between the natural or customary and the culturally constructed, has had a particular history, centered upon the question, as Strathern (1992b) has so succinctly put it, about "what is or is not artefact" (see also Orvell 1989 for exploration of this theme in pre–World War II America). Forms of anthropological representation, I argue, and wider practices of representation within First World contexts have both been strongly shaped in this problematic, in a way that has had implications for Fourth World anthropology at intellectual as well as applied and practical levels.

Western temporal consciousness and dispositions have been partly shaped in the imagining of some societies as traditional and essentially unchanging—originary, not artifact. Some of these depictions are not only commonplaces of anthropology but lie at its very foundations, in which the Aboriginalist literature had a central place. What has perhaps been given less consideration than the traditionalism of anthropological representation are the ways in which traditionalism as ethnographic practice has developed as continuous with wider social practices of compartmentalization of the changing and unchanging. Most recently, I will suggest in relation to Australia, those practices of compartmentalization have played a part in the development of a social technology that, wittingly or unwittingly, to a significant extent has posed itself the challenge of reproducing the indigenous natural or customary.

In this compartmentalization, the changing modern is set against the unchanging traditional, the artificial or constructed against the natural or customary, the built against the natural environment, and nonindigeneity (with its histories of immigration, mixing, heterogeneity, melting pots, multiculturalism) against indigeneity (with its firstness and enormous demand placed upon it for phenotypicality, full-bloodedness, cultural essentialisms). Ethnographic traditionalism is shaped by binarisms of this kind, which also recursively permeate many forms of social action and thought.

For example, the Dreaming has come to be a stereotype concerning Aborigines, a common form of representation of them as oriented to permanence in an unchanging world. Such a construct has also been taken as their sole set of resources with which to meet change. Thus, there has been a great deal of artificial construction of change for Aborigines as the problem of the confrontation of external influences with the mentality of supposed fixity that gave rise to the continental Dreaming imaginary. At the risk of being taken to task, as Myers has been, for saying that the Dreaming is reified projection (Rose 1987, Michaels 1987), one must recognize his contribution in showing a way out of the problems created by identification of the Dreaming as the sum total of means Pintupi had and have for meeting change. He does this by showing something else about them, focusing on the highly negotiated character of the social practices through which the Dreaming was and is perpetuated as a master concept. Many anthropologists viewed the outcome of the encounter of Dreaming world with colonial world as complete social and cultural dissolution (e.g., Sharp 1974)—the "shattered Eden" view (the phrase comes from Errington's and Gewertz' 1995 work in Papua New Guinea)—or as resulting in a life of restive despondency (Stanner 1958). Although this was not far from the truth in many instances, the reason was not that Aboriginal people lived in a condition of Dreaming immutability and inability to meet change, but rather that they were forced to engage socially on conditions of drastic inequality, so that crucial informing dimensions of their social practice were devalued and overridden.

The dialectical resolution to the division is to attempt to cut across radical dichotomies between traditionality and (presumably) non- or posttraditionality, between persistence and change; to assume neither as more fundamental than the other, and to begin in the middle where both are relevant, rather than with notions of separateness and distinctiveness. As far as I can see, the way of doing this must involve problematization, not of difference, which may be socially present and identifiable in various forms, but of the autonomy or independence of the social field as solely indigenous or "Aboriginal," as one observes this from our historical location. Within this field, one nevertheless finds that there are distinctively indigenous, or Aboriginal, perspectives.

Aborigines were long marginalized and devalued as part of their wider exclusion from the Australian nation-state. Until recently, Aborigines were formally the concern of each and every state and territory, but not of the nation-state as it was then. Now, a dimension of Aboriginality has come to be seen, some would say appropriated, as inherent to national identity. Aboriginality as a dimension of national identity is currently more salient, and politically pursued as a matter of unfinished national business, than is true, for example, of the United States. An irony of the dramatic change over the past twenty-five years or so has been that earlier devaluation has been replaced by a situation in which Aborigines are increasingly being brought to a recognition of a divide between their past and the present that is stimulated precisely by intensified national effort to maintain and reconstitute Aboriginality. The demand for Aboriginality to create its innerness out of its past has been linked to the processes of national recognition and reconstitution. Such a demand is of course never complete and never completely acceded to. Also, it is never completely at variance with the demands and visions of Aborigines individually and collectively, now enjoined to be "themselves" under the policy of "self-determination." But the demand for that self to be in the terms of past, imagined identity is a powerful imposed logic with a long and diverse history, as I have indicated, as well as an internal one. If I am correct, it operates with special intensity in relation to Fourth World peoples. There is a palpable sense of disappointment if Aboriginal people are not "really" the way they were; all kinds of special pleading are felt necessary for the way they now appear to be. Some First World nations, liberal Anglo-European democracies, have become emphatic about using their own political and social resources to assist in constructing forms in which and through which the sense of indigenous selfhood can be sustained and experienced. This attitude is in one way benevolent; in other ways it appears hubris-ridden, an acceptance of the challenge of defining and sustaining authentic otherness—that is, something outside of and different from itself, as a problem of social technology.

The question of indigenous recognition has always had at its heart the problem of the prior encumbrance of the land, or put in a more general way, of indigenous firstness (chapter 5). I have taken changing modes of relationship to places as a central substantive issue of this book, since relationship to places is indeed central in Katherine Aborigines' social ordering. Although earlier extermination of Aboriginal people was associated with competition for land (e.g., Wolfe 1994), according of recognition to them in their relation to what Aborigines of Katherine call "country" is by and large a postconquest phenomenon.

We have seen the conditions emerge for a more nationlike status of Aboriginality writ large: recognition as the first *people* of the *land*. As a matter of concrete reconstitution, this has (in land claims and now native title claims) been transacted by foregrounding, and by competition over the legitimacy of, mimetic approximations of the forms of traditional socio-territorial organization.

The reconstitutive effort, well-intentioned though it no doubt is in many respects, has about it some of the same orientation to product rather than process as the essence of culture that is also seen in the exaltation of Aboriginal (indigenous) art, dance, language, and other highly visible, recognized guarantors of genuine difference (Merlan 1989). There is tremendous self-confidence, arrogance, or both in the assumption that cultural products can be sustained *as traditional* under a benevolent reconstitutive regime that itself increasingly suggests the means for displaying those cultural products and assumes the responsibility and the problems—the social technology—of that maintenance and reconstitution.

Indigenous renewal, now distinguishable from former control or mere equalization, has been under implementation for about thirty years in Australia as a developing social technology. One of its important moments, in a climate of benevolence and increasing acceptance of the concept of difference, has been imitation. This has been illustrated in chapter 5 by the example of the Aboriginal Land Rights (Northern Territory) Act 1976, a statute that specifies that findings must be made in terms of what experts had characterized as the form and content of Aboriginal "traditional ownership." Aboriginal relationship to land has been given a fresh form of existence, and indeed considerable material realization, through the invention of the legislation and an associated, complex bureaucratic-administrative machinery. It is also widely assumed that this machinery should be indigenized, run insofar as possible by Aboriginal people, and on organizational bases that some hope may also be seen as indigenous, or at least contrasting distinctively with the way other, nonindigenous institutions are run. It is an important and widely shared assumption that this process be seen as one of reclaiming, giving land-tenure legitimacy in a new context, finding and rescuing from devaluation something already there. It is also considered important that the extent of the artifice in the process, and the difficulties of matching it with a social field of diversity and changed practice, not be explicitly recognized. In other words, it is important (to Aborigines as well as others) that land rights be seen as the recognition of an existing world, rather than an attempt at reconstitution of a world imperfectly known, earlier devalued and discarded as deficient when encountered under different, colonial conditions, and now substantially changed from any such ideal, imaginary model. Imitation is thus a bringing into being through an assumption of externality: the assumption that something exists independent of oneself and the artifice of one's work upon it.

Reproduction of such a world may come close to the center of what Australian legal-legislative culture and other allied Western forms particularly value in this form of enterprise. For value to inhere in reproduction of culture, the condition of possibility must be that a space for imitation be left open, a space between the artificer and that which is reproduced, a space not filled or compromised by too-critical discussion of the economy of cultural values of such reproduction and of historical interrelationship.

Recognition of the absence of this allows us to make a connection between the leaving of this space and traditionalizing forms of representation, which I discussed above. Difference is seen as a positive, independent value, as is acceptance of difference. However, a perspective upon social reproduction as a technology (principally, as we have seen, of the modern nation-state) and upon its processes in terms of an economy of values gives us a critical distance from such unexceptionable, liberal values. We recognize that there is a "class" difference, a different relation to the means of value production, between those who are regarded as different and those who generate the discourses, terms, and social means for the acceptance and implementation of difference. In this sense, even the designation of Aboriginal lands, which has come about so liberally (and, lest I appear to underrate its importance, which may have very significant material and other consequences into the future), does not (yet) significantly tip the balance of this economy of values.

My use of the phrase "social technology" to refer to the dimension of imitation involved in social reproduction is deliberate, for I think the phrase indicates something important about the nature of what is being reproduced: society as thing, rather than as process conceived as requiring its own reproductive life-space and having its own effective reproductive mode. In my view, the effort to reproduce social difference as known, boundable, and manageable gives the social reproductive effort the stamp of cultural continuity with the recent history of Western transformation and its particular local and national realizations. A significant dimension of this transformation has been in the name of concepts of progress; and this progress, in turn, has to a great extent taken the form of technological development and invention, the modeling of other forms, and the very concept of invention upon the technological. I suggest that this "social technology" may be seen as the extension of invention from the material to the social world, the sort of thing we see in the fashioning of a land-rights package that purports to operate as if it were only working to reveal something found and rescued, something old, without necessarily introducing transformation as part of its process. The latter assumption, in its denial of history, is presumptuous.

Going along with this aspect of social technology has been simultaneous recognition of this imitative faculty as something that separates Western social life ever further from its accompanying double: artifice from its other half, nature. The extent to which there has been a doubling, what is often called a sense of "nature-culture divide" has, I think, been a condition of enormous importance in the Western history of externalization (Hegel 1977:479) or the positing of self as object and hence also of self-consciousness and continually amended self-reflexivity. It has also been a condition for the extent of Western openness to otherness.

In short, I suggest that anthropological traditionalism, as well as its correspondences in the wider Western First World, continually involves a tendency toward construction of indigeneity as the natural pole of a natural-cultural binarism. This tendency accounts for a continued rejection of the extent and the nature of processes of change within the indigenous domain as a condition of its definition as something of value. It also involves not only a valorization of one pole as essentially nonartificial, but of the other as artificer in relation to it, with corresponding unequal attribution of agency.

If now, increasingly, models retrieved from their past are selectively taken by Aboriginal people to be central resources for how to live in change, we may again ask where some of that emphasis comes from and—not expecting it to have simply the character of continuity with their past—the extent to which it comes to them from external sources.

It seems to me that one of the fundamental changes in reflexivity that is unevenly proceeding across the Aboriginal domain of Katherine is precisely the coming into being of the form of imaginary that is often associated with modernity (Habermas 1987), the sense of a gulf between past and present. As its penetration proceeds it radicalizes the present and revises the very terms in which the past can be imagined and the social constructs inherited from the past understood, to the point that as Aboriginal persons become differentiated in particular ways, some of these constructs can no longer be communicatively shared. As I illustrated in chapter 7, it now occurs to Aboriginal people to teach Aboriginal "culture" to themselves, on Western models of almost everything being teachable except "culture" in the sense of unreflexive everyday practice.

In a sense then, one of the dilemmas for Aboriginal people of Katherine is having to learn to confront the present through others' conceptions of who and what they are, with all the attribution of value to the re-creation of nonmodern identities that this entails. A related but opposed destructive impulse, which emanates largely from non-Aboriginal persons and governmental domains, is continually present, to the effect that such recreation should be scrapped as a poor job in favor of the renewal of defective others in one's own image.

I referred to Strathern's (1992b) pithy insight that anthropology specializes in revealing the cultural character of the taken-for-granted, naturalisms as cultural constructs. If we can accept that over a long term, self-concepts of openness to change have emerged as Western naturalisms (and what we think of as the "West" has simultaneously been created through them), we are perhaps in a better position to understand the openness, even the vulnerability, of Western culture to others' naturalisms. Those "other" naturalisms may be objects of admiration, material for reflection—but they also have talismanic qualities that both attract and repel, continually stimulating a desire for otherness while also creating barriers against its absorption. But unlike in other cultural orders less self-conscious about a natural-cultural divide, these cannot be incorporated *as* naturalisms, as things about the world that were previously unknown, on the same level as the central naturalism of change.

This brings us again to the question of anthropological representations, their sometime traditionalism, and their employment as I have tried to use them in conceptualizing an intercultural domain through ethnography. The reader may have wondered about the accounts of changing socio-territorial identity in the town and of the appearance of a site: do not both present these situations, which continue to have relevance, in ways that differ from the perspectives of most of the Aboriginal people described in this book? I emphasize perspective*s*, for these are multiple, not singular. I do not want to claim some ultimate transcendence for the sense I have made of the situation; and my approach certainly does not depend on the notion of discovering an ultimate historical "truth" of the situation. Nor do I intend to usurp the cultural authority of the many people, Aboriginal and non-Aboriginal, who shaped my understanding. However, I think that interpretation must not only show what it would mean to be true to the forms of life that are their subject matter, but must also necessarily be somewhat different from them.

In places in chapter 5 I have alluded to some of the dilemmas that confront the anthropologist of the Fourth World, caught up in struggles between indigenous peoples and forces of mainstream society. A typical fate has been a division of anthropological labors into intellectual and practical: theoretical or scholarly versus "applied," the former understood as the principal basis of academic reputation. Both ideally rest on the practice of ethnographic fieldwork, which depends on developing some sort of good practical feel for the tenor of everyday life. The making of this division between scholarly and applied work is sometimes (and sometimes correctly) judged as the suspension of connections between critical work and work on behalf of the people one has come to know in defence of their culture. Where this suspension occurs, it rests on an assumption that it is possible to clearly separate out their valued naturalisms and defend them as having free-standing value as difference. To do this can assist in preserving the notion of "our" capacity for change versus "their" unchangingness. Anthropological work cannot afford the luxury of treating analysis of the situation we refer to as the "Fourth World" and cultural analysis on the home front as if these were two separate domains: Fourth and First World naturalisms have long been constructed in relation to each other.

I return to the question I posed in chapter 7, whether an attempted intercultural account such as this takes unconscionable license with the circulation of cultural representations and thereby limits any effective local control over the circulation of discourse. The ethnographer becomes aware of sensitivities in fieldwork, and these are to be respected. The ethnographer never has sole authority but may in some contexts garner considerable authority and must take responsibility for that. Ethnographic authority is never complete because ethnography is inherently partial and itself perspectival, though its perspectives are shaped in circuits of representation that necessarily differ in some ways from those of our local informants, whoever they may be. Attempts to conceptualize change and continuity within the kind of social field I have dealt with will need to provide ethnographic substance concerning these and show how that enhances understanding.

An issue of importance to me, given the history of my involvements in land claims, sites disputes (Merlan 1991a), and other matters in the Katherine region, is whether Aborigines' relations to place will come to be more widely understood in terms that take account of history and of changes in social practice as these have emerged since outside settlement, or whether these relations will continue to be, as they have often been, an embattled arena of heritage politics in which how Aboriginal people make and remake relations to places remains insufficiently understood for any ethical and practical implications to be drawn out. Continuation of the latter will limit attempts to negotiate a space of and for social reproduction and change on Aboriginal terms in contemporary Australia, despite our best intentions in this pluralist era.

NOTES

One: Places and People of Katherine Town

1. Many Aborigines of Katherine, particularly the regular residents of the town camps as opposed to in-town residential locations, commonly use a tripartite nomenclature of distinctions: they speak of "whitefella," "blackfella," and "yellafella," the latter used to refer to people of mixed Aboriginal and non-Aboriginal descent. (In this area, "Chinese" or "Chinamen," who were numerically dominant in phases of early Territory settlement years and are still present in numbers in Territory towns and in Darwin, tend to be distinguished as such and are not grouped with either "white" or "yellow.") This usage may sound offensive, but one should not immediately impute nuances to it based on other forms of social experience. Even "black" mothers may refer to mixed-blood children they may have had as "yellafella," without necessarily intending offense and despite the oppressive history of efforts to prevent "cohabitation" and "miscegenation" and the removal and institutionalization of "part-caste" children, which in this part of Australia continued into the 1960s (see Cummings 1990, Austin 1993). In Katherine, people of mixed descent not only experienced removal and institutionalization in considerable numbers, but also were subject to schooling and work experience in ways that contributed to setting them off from "blackfellas" (whom some of them still call "natives," following earlier usage). Some older people of mixed descent in the Katherine region still speak of themselves as "colored," and distinguish themselves from both "whites" and "natives," also following earlier usage. But all these designations are temporally as well as socially stratified. Since about the 1970s, acceptable usage nationwide has tended toward a generalized designation, "Aborigine." In place of designations based on degrees of blood or observable color (for fuller accounts of which, see Austin 1993, Tonkinson 1990, Trigger 1989), a Commonwealth definition of 1970 specifies an "Aborigine" as a person descended from the Aboriginal race of Australia, identified as such by himself and so accepted by a relevant community. In southern and eastern Australia, where there are now few people of "full blood" as compared with parts of the north, and with the emergence of forms of historical consciousness still not typical of many northern Aborigines, designations such as "blackfella" and "yellafella," and the very making of such a distinction, are undoubtedly widely regarded as offensive. This note presents common usages as I encountered them in the Katherine region.

2. I would not like to be seen to ignore exceptions to this generalization, and

especially attempts to theorize change in recent ethnography. The "remote-area" Aboriginalist ethnography has tended to be especially traditionalist in character, from classics such as W. L. Warner's *Black Civilization* (1937) onward. Tonkinson's *Victors of the Desert Crusade* (1974) was an exception in the extent to which he considered the effect of missionization in remote Western Australia, though his emphasis remained upon the "triumph" of desert people in sustaining their own culture, seen in terms of autonomous, and largely religiously based, meanings. On the other hand, from the 1940s, studies of what were referred to as "detribalized," "mixed-blood," "half-" or "part-caste" Aboriginal communities of southeastern and "settled" Australia were perforce less focused on precolonial tradition, although the anthropologists were trained to look for and to describe vestiges of traditional culture (kinship and social classification, magical practices, and so on). Writers dealing with these communities wrote about social and cultural transformation under conditions of racially based exclusion in such locations as New South Wales, South Australia, and Victoria (Barwick 1962, 1963; Bell 1961, 1964, 1965; Berndt and Berndt 1951; Calley 1956, 1957; Gale 1972; Kelly 1943, Reay 1945; Reay and Sitlington 1947; Fink 1957; Beckett 1958, 1965a, 1965b; see also the well-known Elkin 1951). Nevertheless, little of this literature came to be known outside Australia, and it was seen (even by some of its authors; see Reay 1964:377) as more social historical than anthropological in character. There finally came pressing recommendations by anthropologists concerning the importance of attempting to conceptualize and somehow study change (Berndt 1982), rather than attempting to reconstruct traditional cultural systems from the memory accounts of aging informants. However, many anthropologists and much of the general public continued in a view in which notions of traditional Aboriginal culture occupied a privileged position as originary and clearly distinct from the culture(s) of mainstream Australia. For more recent ethnographies dealing with change, see Collman's (1988) discussion of the effect of welfare bureaucracy upon Aborigines' lives in Alice Springs and a variety of work influenced by Marxist political-economic perspectives and theorization of the state (Beckett 1977, 1987, 1988; Hartwig 1977; Anderson 1984). Recently, Macdonald's (1986) study of fighting and expressive action in central New South Wales, Morris' (1989) account of Aboriginal-white interaction in northern New South Wales, and Trigger's (1992) treatment of a mission regime in remote Queensland are notable for the extent to which they examine the conditions and processes of Aborigines' interaction among themselves and with others at a variety of levels, while keeping in view the specificities of Aboriginal life under those circumstances.

3. Aboriginal people of the region refer to social collectivities as "mobs," adopting a term of pastoral origin. For insightful discussion of their time- and experience-bound nature, see Sansom 1980, chapter 1.

4. Native Affairs Branch was officially established in the Northern Territory on February 10, 1939, an implementation of one of the recommendations to

emerge from a 1937 Aboriginal Welfare Conference (Cummings 1990:40–41), at a time when direct control of "native" affairs was principally exercised by the states and territories, not by the Commonwealth of Australia.

5. The 1964 bill did, however, retain provisions for the restriction of entry to reserves of persons other than Aborigines (including part-Aboriginal people, one of the ways in which the latter were treated differently from "full-blooded" Aborigines; see n. 1). See Giese 1990:4–5 on the strength of demands by the Half-Caste Association based in Darwin not to be included within the terms of restrictive legislation on the same basis as full-blooded Aborigines (and on general grounds of objection to a universally applicable notion of "wardship"). Such objection is understandable in terms of the contemporary disabilities under which "full-blooded" people were made to labor, the opprobrium attached in many circumstances to being considered Aboriginal, and general governmental policy objectives of "assimilation" of those deemed acceptable into the notional Australian mainstream. Before the Social Welfare Ordinance of 1964, "wards" who specially petitioned and who showed evidence of responsible behavior and good character were given individual permission to drink alcohol (otherwise prohibited), but this could be revoked. The dismantling of "ward" status was part of a set of legislative moves within Australia to deliver civic parity to Aborigines, or at least to revoke obviously discriminatory measures that targeted them. As part of the 1964 ordinance, Aborigines (here, referring both to those considered to be "full-blooded" and "part-caste") became entitled to drink alcohol.

6. The Commonwealth Department of Aboriginal Affairs was created during the term of Labor government headed by Prime Minister Gough Whitlam (1972–1975). In 1987, the department was remodeled and renamed the Aboriginal and Torres Strait Islander Commission, with the creation of a complex structure of regional Aboriginal constituencies and the devolution of some powers to them.

7. For description of this north Australian, English-based Kriol, see Sandefur 1979. In subsequent chapters where I quote any significant amount of Kriol, I pair it with a free English translation for the reader's convenience.

8. This incident can be dated to 1936, and related historical records give a somewhat different picture of what the main problem was than do contemporary Aboriginal accounts (see Ogden 1992:17). The incident seems to have been linked to Bartlam's decision to dismiss Brumby, previously the manager's "boy." Brumby was Claude Manbulloo's father, and thus a person who would have considered Willeroo homestead to be his own country.

9. Since one of their considerations in choosing an area was, naturally enough, that it have a dependable water source, these requests were unfavorably regarded by the station, and none came to anything at that time (though an excision area on Willeroo has since been established at Johnstone Waterhole for Elsie's immediate family and was surveyed in 1990).

10. Locally, and on the sign on the road pointing to the community, this name

is spelled "Binjara." Alternatively, the name is sometimes spelled "Binjari." It is pronounced "Bunjarri" by older Wardaman speakers, a pronunciation reflected in the spelling I use here. On maps, I have used the common spelling, "Binjara."

11. The term "Mayali" is used for these northerners by Aborigines of the Katherine area. But the people from that northern area make a finer set of distinctions, sometimes use additional terms including "Kunjey'mi," "Kunwinyku," and others, to refer within a social field characterized by general cultural and linguistic commonality.

12. The yearly round was roughly as follows. Ploughing and harrowing would take place around the early wet. It was best to have several annual plantings, the first about the first part of December, the second about New Year's, and the third in the first half of January. The plants would take about sixteen or eighteen weeks to grow before they would be dug and "stooked" (heaped) and left to dry for two or three weeks. They would then be thrashed, bagged, rumbled to get rid of any unwanted dirt and other matter, sorted on tables, and then bagged for the last time to make up a certain weight. Aborigines' labor was used for various parts of the process, but especially in pulling the plants, stooking, and loading the stooks onto the thrasher. Both men and women might pull and stook, but the men tended to put the peanuts through the rumbler, the women to sort them, and the men to handle the loaded bags. I am grateful to Wally Christie for having taken the time to talk with me in detail about peanut farming around Katherine.

13. For instance, in the tourist season, people from the Gorge and from Mayali-Brumby camp would dance a "traditional Aboriginal corroboree" at Springvale Homestead. They were picked up by the tourist operator and returned to their camp at the end of the evening. The relationship, from the operator's point of view, was attended by problems of the dancers' lack of punctuality and with regulating the role of grog in the contractual relationship.

14. In my experience, older Aboriginal people elsewhere also commonly say this or similar things. As I understand it, their focus is upon the loss of known persons now gone, not upon what might be called a general sense of culture loss.

15. Indeed, the Phillipses have a family connection with the Drysdales, who were missionaries at remote Maningrida in northeast Arnhem Land when Aborigines in that area were first sedentized in the 1950s (see Drysdale and Durack 1974). A religiously informed ethic of social uplift and equalization was present in some measure in the CSIRO environment.

Two: From Place to Town

1. Its valley first became known to Europeans through the exploring expedition of 1855–1856 led by A. C. Gregory (Gregory 1884), but pastoral settlement did not take place until the 1880s.

2. On first hearing, Kriol is not easily understood by English speakers unfa-

miliar with it and is sometimes not recognized as a form of English at all. Many of the Aboriginal people quoted in the book also speak Aboriginal languages with varying degrees of proficiency. I have taken readers' advice to minimize the inclusion of native-language quotations but attempt to preserve something of the prosody and "line" structure of Kriol, as in this quotation, lightening the reader's task by free English glossing.

3. It is common for those socialized in Aboriginal kinship usage and practice to refer from the perspective of the addressee on many occasions. This is done in a much more thoroughgoing way than it is in English (where, for example, such usages as "your mother" to an addressee tend to index his or her juniority). See McConvell 1982; Merlan 1982, 1990.

4. On reading this chapter, Lowell Lewis observed to me that I have included a much fuller picture of the life of Henry Scott further on. I retain Julie's account here as reflecting the different modes of self-presentation I take to be characteristic of each. Julie allowed me to participate in many aspects of her and her family's daily lives in Katherine, gradually making herself known to me in greater biographical depth as I became familiar with her and her social scene, including the places she had lived. On the other hand, the first time I met him, Henry Scott gave me a comprehensive summary of his background, upbringing, education, and wartime career in the Northern Territory, also giving me a copy of a short biographical account of himself already written as part of a family history.

5. For instance, a plan formulated in the 1920s to develop the Territory's capital at Elliott, still a small road-stop in the orange center along the Stuart Highway, was rumored to have been conceived to favor certain politicians' interests in real estate.

6. The main street of town was a narrow two-lane strip until 1968, when the development of the present, distinct south- and north-bound lanes, divided by a median green strip, began. That work was carried out in stages from 1968 to 1971; and the last section completed, between the Crossways Hotel and the High Level bridge, was the last section to be made over (between location 2 and the river in the inset, map 3). As part of the last stage, the limestone sinkhole was capped. A slab of reinforced concrete was poured over the top of the hole. Two or three meters of sand were layered between the slab and the roadbed built on top of it. At first, stormwater was allowed to run into the sinkhole, and thence into the river (so they did connect, despite Scott's belief otherwise). But this drainage was inadequate, and water flooded portions of the main street, causing some residents to call the project "Darben's debacle." Because of this problem, stormwater pipes were laid so that there was a discharge route running straight into the river, between the vehicular and railway bridges.

7. Henry Scott was Katherine's longest-term white resident in the early 1990s. He had first come to Katherine during the war and had lived there for more than fifty years. Consequently, his sense of the town's history was detailed and compre-

hensive in ways that the views of more recent arrivals—for example, the Tindal RAAF personnel—would not be. Recognition of the particular nature of Scott's view of the town, I think, reinforces rather than detracts from the general contrast drawn here between person-relative concepts of town spaces and white residents' concerns with change and development.

8. I suggested "Dr. Fenton" because, to Aborigines who grew up around Katherine from the wartime, Clyde Fenton, known as the "flying doctor" (Woldendorp 1994), is the unmarked "doctor" of their early experience. An Aboriginal man who worked as his assistant is still proudly referred to by his widow as "Dr. Fenton George."

9. Aboriginal representation of whites' insertion of themselves into, and convergence with, their own purposes, seems quite common. To give another example, in talking about his life on a cattle station remote from Katherine, an old man, Julie's husband's close father, represented the "boss," a white man named Joe Callanan, as having decided it was time for him and another young man to be initiated: "Old Joe been talk" (Jawoyn [Gimbat Area] Land Claim Transcript 1992:597).

10. Australian currency was changed from pounds to dollars in February 1966.

11. For another source on the significance of sweat in relation to sentient country, see Povinelli (1993:45–46, 151–160), who discusses this in relation to the Belyuen community, near Darwin.

12. The process of head watering was no doubt performed more frequently and unselfconsciously than it is today. In the present, a great many returns to country, and the introduction of newcomers to country, have often occurred in the context of preparations for land claims or in other situations where there is an explicit focus upon Aboriginal culture and traditionality. When head watering is done, it becomes clear that even notions of traditional attachment to country are not sufficient to overcome the sense of people's strangeness. Even those closely connected to an area in other terms must have their heads watered if they have not been there before.

Three: We Useta Walk Around, All the People

1. Confirming evidence of this kind of patterning, particularly of the bodily distribution of the creative figure over a number of places in an area, can be found in regions where settler impact was less intense. For example, Tamisari (1995, chapter 4) stresses for Arnhem Land the notion of ancestral movement as connection (cf. Swain 1993), and she also (chapter 5) explores imagery of the dissection of ancestral bodies through which people and social categories at different levels may be, variably and negotiatedly, linked to specific landscape features and to various feeling complexes elaborated in song, painting, and dances: "The image of the body as a whole made up of parts expresses the dialectic articulation of Yolngu

group and individual identity accommodating the underlying discourse of autonomy and relatedness, unity and separation, uniqueness and similarity in the context of shifting political interest and circumstances" (182). By this Tamisari seems to indicate that the individual clan member is to the whole clan as body part is to the whole body, in a way that may be too systematizing of the relationships as indigenously understood. The example of the emu body distributed over places in the vicinity of Wetji Namurrgaymi suggests that individual places are to some notion of the totality of clan places as body part is to body.

2. She was one of two Aboriginal people I have known who recounted to me in detail their experience of having encountered whites for the first time. Fanny remembered with particular clarity how the first white she saw when a child while "walking around" with close relatives offered to show them how to use matches.

3. Generally referred to locally as "diver duck," *barrakbarrak* is *Anhinga melanogaster*, a water bird with a long, snakelike neck.

4. Among other things, he vehemently objected to the situation of the settlement at one location, which was abandoned after a time, ostensibly (from the superintendent's point of view) because the water supply was poor. Clearly, however, for Aborigines, such "practical" problems were meaningful indications of the profound unsuitability of the place.

5. Of the forty-three clans I documented, the localization of those with no living members was often indeterminate, vague, or obscure, sometimes despite the persistence of shared knowledge of the name of a significant clan place.

6. These, however, are not always clearly clan-level places. In some instances, such an association may be made on the basis that the senior person lived or worked in a place. As this suggests, younger people typically make no clear distinction between such an association as one at the clan level or of some other kind. The place is enshrined in memory as one with which one's forebears had to do; and especially if the sense of Dreaming association is attenuated, the place-person link seems more exclusively genealogical.

7. One of Fanny's brother's sons has said that he thinks of Yurl'mayn as associated with "Mainoru," a cattle station in the area just south of the border of central Arnhem Land. Certain other places commonly mentioned among family and camp mates have become significant mainly because his father worked and lived at them. But as might be expected given the actualities of his experience, his most enduring personal attachments are to Barunga, the environs of Jabiru township, and a number of other places where he has been living. Fanny's centering identification of herself as emu, as Wetji—for her, ordinary and integral to her sense of self and in her view, also inherent in her nephew, as well as extensible over space-time—is not reproduced. Distant places such as Wetji are a horizon of significances deeply felt in that way by fewer and fewer. There may be greater vitality, and potential for continuing transformation, among the contemporary forms of such

clan-level and other connections with places around points of major settlement, such as Barunga, and around Katherine town, where Julie's children, for example, are still being shaped by events of the recent, more liberal period of Aboriginal recognition.

8. Literally *-beng-* "mind, mentation"; *gapoyn* "old"; *-ji-* "become": "I've become stale of mind," or the like.

9. Phyllis too described that she first encountered her daughter in the form of a bullock when she was out looking around for food. As far as I know, no names were ever given to children as a result of these events, and the form in which the child appeared does not seem to give rise to any idea of lasting connection between the child and that *kind* of animal (in contrast to some other regions; Merlan 1986a).

10. Other common ways of naming, which depend not only on Jawoyn-language use but also continuity in patterning, include the use of nicknames. One type of name, formerly widespread but now largely restricted to "old people," designates the person by a term that alludes to some accident or similar episode that has left a mark upon the body (the name of a woman referred to in chapter 1, Barrak-jowotj [scorpion hand] is an example of this). One man was known as Na-Bam-Wowotj (possum head). In this case, "head" is not a metaphor for birth but a literal reference to head: this man had been bitten on the head by a possum and was scarred as a result. Nipper Brown's father was called Na-Ngalk-wik-waruk (dog lip; lit. "mouth-skin-dog"), from a dog's bite having scarred his lip. Another old man at Pine Creek was known as Na-Barrak-golotok (pigeon hand; "hand" and "dove"), from a gnarled hand (very likely the result of leprosy). The father of Roy Anderson, Julie's "brother," was called Na-Bok-deren (rump and train), the last part allegedly from English "train," because he had been bumped on the railway track. All of these people, of course, also had other personal names, which were recycled within kindred groups and were much less commonly used (often, because of their resonance with Dreaming stories or ceremony), than birthplace names or nicknames. Because their use was restricted, people sometimes find it hard to remember these names when thinking of the person and may more easily remember an individual by one of the more publicly used kinds of names.

11. This may be best analyzed as syntactically possessive, "Dr. Fenton's George." Possessives marked by 's are not present in Kriol; and in most Aboriginal languages, some forms of possession are expressed simply by juxtaposition of possessor and possessed. The social origin of the construction is, however, uncertain. Interpreted as above, the phrase would be comparable to entries I have seen in old station record books, where (sometimes because several people have the same name) a woman may be designated as "Billy's Maggie," or more rarely, a man as "Violet's Tommy." I have never noted such "human" possessive constructions in use in Aboriginal languages.

12. As far as I know, this naming pattern first appeared in the region among politically activist and prominent families at Roper River (Ngukurr), initially a mission community, to the east of Katherine (see map 1). Aboriginal people of Katherine are certainly aware of its use there, and its implementation, it seems to me, is an expression both of "being modern" and of familial pride.

13. Some Aborigines use "culture" as a near-synonym for "(Aboriginal) Law," and its associated secret-sacred ritual practice. In such usages, no assumption of ready and easy transmission is implied.

14. This central meaning is perceptible in another answer she gave, to the question why was she telling her grandchildren Dreaming stories? She said, "He's going to be understand. Him going to learn or him teach himself. 'Oh, yeah; that what I going to do when I big man.'" (KALCT 1982:596).

Certain other witnesses, perhaps more conversant with Western styles of formal instruction, responded to questions about teaching in a way that signaled acceptance of some of its typical elements of meaning in other cultural settings. Principal among these were "to make someone know" or "to create the conditions for someone else to learn." For example, Julie's old friend, Margaret Katherine, asked whether she teaches her children the Jawoyn language, said, "Yes, I talk to them and teach them" (KALCT 1982:756). In all Katherine-area Aboriginal languages, the primary sense of native-language words that may be, contextually, translated as "teach" is "show," "demonstrate to."

15. Some readers may see this chapter as portraying social and cultural "loss" in a way that will disadvantage Aboriginal people. I think of my own position with respect to this problem as empathetic but not oversentimentalized and as a general problem of positioning that anthropologists, perhaps especially those who work with indigenous peoples, share. Empathy and forms of modernist social radicalism have always been important anthropological motivations; but they have tended to be fragmented into a theoretical activity generally more oriented toward presentation of enduring forms of otherness and toward practical activity concerned with the contemporary situation of colonized and encapsulated peoples, in which issues of sometimes dramatic transformation can more easily be recognized and, from a strategic point of view, often must be.

My view is that the perspectives to be gained from critical anthropological examination outweigh objections to examining issues in ways that initially may seem disadvantageous to the people concerned. For instance, the onus of demonstrating sufficient social and cultural traditionalism to meet requirements as written into some forms of land-rights legislation (see chapter 5) invariably affects Aboriginal people. Burdens of demonstration fall most heavily upon them, and they stand to lose much. One of my aims in discussing socio-spatial transformation is to suggest the need for some shift in the public sense of how the burden of proof concerning ties to country might be formulated and where it might lie. This is especially important with respect to measures such as land rights, which create and sometimes exacerbate a sense of divided interest between Aborigines and others. I discuss this position further in chapter 8.

Four: Tribes and Town

1. For many Kriol-speaking Aborigines the words "stripe" and "tribe" are homophonous (generally, [traip]), since the initial cluster /st/ is not distinct from /t/ for many). Thus, Aborigines talk about two people, for example, as /jem traip/, in English best rendered as "same stripe." Both "stripe" and "tribe" signify something like "differentiating mark." In no language that I know of in the Katherine area is there a generic, monolexemic term for the level of organization designated in English by "tribe."

2. His principal Djauan (my spelling, Jawoyn) informant was Soupy Marrapunya (my spelling, Marapunyah) who, Arndt came to recognize, originated from Gimbat Station well to the north of Katherine; see Arndt 1962, 1966.

3. Arndt (1961–1962) recorded Nolgoyma's self-identification as "Tagoman" in a paper he wrote on indigenous sorghums and the associated mythic traditions in terms of which Nolgoyma explained local Katherine rock-art sites.

4. The terms "Dalabon" and "Ngalkbon" appear to be used synonymously by Aborigines of the southern Arnhem fringe. Whether these terms had or have different connotations or varying distributions is not presently clear.

5. An example of questioning concerning dual identity, and the tendency to narrow the range of identification in terms of immediate parental identity, sometimes attributed to the grandparental level, is shown by this exchange, which occurred during the Katherine Area Land Claim, between Julie Williams' childhood friend, Margaret Katherine, and senior counsel for the claimants:

> Margaret, can you tell us when you were born—how long ago?
> *MK:* I can't tell you that.
> You cannot tell me. Whereabouts were you born?
> *MK:* Maranboy.
> Were you born in the bush?
> *MK:* Yes.
> What was your father? What mob was he from?
> *MK:* Jawoyn.
> What about your mother? What mob was your mother from?
> *MK:* Ngalkbon.
> What are you? What mob are you from?
> *MK:* Jawoyn.
> You are Jawoyn?
> *MK:* Yes.
> For what reason do you say you are Jawoyn?

MK: Because my father Jawoyn.
Do you speak Jawoyn?
MK: Yes.
Are you married?
MK: Yes.
Do you have children?
MK: Yes.
What is your husband? What mob is he from?
MK: Mayali . . .
What about your children? What are they?
MK: Jawoyn.
How do you say your children are Jawoyn?
MK: They follow me. (KALCT 1981:750–751)

Perhaps in this context Margaret tended to foreground Jawoyn connections, but in her claiming to follow her father, she adheres to a pattern that has some strength among southern Arnhem Land people. And though here she also identifies her children as Jawoyn, she went on to note that they belong to Gartbam, their father's Mayali clan; so, on many occasions, she would also identify her children as Mayali.

6. Ties to known grandparents, insofar as they bore on links to country, tended to be subsumed within identities that one attributed to one's parents and to oneself. "Following up" ties was strongly determined by actual distributions of people recognized as close family—in the recent past, at least—over what had come to be a number of major residential locations in the region. For example on the basis of close kin ties and a sense of wider, shared identity, someone like Dick would gravitate to specific camps and people around Katherine; to Barunga, Beswick, and Bulman; or to some combination of these over time.

7. In the context of the Katherine Land Claim, an issue was raised in the case of a few people of known Jawoyn parentage (in all cases, given the racially defined sexual asymmetries that prevailed, their mothers rather than fathers had been Jawoyn) who had been taken away by Native Affairs and later by Welfare Branch as "half-castes." Such people had generally been institutionalized, had been sent to school often well out of the Katherine region, and had spent much time away (see also n. 26). A few such people are well known, having returned periodically to Katherine and reestablished and then maintained ties particularly with close family. Their ties to the local Aboriginal community tend to be more single-stranded, dependent on a particular kin link or several for personal and wider social recognition, than is the case for those, whether of "full" or "mixed" descent, who live out their lives locally. Their children, if they live outside the Katherine area, tend to have diminished relationships to the majority of those recognized as Jawoyn within the Katherine region. Several such people had reestablished family contacts

in years preceding the Katherine Land Claim, with varying measures of subsequent integration into the lives and rounds of local people. Questions of their identity, however, were more formally considered in relation to the Katherine Area Land Claim. During the Katherine Land Claim, the claimants were asked to give opinions about including such people and their descendants as co-claimants. As might be expected, the answers were not definitive of any general principles in terms of which decisions might be made. The claimants universally answered Yes to including people whom they knew themselves or whose parents or other close relatives they knew. Beyond this—for example, regarding the children and grandchildren of people who had been taken away—there was uncertainty. What *were* people whom one did not know? Were they Jawoyn? Did identities understood heretofore to entail presence and mutual knowledge, as well as attachment to locality, apply to them, or not? Some claimants found it "hard" not to include them: it was not their fault that their parent(s) had been taken away; still, many of them were not familiar people. Family connection in these cases was not one aspect of wider belonging within the local scene: it was everything, it was all local people had to work with. Still, it was not decisive, but depended to some extent on the actualization and current affective content of those ties. In some of these cases, the non-Aboriginal "father" was, as Aborigines would say, "father for nothing," the basis for no continuing connection at all. One claimant made a joke about this, saying that since it was thought his father was Chinese, he would have to "claim Hong Kong." This comment shows the understanding of the parental link as the basis for connection to country—in this case, laughable.

With respect to these people in particular, some Aborigines conceive the problem as one of the acceptability of being identified "mother way" versus "father way." This issue does not seem to be raised as strongly in relation to Aboriginal people who are seen as part of the local or regional scene. But sometimes this issue is posed in the available terms of clan, formally bounded by the notion of patrifiliation. For some Jawoyn, but even more strongly for some neighboring and co-resident southern Arnhem people of other social affiliations, the clan as demarcation of social difference continues to be important. For one thing, clan affiliation is assumed by many Arnhem Landers to be an important element in defining one's place in ceremony. For some, resonances of clan may also be important in other aspects of social life. Neither was strongly the case for many Jawoyn. For some Jawoyn men, however, clan affiliation had salience in relation to their (often earlier, that is, not current) ritual participation.

8. Gordon's own name was actually Gulambarra, but at Barunga the form "Bulumbara," probably originally deriving from some administrator's or welfare officer's attempt to transcribe it, has come to be used by his family as their surname; see chapter 3 on naming.

9. Writings pointing to the significance of indigenous concepts of language as a dimension of social difference in Australia include Schebeck 1968, Morphy 1977, Merlan 1981, Sutton and Palmer 1981, Trigger 1987, Sutton 1991.

10. These are also objectively quite distinct languages. Sometimes language varieties that are socially distinctive may be objectively very similar, in some cases (as, for example, among Western Desert dialects), almost identical.

11. The identity "Yangman" has greatest currency today among Aboriginal people living at Jilkmingan (Jilgmirn.gan) community on Elsey Station, the pastoral property with which the largest number of Yangman people and their descendants have been continuously associated since early pastoral settlement days. It is in Katherine that this identity has become obsolete.

12. The Turtle Dreaming place mentioned by Arndt is Wubilawun, the place to which Julie claims ties through her second father, Fortymile, her mother's second husband who raised Julie.

13. Some corroborating evidence of this complex could be gathered from a range of informants on visits to places along the river in the early 1980s, and there is still a diminishing number of such people today. Publication of specific information collected by Arndt about this complex would be considered offensive by Aborigines of the Katherine region, regardless of their specific familiarity with it.

14. A large hill in the area of the Two Mile is known to the Gorge Jawoyn and Mayali as Gumbitjbay, clearly Arndt's Kumbidgee. On maps, the hill is designated Mt. Peckham. A European pastoral property nearby, on the Katherine River, is also called Kumbidgee. In Jawoyn, *gumbitj* means "lancewood," which as Arndt noted refers to a patch of lancewood on the hill's ridges. The suffix *-bay* is found in some other place-names of the immediate Katherine area, and together with two other suffixes— *-la* and *-jang~-yang*—appears to be especially characteristic of Dagoman place-names (though *-la* is found, with much lesser frequency, for a considerable distance northward).

15. The former owner of Kumbidgee, Frank Lansdowne, was one of the first white residents I met in Katherine. Interested in local history, including Aboriginal history, he told me that the area had been a "tribal boundary." But he did not mention a basalt column in connection with it (and I did not know enough at the time to specifically ask him about this). I have no idea what may have happened to this column. Among Arndt's papers there was no photograph of it, but there was a photograph of about a dozen apparently very similar, standing, phallic-shaped stones on Manbulloo Station, which one may surmise were connected with the subincision complex. I have seen other stones of exactly this kind at a number of places to the south and southwest of Katherine; some of them were linked by informants to subincision mythology and practice, while others were not.

Concerning Arndt's Wallan-luk, there is a place on the Katherine River close by which was known to Gorge campers as Warlang-luk. They said it was *warlang* (Bat) Dreaming; but I was unable to elicit any substantial mythology concerning the bat. In general, for them, sites somewhat farther upstream, that is, farther away from the township, were mythologically more vivid and generally more significant (with the exception of certain ceremony grounds near the old peanut farms).

16. After the war, one of the Army's priorities was to relocate concentrations

of Aboriginal people away from town. However, in the postwar period, despite official discouragements, Aboriginal interests focused with increasing intensity upon the town. "Army time," with its more benevolent work and rationing regime than most Aborigines had known and the number of camps established in the vicinity of the town, must have contributed to familiarization with it for many. As to CSIRO, it should be noted that claim to its wages, rationing, and other attractions was largely made by those Aboriginal people and their close associates who had a particular sense of their attachment to the immediate Katherine area. Their first real work season, according to L. J. Phillips, was in 1948–1949, when they cleared stumps and otherwise prepared the ground at the new experimental farm.

17. Though some Aboriginal people from farther afield were also at CSIRO, in certain crucial cases (Soupy Marapunyah and his male cousins) this was clearly conditioned by in-marriage with people identified then as (or with) Dagoman.

18. Wardaman people today, though the most knowledgeable about this area in the mythic terms that were a major focus of Arndt's inquiries, have what appear, next to his accounts, to be highly attenuated versions of the mythological significances and wider regional linkages of any of these sites and their associated Dreamings. They appear to have learned about these mainly in traveling through the area to and from Willeroo and farther south (many of the known names are along the Victoria Highway or not far off it) and in doing stock work on Manbulloo Station (some places, often more remote from the road, focus on waters). At one level, information about these places is limited to a site name (e.g., Barngunyang), often a simple mythological association ("possum"); sometimes there is also a notion of links to the general area on the part of a particular mob (including certain descendants of the CSIRO families who do not themselves recognize these associations). Wardaman refer to this relation between people and country in this subarea of what they consider Dagoman country by the term "Wungayajawun," attributing the area to patrifiliatively defined members of a particular kin cluster (of whom Dodger, the sole fatality of the 1942 Japanese bombing, was one). At another level, those people who were stock workers on Manbulloo (most of those who remain are Wardaman) have extensive practical knowledge of some of this country, are able to navigate around it, and discuss its place as part of a wider region of creeks, rivers, and other formations. Assertion by certain older Wardaman that this is Wungayajawun country and is that of particular persons of Dagoman background remains strong despite those people's limited knowledge, in some cases amounting to complete lack of recognition, of the situation in those terms.

19. Wardaman and Dagoman are also objectively closely related to Yangman; all three are dissimilar to Jawoyn, which belongs with certain other Arnhem languages. Paralleling the evanescence of Dagoman identity has been the obsolescence of the language. When I first came to Katherine area, I was able to do some work on Dagoman language with two old women, but since their deaths it is no longer known by anyone, as far as I have been able to ascertain. Jawoyn is now spo-

ken fluently only by a small number of middle-aged and older people and is in an advanced state of obsolescence, particularly in the town area (as compared with Barunga, where a number of younger people at least understand it).

20. *Gany-* is found prefixed to a number of the names of clans that appear to have been associated with the lower Katherine Gorge area and the Edith River.

21. I am aware of some place-names from their hinterlands having been applied, or transferred, by Jawoyn people to places near the town.

22. This is a fascinating case of personal reidentification that went in the opposite direction from the predominant trend discussed in this chapter. On the basis of wide-ranging inquiry among Aboriginal people of the region, it appears to me likely that this man originated from the northern Jawoyn area. But he came and worked for many years at Manbulloo Station at a time when, it seems, Dagoman identity was still prevalent there. Apparently in the course of his long-term presence at Manbulloo, he became known as Dagoman to at least some Aborigines in Katherine. His wife was from Daly River, and as hers continued to be recognized as a nonlocal identity, it is in terms of the father's "Dagoman" identification that this family is now thought of, but selectively, and mainly by "western siders." Certain older Jawoyn people who firmly assert his Jawoyn identity confidently give upper-generation relations of kinship to establish their version of his identity and name some people who live at Pine Creek as his close kin. There is at least one other version of his background, which would have him originate from Wagiman country, generally to the east of Pine Creek.

23. The place-name "Garlirliwa," for instance, is clearly associated by Wardaman speakers with *garlirlin* (mosquito), common to Wardaman and Dagoman languages.

24. Now, after many years, some of the children of Wardaman who lived at Manbulloo back then have some sense of it not only as familiar country where they grew up, where relatives are buried, and where many still live today in the new community at Bunjarri, but for all of these reasons as an area to which they feel close personal attachments, even though some of their elders may still observe that it is not Wardaman country. There is a tension between lived experience and the tenacity of earlier sedimentations (see Povinelli 1993, a book that may also be seen in part as about such a tension).

25. Given the success of land claims to the north of town on behalf of the Jawoyn and the rise of the Jawoyn Association with its capacity to build a business arm in relation to Katherine Gorge and to negotiate in respect to mining and other ventures in the Katherine vicinity, there has grown a certain feeling that the Jawoyn, as represented by the association, have gained more than others in the recent period. In the last few years, questions have also arisen about possible development, control, title and management, of new Aboriginal living areas in and around Katherine town. This issue has no doubt stimulated greater attention to the town situation as a "historical" one, rather than one couched only in the terms

of traditional associations with country. Heretofore, debate about the development of town living areas had not been cast so fully in terms of traditional association, but the rise of Jawoyn and Wardaman Associations seems to have been one catalyst for change in this regard.

26. This person has subsequently been part of a High Court action, commonly referred to as the "Stolen Generations," that seeks to have the earlier removal of children from their parents found unconstitutional. If this is the outcome (the action is in process), then no doubt other cases will follow.

27. For reference to the legislation of 1953 by which Aborigines (unless exempted) came to have the status of "wards," see chapter 1, n. 4, and discussion in the chapter.

28. A number of women from that area had or have the same name, and its transmission can be traced within broad regional kin networks.

Five: Imposition and Imitation: Changing Directions in Aboriginal Affairs

1. There is current debate concerning whether or not Australia will become a republic, again often posed as a question of national maturity (Rowse 1978, Hage 1993) within a country whose inhabitants are notorious for seeing themselves as socially and culturally dependent on other countries (viz. frequent accusations of Australian "cultural cringe" or references to its being overcome) and also seem to have resented this sense of their own dependence. It is perhaps significant that Britons, too, have begun to debate more openly the question of the future of the monarchy and the possibility of republicanism.

2. Though this legislation well precedes the referendum of 1967, existing restrictive legislation continued to deprive many Aborigines of citizenship rights, state by state, even after the passage of the act.

3. There had long been a federal "three mines" policy, that is, limitation of the opening of additional uranium mines. This changed in latter 1996 with an electoral win by the Liberal-National party coalition.

4. Considerations of political pragmatism and philosophy obviously played a substantial role. In the final draft, the Fraser government disposed of any "needs" dimension, arguing that any such dimension would create an invidious distinction between Aborigines and others and would amount to special treatment on the basis of race. Prime Minister Fraser averred that "the same conditions of hardship" apply to all those in need (Merlan 1995:16). I argue (in Merlan 1995) that this singular conception of need, apparently egalitarian, is not the only one possible. I compare it with R. H. Tawney's (1938) concept of "equal care in meeting needs which may differ," which appears to allow greater scope for measure of social justice.

5. When the legislation was implemented, all gazetted Aboriginal Reserve land, amounting to about 18 percent of the Territory, was scheduled as Aboriginal

land without inquiry. Under successful claims processes, land comes to be held by Aboriginal land trusts under "inalienable communal freehold" title. Unlike ordinary freehold, it cannot be sold or otherwise alienated, on the (mimetic) basis that Aboriginal relationships to country involve inalienability. There has been unfavorable comment on this unique form of title by those opposed to land rights, who claim that it "locks land up" or at least has the potential to remove it from ordinary processes of finance and productive usage. Currently, in this year when the "sunset" clause on land claims is due to come into effect, about 45 percent of the Northern Territory has been gazetted as Aboriginal land.

Six: Struggles in Town Space

1. The Northern Territory has very high recorded levels of alcohol consumption, abuse, and related domestic violence and other issues within its population, both Aboriginal and non-Aboriginal. See Bolger (1990) and references therein.

2. Before the implementation of local government in 1978, Katherine had no mayoral office. Here, Scott is attempting to find terms in which to convey a feeling for the position McGinness occupied in town.

3. That is, from about the time of implementation of the rural pastoral award wage, resulting in movement of many Aborigines away from stations and properties into towns, and the gradual expansion of a welfare economy as their principal means of support.

4. Insistence upon self-direction, being "boss" for oneself as an obvious Aboriginal social value, has been a subject of considerable ethnographic comment, most clearly beginning with Goodale (1971), elaborated in Myers (1986), Rose (1992), and Martin (1993). Examination of this dimension has helped to alter the earlier anthropological view of Aborigines as custom-bound, their actions as "determined" within given social structures (see the discussion in Myers 1986, chapter 5).

5. Sansom (1980) emphasizes the processual nature of Aboriginal social life and the formation of social determinations in social action, deemphasizing notions of achieved structure. He writes of running assessments of "worth" in the Darwin camps and rejects the notion of more permanent "status." In my observation, however, there is no doubt of the relatively enduring character of some of these place- and family-linked social positions which, as discussed here, allow the ascription of current worth to incumbents who may be personally "impaired" in some ways and for some time. In the case of the man I have referred to, there is no doubt that his father was relatively prominent in his station community of origin and that renown earlier attached to him extended to his son. There is also little doubt that the man described here had been, and could be on occasion even during his years of intensive grogging, a formidable worker and that he was, generally, a "western-side" person of considerable renown.

6. In the Northern Territory, dry areas have been supported by the Liquor Commission. The Northern Territory Liquor Act (version of 1990) provides for the declaration of "restricted areas" (Part VIII, sec. 73), into which no liquor may be brought and within which no liquor may be kept, consumed, sold, or otherwise disposed of. The commission consults with communities to ascertain whether they wish to apply for a declaration to be made. Upon such a declaration's being made, the commission must make public notification (newspaper, etc.) and may post signs and other notices that the restrictions now apply. Offenders can be prosecuted under the Liquor Act.

Around Katherine, Bunjarri has recently been posted as a dry area. A sign at the turnoff to Bunjarri from the Victoria Highway reads: "Private Property! Trespassers prosecuted—NO GROG—NO DRUNKS OR HALF SHOT NOT [*sic*] UNDER THE INFLUENCE OF ALCOHOL OR DRUGS. By order COUNCIL, Binjari Aboriginal Community Corp."

Rockhole was intended as a dry camp from its inception in the early 1970s. It also has a set of community rules, many of which relate to drinking and restrictions on alcohol, including the following:

Possession of and/or consumption of alcohol is prohibited.

Tenants shall not permit the consumption or possession of alcohol.

No person shall enter Rockhole under the influence of alcohol or drugs.

Main gate is to be locked at 10 P.M.

Given the centrality of spatial ordering in Aboriginal social action, dry areas and distancing will no doubt continue to be useful strategies for many Aboriginal people. It may be possible to develop better support-group strategies that do not depend (as do some Western ones, e.g., that of Alcoholics Anonymous) on negative definitions of drinkers as diseased or alcoholic or on the opposition between personal control and loss of control. This, I have suggested, is a Western problematic not easily referrable to practices and understandings of the Katherine Aboriginal social environment. Such support strategies might make more explicit use of the strength of familial connections, while recognizing their particular nature. It is unlikely that people seeking to quit drinking would be willing or able to respond to people within their own kin networks as "authority figures," in the sense of taking commands from them, and indeed unlikely that many of those people would attempt to give and enforce commands. But given the recognition of older people as having a leadership role, such that younger people look to them for signs of their intentions and projects, it might be possible to develop effective grog-free camps if some older people regularly assumed an exemplary role, taking responsibility for organizing, or probably better put, facilitating, everyday activities consonant with a grog-free location. Even such a simple thing as the continuous presence of such a person at a camp and his or her stable engagement in mundane activities there would provide considerable support for those trying to stay put in a grog-free location. Such possibilities, although they may rely on the importance of place, thereafter depend upon persons for their implementation, and require hard work. There is, in any case, no quick fix. See Brady 1994, 1995.

7. Most yards are now fenced, in an effort by town camp management to restrict debris to the yard where it is produced and to try to encourage residents to feel a sense of responsibility for maintaining their own houses and yards. The building of fences, however, occasioned bewilderment among some camp residents to whom the official motive was mysterious because, they reasoned to me, if one had no fences then the litter would eventually blow away.

8. See Sansom 1980 on the dangers of "mystical contamination" (for example, introduction of poisons into drink) and the precautions drinkers may take in relation to this; also comments on the existence of informal conventions or rules of drinking in Brady (1992:707).

Seven: Do Places Appear? Further Struggle in Space

1. Both the Alice Springs dam and Hindmarsh Island controversies have involved questions of the significance of places to women. Hindmarsh has been characterized in the press as involving "secret women's business." In 1994, the federal minister for Aboriginal Affairs imposed a twenty-five-year ban on the construction of a proposed bridge from the mainland to the island without opening certain envelopes, which allegedly contained details of the secret business. A male Opposition minister who did open the envelopes, reportedly marked as restricted to women only, was compelled to resign. In early 1995, other Aboriginal women from the area came forward who said they had no knowledge of the "secret business," and there were expressions of doubt by them and others concerning its authenticity. A South Australian Royal Commission was constituted to address the question whether the initial accounts of the area's significance were "fabrications," and if so, when they had been made and for what purposes. The commission's conclusion was that the secret business was a complete fabrication (Hindmarsh Island Bridge Royal Commission 1995), a finding firmly rejected by the federal minister. A federal commission of inquiry was formed to consider submissions on the significance of the place and other matters (Mathews 1996). However, the appointment of a federal court judge, Jane Mathews, as commissioner was found by the High Court to breach separation of powers. The report was quashed.

2. Casey (1993:65) observes that a place becomes a "site" when it has been subjected to "simple location," that is, is specified merely as in some definite portion of space. "Site," in other words, is place reduced to being "just there," in Casey's terms, existing "in splendid isolation" from other objects. Many investigative procedures aim to establish the significance of a site in this sense, a specific and delimited area, apart from consideration of how it may relate to other places in terms

of Aboriginal concepts of connections. Concepts of linkage among places and of shared and widely distributed responsibilities resulting from this may be contentious and, from Aboriginal perspectives, often crucial.

3. Essential Aboriginalist writings on the concept of places, or "country," include Munn 1970 and Myers 1986; see also next section. On innovation in Aboriginal religious life, see Stanner 1966, Kolig 1981, Maddock 1982, Stanton 1983, Tonkinson 1991, Myers 1986, Rose 1992.

4. It will become clear that the significance of the place was partly built up in light of previous human association with it. To that extent, and in terms of other factors explored here, Aboriginal people concerned would reject any notion of its complete novelty.

5. Alternatively, she referred to it as *morroporl*, a term that refers to (apparently, medium-sized), fork-tailed catfishes.

6. This was a reference to the young man's death in a mysterious road accident that, while clearly being alcohol-related, was also seen by some members of his family as due to inimical relations with certain other Aborigines with whom he had been driving around, people who were not of the immediate town area.

7. Area 3 adjacent to the Rockhole was excluded from the Katherine Area Land Claim of the early 1980s because it was understood that any claim to it would necessarily be complex and would have to involve some subset of claimants for the other areas, perhaps together with some different personnel.

8. Mayali people from the north had worked on peanut farms in the vicinity of the Rockhole; so had Ngalkbon, from the southern fringe of Arnhem Land; so had Wardaman, many of them also having lived at nearby Manbulloo Station on the river. As noted in chapter 1, Willeroo and Delamere stations farther south, together with Manbulloo, were owned by the same cattle company, Vestey's, for a considerable time. Many Wardaman were brought to Manbulloo as workers.

9. The woman of whom she was speaking as having been married to her grandfather, Nolgoyma, was with us on this occasion. Thus Julie's remarks not only were intended to establish a claim on her own behalf, but also were sensitive to norms of etiquette concerning positive inclusion of persons present in the formulation of the relevance of the current speech situation to ongoing issues. Such a remark often also elicits support from the person mentioned who is present on the scene and is thus a significant dimension of opinion management.

10. The Aboriginal Sacred Sites Protection Authority (now renamed the Aboriginal Areas Protection Authority; see n. 2 for indication of the significance of this change from pinpointed "site" to "area") is a Northern Territory agency, established under complementary legislation at the time of the passage of the federal Aboriginal Land Rights (Northern Territory) Act 1976.

11. The area of Mt. Todd was not recommended for grant on the grounds, as the land commissioner wrote in his report, that "the evidence does not establish

any considerable strength of attachment to that land" (Aboriginal Land Commissioner 1988:34, para. 165).

12. Along with Eva Valley Station, another property that was to be the eventual object of further claim, just to the east of land won during the Katherine Area Land Claim.

13. Part of my point is to illustrate the much-expanded circuitry and implications of issues such as this one. In light of this, it is worth noting that the handover was organized as part of the confirmation of a "sister city" arrangement between the Sutherland Shire Council (relevantly, the Sydney electorate of the incumbent federal minister for Aboriginal affairs) and what was called on the invitations the "Jawoyn nation"—the identity that had been emphasized in events of the previous fifteen years and that had become a principal term of the Katherine region's and the Australian nation's recognition of much that went on in terms of development and other issues around Katherine, including the Coronation Hill sites dispute.

14. I am not aware that such a connection existed previously.

REFERENCES

Aboriginal Land Commissioner. 1988. *Katherine Area (Jawoyn) Land Claim.* Canberra: Australian Government Printing Service.

Anderson, B. 1983. *Imagined Communities: Reflections on the Origin and Spread of Nationalism.* London and New York: Verso.

Anderson, C. 1984. The Political and Economic Basis of Kuku-Yalanji Social History. Ph.D. Thesis. University of Queensland.

Arndt, W. 1961–1962. Indigenous Sorghum as Food and in Myth: The Tagoman Tribe. *Oceania* 32(2):109–112.

———. 1962. The Nargorkun-Narlinji Cult. *Oceania* 32(4):298–320.

———. 1966. Seventy-Year-Old Records and New Information on the Nargorkun-Narlinji Cult. *Oceania* 36(3):231–239.

———. n.d. Notes and papers. Unpublished. Canberra: Australian Institute of Aboriginal and Torres Strait Islander Studies.

Asad, T. 1979. Anthropology and the Analysis of Ideology. *Man* 14:607–627.

Atkinson, J. 1989. Violence in Aboriginal Australia. Ms. prepared for the National Committee on Violence.

Attwood, B. 1989. *The Making of the Aborigines.* Sydney: Allen and Unwin.

Austin, T. 1993. *I Can Picture the Old Home So Clearly: The Commonwealth and "Half-Caste" Youth in the Northern Territory, 1911–39.* Canberra: Aboriginal Studies Press.

Australia. 1977. *Ranger Uranium Environmental Inquiry: Second Report.* Canberra: Australian Government Publishing Service.

Bandler, F. 1983. *The Time Was Ripe: A History of the Aboriginal-Australian Fellowship (1956–69).* Chippendale: Alternative Publishing Cooperative.

Barsh, R. 1990. Indigenous Peoples, Racism and the Environment. *Meanjin* 49:723–731.

Bartlett, R. 1993. *The Mabo Decision.* Sydney: Butterworths.

Barwick, D. 1962. Economic Absorption without Assimilation? The Case of Some Melbourne Part-Aboriginal Families. *Oceania* 33(1):18–23.

———. 1963. A Little More Than Kin: Regional Affiliation and Group Identity among Aboriginal Migrants in Melbourne. Ph.D. Thesis. Australian National University.

Beckett, J. 1958. Marginal Men: A Study of Two Half-caste Aborigines. *Oceania* 29(2):91–108.

———. 1965a. The Land Where the Crow Flies Backward. *Quadrant* 9(4):38–43.

———. 1965b. Kinship, Mobility and Community among Part-Aborigines in Rural Australia. *International Journal of Comparative Sociology* 6(1):7–23.

———. 1977. The Torres Strait Islanders and the Pearling Industry: A Case of Internal Colonialism. *Aboriginal History* 1:77–104.

———. 1987. *Torres Strait Islanders: Custom and Colonialism.* Cambridge and New York: Cambridge University Press.

———. 1988. Aborigines and the State in Australia. *Social Analysis* 24:3–18.

Bell, D. 1983. *Daughters of the Dreaming.* Melbourne: McPhee Gribble/George Allen and Unwin.

Bell, J. H. 1961. Some Demographic and Cultural Characteristics of the La Perouse Aborigines. *Mankind* 5(10):425–438.

———. 1964. Assimilation in New South Wales. In *Aborigines Now: New Perspectives in the Study of Aboriginal Communities,* ed. M. Reay, 59–71. Sydney: Angus and Robertson.

———. 1965. The Part-Aborigines of New South Wales: Three Contemporary Social Situations. In *Aboriginal Man in Australia,* ed. R. M. and C. H. Berndt, 396–418. Sydney: Angus and Robertson.

Bennett, S. 1989. *Aborigines and Political Power.* Sydney: Allen and Unwin.

Bern, J. 1979. Ideology and Domination: Toward a Reconstruction of Aboriginal Social Formation. *Oceania* 50(2):118–130.

Berndt, R. M. 1959. The Concept of "the Tribe" in the Western Desert of Australia. *Oceania* 30(2):81-107.

———. 1982. The Changing Face of Aboriginal Studies: Some Personal Glimpses. In *Anthropology in Australia: Essays to Honour 50 Years of "Mankind,"* ed. F. McCall, 49–65. Sydney: Anthropology Society of New South Wales.

Berndt, R. M., and C. H. Berndt. 1951. *From Black to White in South Australia.* Melbourne: F. W. Cheshire.

———. 1987. *The End of an Era: Aboriginal Labour in the Northern Territory.* Canberra: Australian Institute of Aboriginal Studies.

Bhabha, H. K. 1990. *Nation and Narration.* London and New York: Routledge.

Birdsell, J. 1953. Some Environmental and Cultural Factors Influencing the Structuring of Australia's Aboriginal Population. *American Naturalist* 87:101–207.

———. 1970. Local Group Composition among the Australian Aborigines: A Critique of the Evidence from Fieldwork Conducted since 1930. *Current Anthropology* 11:115–141.

———. 1976. Realities and Transformations: The Tribes of the Western Desert of Australia. In *Tribes and Boundaries in Australia,* ed. N. Peterson, 95–120. Canberra: Australian Institute of Aboriginal Studies.

Blainey, G. 1982. *The Tyranny of Distance.* Melbourne: Sun Books.

Bolger, A. 1990. *Aboriginal Women and Violence: A Report for the Criminology Research Council and the Northern Territory Commissioner of Police.* Darwin: Australian National University, North Australia Research Unit.

Bourdieu, P. 1977 [1972]. *Outline of a Theory of Practice*. Cambridge: Cambridge University Press.

Brady, M. 1992. Ethnography and Understandings of Aboriginal Drinking. *Journal of Drug Issues* 22(3):699–712.

———. 1994. Marching against Grog: Women, Culture and Indigenous Approaches to Alcohol Abuse in Australia. Paper presented at the J.W. Goethe Institute für Historische Ethnologie, Frankfurt am Main.

———. 1995a. Culture in Treatment, Culture as Treatment: A Critical Appraisal of Developments in Addictions Programs for Indigenous North Americans and Australians. *Social Science and Medicine* 41(11):1487–1498.

———. 1995b. *Giving Away the Grog: Aboriginal Accounts of Drinking and Not Drinking*. Canberra: Commonwealth Department of Human Services and Health.

———. n.d. Broadening the Base of Intervention for Aboriginal People with Alcohol Problems. Technical Report no. 29. Sydney: National Drug and Alcohol Research Centre.

Braroe, N.W. 1975. *Indian and White: Self-Image and Interaction in a Canadian Indian Community*. Stanford, Calif.: Stanford University Press.

Brennan, F. 1991. *Sharing the Country: The Case for an Agreement between Black and White Australians*. Ringwood, Victoria: Penguin.

———. 1995. *One Land, One Nation: Mabo—Towards 2001*. St. Lucia: University of Queensland.

Briggs, C. 1996. The Politics of Discursive Authority in Research on the "Invention of Tradition." *Cultural Anthropology* 11(4):435–469.

Briscoe, G. 1991. A Social History of the Northern Central Region of South Australia, 1950–79. M.A. Thesis. Australian National University.

Brunton, R. 1991. *Aborigines and Environmental Myths: Apocalypse in Kakadu*. Environmental Backgrounder, no. 4. Canberra: Institute of Public Affairs.

———. 1996. The Hindmarsh Island Bridge and the Credibility of Australian Anthropology. *Anthropology Today* 12(4):2–7.

Burke, E. 1960. *Selected Writings of Edmund Burke*. New York: Modern Library.

Calley, M. 1956. Economic Life of Mixed-Blood Communities in Northern New South Wales. *Oceania* 26(3):200–230.

———. 1957. Race Relations on the North Coast of New South Wales. *Oceania* 27(3):190–209.

Carter, P. 1987. *The Road to Botany Bay: An Essay in Spatial History*. London and Boston: Faber and Faber.

Casey, E. S. 1993. *Getting Back into Place: Toward a Renewed Understanding of the Place-World*. Bloomington and Indianapolis: Indiana University Press.

Cohn, B. 1996. *Colonialism and Its Forms of Knowledge: The British in India*. Princeton, N.J.: Princeton University Press.

Collman, J. 1988. *Fringe-dwellers and Welfare: The Aboriginal Response to Bureaucracy*. Brisbane: University of Queensland Press.

Commonwealth Archives. Darwin, N.T. F1 52/648 Pt. 1 (1952): Aborigines in the

Katherine Area (by J. R. Ryan); F1 52/615 (1935): Conviction of Aborigines, Katherine Prohibited Area; F1 48/98: Town of Katherine, Post-War Planning 1944–50.

Connell, R. W. 1974. Images of Australia. In *Social Change in Australia*, ed. D. E. Edgar, 29–41. Melbourne: Cheshire.

Cowlishaw, G. 1982. Socialisation and Subordination among Australian Aborigines. *Man*, n.s., 17:492–507.

———. 1988. *Black, White or Brindle*. Melbourne: Cambridge University Press.

Crawford, R. M. 1975. *"A Bit of a Rebel": The Life and Work of George Arnold Wood*. Sydney: Sydney University Press.

Creamer, H. 1988. Aboriginality in New South Wales: Beyond the Image of Cultureless Outcasts. In *Past and Present: The Construction of Aboriginality*, ed. J. Beckett, 45–62. Canberra: Aboriginal Studies Press.

Cummings, B. 1990. *Take This Child: From Kahlin Compound to the Retta Dixon Children's Home*. Canberra: Aboriginal Studies Press.

d'Abbs, P. 1990. *Dry Areas, Alcohol and Aboriginal Communities: A Review of the Northern Territory Restricted Areas Legislation*. Darwin: Drug and Alcohol Bureau, Department of Health and Community Services and the Racing, Gaming and Liquor Commission.

Dagmar, H. 1978. Aborigines and Poverty: A Study of Inter-Ethnic Relations and Culture Conflict in a Western Australian Town. Ph.D. Thesis. Katholieke Universitet.

Davidson, B. R. 1966. *The Northern Myth*. Melbourne: Melbourne University Press.

Deleuze, G., and F. Guattari 1987. *A Thousand Plateaus*. Minneapolis: University of Minnesota Press.

Dodson, M. 1995. Third Report of the Social Justice Commissioner. Canberra: Australian Government Printing Service.

Doolan, J. 1977. Walk-off (and Later Return) of Various Aboriginal Groups from Cattle Stations: Victoria River District, N.T. In *Aborigines and Change: Australia in the 1970s*, ed. R. M. Berndt, 106–113. Canberra: Australian Institute of Aboriginal Studies.

Donovan, P. F. 1981. *A Land Full of Possibilities: A History of South Australia's Northern Territory*. St. Lucia: Univesity of Queensland.

Drysdale, I., and M. Durack. 1974. *End of Dreaming*. Adelaide: Rigby.

Elkin, A. P. 1951. Reaction and Interaction: A Food-Gathering People and European Settlement in Australia. *American Anthropologist* 53:164–186.

———. 1963 [1938]. *The Australian Aborigines: How to Understand Them*. 4th ed. Sydney: Angus and Robertson.

Errington, F. and D. Gewertz. 1995. *Articulating Change in the Last Unknown*. Boulder, Colo.: Westview Press.

Eylmann, E. 1908. *Die Eingeborenen der Kolonie Suedaustralien*. Berlin: D. Reimer.

Fink, R. 1957. The Caste Barrier: An Obstacle to the Assimilation of Part-Aborigines in North-west New South Wales. *Oceania* 28(2):100–110.

Fried, M. 1975. *The Notion of Tribe.* Menlo Park, Calif.: Cummings.

Gale, F. 1972. *Urban Aborigines.* Canberra: Australian National University Press.

Gibbins, R. 1987. *Federalism in the Northern Territory: Statehood and Aboriginal Political Development.* Darwin: North Australia Research Unit.

Giddens, A. 1990. *The Consequences of Modernity.* Cambridge: Polity Press.

Giese, H. 1990. *Planning a Program for Aborigines in the 1950s.* Occasional Papers no. 16. Darwin, N.T.: Northern Territory Library Service.

Giles, A. 1928. The First Pastoral Settlement in the Northern Territory (compiled 1928). Adelaide: South Australian Archives.

Goffman, E. 1959. *The Presentation of Self in Everyday Life.* New York: Doubleday Anchor Books.

Goodale, Jane 1971. *Tiwi Wives.* Seattle: University of Washington Press.

Gottdiener, M. 1985. *The Social Production of Urban Space.* Austin: University of Texas Press.

Graburn, N. 1981. 1, 2, 3, 4 . . . : Anthropology and the Fourth World. *Culture* 1(1):66–70.

Gregory, A. 1884 [facsimile edition 1881]. *Journals of Australian Explorations 1846–58.* Victorian Park, W.A.: Hesperian Press.

Gregory, D., and J. Urry, eds. 1985. *Social Relations and Spatial Structures.* Basingstoke: Macmillan.

Guss, D. 1995. *"Indianness" and the Construction of Ethnicity in the Day of the Monkey.* Latin American Studies Center Series 9. College Park: University of Maryland at College Park.

Habermas, J. 1987. *The Philosophical Discourse of Modernity.* Cambridge: Massachusetts Institute of Technology Press.

Hage, G. 1993. Republicanism, Multiculturalism, Zoology. In *Republicanism, Citizenship, Community,* ed. L. Johnson, 113–137. Nepean: University of New South Wales.

Hall, R. A. 1989. *The Black Diggers: Aborigines and Torres Strait Islanders in the Second World War.* Sydney: Allen and Unwin.

Hancock, W. K. 1930. *Australia.* London: Ernest Benn.

Hanson, A. 1989. The Making of the Maori: Culture Invention and Its Logic. *American Anthropologist* 91:890–902.

Hardy, F. 1968. *The Unlucky Australians.* Melbourne: Nelson.

Harris, S. 1984. *Culture and Learning: Tradition and Education in North-East Arnhem Land.* Canberra, and Atlantic Highlands, N.J.: Humanities Press.

———. 1990. *Two-Way Aboriginal Schooling: Western Education and the Survival of a Small Culture.* Canberra: Aboriginal Studies Press.

Hartwig, M. C. 1977. Capitalism and Aborigines: The Theory of Internal Colonialism and Its Rivals. In *Political Economy of Australian Capitalism,* ed. E. L.

Wheelwright and K. Buckley, 3:119–141. Sydney: Australian and New Zealand Book Company.

Harvey, D. 1985. *Consciousness and the Urban Experience*. Oxford: Basil Blackwell.

Hawke, S., and M. Gallagher. 1989. *Noonkanbah: Whose Land, Whose Law*. Fremantle: Fremantle Arts Centre Press.

Hegel, G. F. W. 1977. *Phenomenology of Spirit*. Oxford: Oxford University Press.

Hiatt, L. R. 1965. *Kinship and Conflict*. Canberra: Australian National University Press.

———. 1967. Authority and Reciprocity in Australian Aboriginal Marriage Arrangements. *Mankind* 6(10):468–475.

Hobsbawm, E., and F. Ranger. 1983. *The Invention of Tradition*. Cambridge and New York: Cambridge University Press.

Horne, D. 1980. *Time of Hope: Australia 1966–72*. Sydney: Angus and Robertson.

House of Representatives Standing Committee on Aboriginal Affairs. 1981. Fringe-Dwellers: Submission. MS.

Hunter, E. 1993. *Aboriginal Health and History*. Cambridge: Cambridge University Press.

Jackson, J. 1989. Is There a Way to Talk about Making Culture without Making Enemies? *Dialectical Anthropology* 14:127–143.

———. 1995a. Culture, Genuine and Spurious: The Politics of Indianness in the Vaupes, Colombia. *American Ethnologist* 22:3–27.

———. 1995b. Preserving Indian Culture: Shaman Schools and Ethno-Education in the Vaupes, Colombia. *Cultural Anthropology* 10:302–329.

Jawoyn (Gimbat) Land Claim Transcript. 1992. Canberra. Australian Government Printing Service.

Jones, D., and J. Hill-Burnett. 1982. The Political Context of Ethnogenesis: An Australian Example. In *Aboriginal Power in Australian Society*, ed. M. Howard, 214–246.

Jull, P. 1992. *The Politics of Northern Frontiers in Australia, Canada and Other "First World" Countries*. Darwin: Australian National University, North Australia Research Unit.

Katherine Area Land Claim Transcript [KALCT]. 1982–1985. Canberra: Australian Government Printing Service.

Katherine Historical Society Files. Katherine, N.T.

Keen, I. 1994. *Knowledge and Secrecy in an Aboriginal Religion*. Oxford: Clarendon.

Keesing, R. 1989. Creating the Past: Custom and Identity in the Contemporary Pacific. *Contemporary Pacific* 1:19–42.

Kelly, C. 1943. The Reaction of White Groups in Country Towns of New South Wales to Aborigines. *Social Horizons* 1:34–40.

Kolig, E. 1981. *The Silent Revolution: The Effects of Modernization on Australian Aboriginal Religion*. Philadelphia: Institute for the Study of Human Issues.

———. 1987. *Noonkanbah Story*. Dunedin: University of Otago.

———. 1995. *Darrugu:* Secret Objects in a Changing World. In *Politics of the Secret*, ed. C. Anderson, 27–42. Oceania Monograph 45. Sydney: University of Sydney Press.

Lea, John P. 1987. *Government and the Community in Katherine, 1937–78.* Darwin: North Australia Research Unit.

Lefebvre, H. 1991 [1974]. *The Production of Space.* Oxford: Basil Blackwell.

Lemert, E. 1951. Alcoholism and the Sociocultural Situation. *Quarterly Journal of Studies on Alcohol* 17(2):306–317.

Lévi-Strauss, C. 1966. *The Savage Mind.* Chicago: University of Chicago Press.

Linnekin, J. 1991. Cultural Invention and the Dilemma of Authenticity. *American Anthropologist* 93:446–449.

London, H. I. 1970. *Non-White Immigration and the "White Australia" Policy.* Sydney: Sydney University Press.

Loveday, P. 1987. *Two Years On: Aboriginal Employment and Housing in Katherine, 1986.* Darwin: North Australia Research Unit.

Loveday, P., and J. P. Lea. 1985. *Aboriginal Housing Needs in Katherine.* Darwin: North Australia Research Unit.

MacAndrew, C., and R. B. Edgerton. 1969. *Drunken Comportment: A Social Explanation.* Chicago: Aldine.

Macdonald, G. M. 1986. The Koori Way: The Dynamics of Cultural Distinctiveness in Settled Australia. Ph.D. Thesis. University of Sydney.

Maddock, K. 1970. Imagery and Social Structure at Two Dalabon Rock Art Sites. *Anthropological Forum* 2:444–446.

———. 1982. *The Australian Aborigines: A Portrait of Their Society.* Ringwood, Vic.: Penguin Books.

Maff, W. n.d. *Katherine's No Lady.* Perth: Advance Press.

Makin, J. 1987. *The Big Run: The Story of Victoria River Downs Station.* Adelaide: Rigby.

Manuel, G., and M. Posluns. 1974. *The Fourth World: An Indian Reality.* New York: Free Press.

Marcus, J. 1988. The Journey out to the Centre: The Cultural Appropriation of Ayers Rock. In *Aboriginal Culture Today*, ed. A. Rutherford, 254–274. Kunapipi special edition 10, 1 and 2. Sydney: Dangaroo Press.

Martin, D. 1993. Autonomy and Relatedness: An Ethnography of Wik People of Aurukun, Western Cape York Peninsula. Ph.D. Thesis. Australian National University.

Mathews, J. 1996. Commonwealth Hindmarsh Island Report. Report to the Minister for Aboriginal and Torres Strait Islander Affairs.

McConnell, U. 1930. The Wik-Munkan Tribe of Cape York Peninsula. *Oceania* 1(1):97–104, 1(2):181–205.

McConvell, P. 1982. Neutralisation and Degrees of Respect in Gurindji. In *Languages of Kinship in Aboriginal Australia*, ed. J. Heath, F. Merlan, and A. Rumsey,

86–106. Oceania Linguistic Monographs, no. 24. Sydney: Sydney University Press.

———. 1991. Cultural Domain Separation: Two-way Street or Blind Alley? Stephen Harris and the Neo-Whorfians on Aboriginal Education. *Australian Aboriginal Studies* 1:13–24.

Mead, G. 1995. *A Royal Omission: A Critical Summary of the Evidence Given to the Hindmarsh Island Bridge Royal Commission with an Alternative Report.* Adelaide: Self- published.

Memmott, Paul. 1991. Queensland Aboriginal Cultures and the Deaths in Custody Victims. In *Royal Commission into Aboriginal Deaths in Custody Regional Report of Inquiry in Queensland,* 171–278. Canberra: Australian Government Publishing Service.

Mencken, H. L. 1947. *The American Language: An Inquiry into the Development of English in the United States.* 4th ed. New York: Knopf.

Merlan, F. 1981. Land, Language and Social Identity. *Mankind.*13:133–148.

———. 1982. "Egocentric" and "Altercentric" Usage of Kin Terms in Mangarrayi. In *Languages of Kinship in Aboriginal Australia,* ed. J. Heath, F. Merlan, and A. Rumsey, 125–140. Oceania Linguistic Monographs, no. 24. Sydney: University of Sydney.

———. 1986a. Aboriginal Conception Beliefs Revisited. *Man,* n.s., 21(3):474–493.

———. 1986b. *Mataranka Land Claim.* Darwin: Northern Land Council.

———. 1989. The Objectification of "Culture": An Aspect of Current Political Process in Aboriginal Affairs. *Anthropological Forum* 6(1):105–116.

———. 1990. Jawoyn Relationship Terms: Interactional Dimensions of Australian Kin Classification. *Anthropological Linguistics* 31(3–4):227–263.

———. 1991a. The Limits of Cultural Constructionism: The Case of Coronation Hill. *Oceania* 61(4):1–12.

———. 1991b. Women, Productive Roles and Monetisation of the "Service Mode" in Aboriginal Australia: Perspectives from Katherine, Northern Territory. *Australian Journal of Anthropology* 2(3):259–292.

———. 1992b. *Jawoyn (Gimbat Area) Land Claim.* Darwin: Northern Land Council.

———. 1994. Entitlement and Need: Concepts Underlying and in Land Rights and Native Title Acts. In *Claims to Knowledge, Claims to Country: Native Title, Native Title Claims and the Role of the Anthropologist,* ed. Mary Edmunds, 12–26. Canberra: Australian Institute of Aboriginal and Torres Strait Islander Studies.

———. 1995. The Regimentation of Customary Practice: From Northern Territory Land Claims to Mabo. In *Australian Journal of Anthropology* 6 (1–2):64–82. Special issue, ed. G. K. Cowlishaw and V. Kondos.

Merlan, F., and A. Rumsey. 1982. Jawoyn (Katherine Area) Land Claim. Darwin: Northern Land Council.

Merleau-Ponty, M. 1994 [1962]. *Phenomenology of Perception.* London: Routledge.

Michaels, E. 1987. If "All Anthropologists Are Liars. . . ." *Canberra Anthropology* 10(1):44–58.

Milirrpum vs. Nabalco Pty. Ltd. and the Commonwealth of Australia. 1971. Darwin: Northern Territory Supreme Court.

Miller, D. 1994. *Modernity, An Ethnographic Approach: Dualism and Mass Consumption in Trinidad.* London: Berg.

Morphy, F. 1977. Language and Moiety: Sociolectal Variation in a Yu:lngu Language of North-east Arnhem Land. *Canberra Anthropology* 1:51–60.

Morris, B. 1989. *Domesticating Resistance: The Dhan-Gadi Aborigines and the Australian State.* London: Berg.

Morton, J. 1985. Sustaining Desire: A Structuralist Interpretation of Myth and Male Cult in Central Australia. Ph.D. Thesis. Australian National University, Canberra.

Munn, N. 1970. The Transformation of Subjects into Objects in Walbiri and Pitjantjatjara Myth. In *Australian Aboriginal Anthropology*, ed. R. Berndt, 141–156. Perth: University of Western Australia.

———. 1992. The Cultural Anthropology of Time: A Critical Essay. *Annual Review of Anthropology* 21:93–123.

———. 1996. Excluded Spaces: The Figure in the Australian Aboriginal Landscape. *Critical Inquiry* 22:446–465.

Myers, F. R. 1986. *Pintupi Country, Pintupi Self: Sentiment, Place and Politics among Western Desert Aborigines.* Canberra, and Washington, D.C.: Australian Institute of Aboriginal Studies and Smithsonian Institution.

———. 1988. Locating Ethnographic Practice: Romance, Reality and Politics in the Outback. *American Ethnologist* 15(4):609–624.

Neate, G. 1989. *Aboriginal Land Rights Law in the Northern Territory.* Vol. 1. Chippendale: Alternative Publishing Co-operative.

O'Connor, R. 1984. Alcohol and Contingent Drunkenness in Central Australia. *Australian Journal of Social Issues* 19(3):173–183.

Ogden, Pearl 1992. *From Humpy to Homestead: The Biography of Sabu.* Darwin: P. Ogden.

Ordinances of the Territories of the Commonwealth made from 1917 to 1924 inclusive in 2 volumes. Includes Aboriginals Ordinance No. 9 of 1918. State of Victoria: H. S. Green, Government Printer.

Orvell, M. 1989. *The Real Thing: Imitation and Authenticity in American Culture, 1880–1940.* Chapel Hill, and London: University of North Carolina Press.

Palmer, K. 1978. *Somewhere between Black and White: The Story of An Aboriginal Australia.* South Melbourne: Macmillan.

Pearson, N. 1997. The Concept of Native Title at Common Law. In *Our Land Is Our Life: Land Rights Past, Present and Future*, ed. G. Yunupingu, 150–161. St. Lucia: University of Queensland.

Perkins, C. 1975. *A Bastard like Me*. Sydney: Ure Smith.

Peterson, N. 1993. Demand Sharing: Reciprocity and the Pressure for Generosity among Foragers. *American Anthropologist* 95(4):860–874.

Povinelli, E. A. 1993. *Labor's Lot: The Power, History, and Culture of Aboriginal Action*. Chicago: University of Chicago Press.

RAC. *See* Resource Assessment Commision.

Radcliffe-Brown, A. R. 1913. Three Tribes of Western Australia. *Journal of the Royal Anthropological Institute* 43:143–195.

———. 1930a. The Rainbow-serpent Myth in South-east Australia. *Oceania* 1(3):342–347.

———. 1930b. The Social Organization of Australian Tribes, parts 1 and 2. *Oceania* 1(1):34–63, 1(3):206–246, 322–341.

———. 1931. The Social Organization of Australian Tribes, part 3. *Oceania* 1(4):426–456.

Reay, M. 1945. A Half-caste Aboriginal Community in North-western New South Wales. *Oceania* 15(4):296–323.

Reay, M., ed. 1964. *Aborigines Now: New Perspectives in the Study of Aboriginal Communities*. Sydney: Angus and Robertson.

Reay, M., and G. Sitlington. 1947. Class and Status in a Mixed-blood Community (Moree, New South Wales). *Oceania* 18(3):179–207.

Resource Assessment Commission [RAC]. 1991. *Kakadu Conservation Zone Inquiry Final Report*. Vols. 1 and 2. Canberra: Australian Government Publishing Service.

Reynolds, H. 1987. *The Law of the Land*. Ringwood, Victoria: Penguin.

Riches, D. 1990. The Force of Tradition in Eskimology. In *Localizing Strategies: Regional Traditions of Ethnographic Writing*, ed. Richard Fardon, 71–89. Edinburgh, and Washington, D.C.: Scottish Academic Press and Smithsonian Institution.

Roberts, S. H. 1968. *History of Australian Land Settlement 1788–1920*. Melbourne: Macmillan.

Robinson, R. 1956. *The Feathered Serpent*. Sydney: Edwards and Shaw.

Room, R. 1984. Alcohol and Ethnography: A Case of Problem Deflation? *Current Anthropology* 25(2):169–191.

Roosens, E. E. 1989. *Creating Ethnicity: The Process of Ethnogenesis*. Newbury Park, Calif.: Sage.

Rosaldo, R. 1989. *Culture and Truth: The Remaking of Social Analysis*. Boston: Beacon Press.

Rose, D. 1987. Representing the Pintupi. *Canberra Anthropology* 10(1):35–43.

———. 1992. *Dingo Makes Us Human: Life and Land in an Aboriginal Australian Culture*. Cambridge and Melbourne: Cambridge University Press.

Rowse, T. 1978. *Australian Liberalism and National Character*. Melbourne: Kibble.

———. 1983. Liberalising the Frontier: Aborigines and Australian Pluralism. *Meanjin* 42:71–84.

Rumsey, A. 1989. Language Groups in Australian Aboriginal Land Claims. *Anthropological Forum* 6(1):69–79.

———. 1993. Language and Territoriality in Aboriginal Australia. In *Language and Culture in Aboriginal Australia*, ed. M. Walsh and C. Yallop, 191–206. Canberra: Aboriginal Studies Press.

Sackett, L. 1988. Resisting Arrests: Drinking, Development and Discipline in a Desert Context. *Social Analysis* 24 (December):66–77.

———. 1991. Conservationist Depictions of Aborigines. *Australian Journal of Anthropology* 2(2):233–246.

Sahlins, M. 1976. *Culture and Practical Reason*. Chicago and London: University of Chicago Press.

———. 1993. Goodbye to Tristes Tropes: Ethnography in the Context of Modern World History. *Journal of Modern History* 65:1–25.

Sandefur, J. 1979. *Australian Creole in the Northern Territory: A Description*. Darwin: Summer Institute of Linguistics.

Sanders, W. 1982. From Self-determination to Self-management. In *Service Delivery to Remote Communities*, ed. P. Loveday, 4–10. Darwin: North Australia Research Unit.

Sansom, B. 1980. *The Camp at Wallaby Cross*. Canberra: Australian Institute of Aboriginal Studies.

———. 1981. Processual Modelling and Aggregate Groupings in Northern Australia. In *The Structure of Folk Models*, ed. L. Holy and M. Stuchlik, 257–280. London: Academic Press.

———. 1982. The Aboriginal Commonality. In *Aboriginal Sites, Rights and Resource Development*, ed. R. M. Berndt, 117–138. Perth: University of Western Australia.

Saunders, C. 1994. *Report to the Minister for Aboriginal and Torres Strait Islander Affairs on the Significant Aboriginal Area in the Vicinity of Goolwa and Hindmarsh (Kumarangk) Island*. Melbourne: University of Melbourne, Centre for Comparative Constitutional Studies.

Schebeck, B. 1968. Dialect and Social Grouping in North-east Arnhem Land. Typescript. Library, Australian Institute of Aboriginal and Torres Strait Islanders Studies, Canberra.

Sharp, L. 1958. People without Politics: The Australian Yir-Yoront. In *Systems of Political Control and Bureaucracy in Human Societies*, ed. R. F. Ray, 2–8. American Ethnological Society Monographs. Seattle: University of Washington Press.

———. 1974. Steel Axes for Stone Age Australians. In *Cultures of the Pacific: Selected Readings*, ed. T. G. Harding and B. J. Wallace, 69–90. New York: Free Press.

Sider, G. 1987. When Parrots Learn to Talk, and Why They Can't: Domination, Deception, and Self-deception in Indian-White Relations. *Comparative Studies in Society and History* 29:3–23.

Spencer, B. 1914. *Native Tribes of the Northern Territory of Australia*. London: Macmillan.

Spencer, B., and F. J. Gillen. 1899. *Native Tribes of Central Australia.* London: Macmillan.

Stanner, W. E. H. 1937. Aboriginal Modes of Address and Reference in the North-west of the Northern Territory. *Oceania* 7(3):300–315.

———. 1958. Continuity and Change among the Aborigines. *Australian Journal of Science* 21:99–109.

———. 1965. Religion, Totemism and Symbolism. In *Aboriginal Man in Australia: Essays in Honour of Emeritus Professor A. P. Elkin,* ed. R. M. and C. H. Berndt, 207–237. Sydney: Angus and Robertson.

———. 1966. *On Aboriginal Religion.* Oceania Monographs. Sydney: Sydney University Press.

———. 1979. *White Man Got No Dreaming.* Canberra: Australian National University Press.

Stanton, J. 1983. Old Business, New Owners: Succession and "the Law" on the Fringe of the Western Desert. In *Aborigines, Land and Land Rights,* ed. N. Peterson and M. Langton, 160–171. Canberra: Australian Institute of Aboriginal Studies.

Stevens, F. 1974. *Aborigines in the Northern Territory Cattle Industry.* Canberra: Australian National University.

Strathern, M. 1990. Negative Strategies in Melanesia. In *Localizing Strategies,* ed. R. Fardon, 204–216. Edinburgh, and Washington, D.C.: Scottish Academic Press and Smithsonian Institution Press.

———. 1992a. *After Nature: English Kinship in the Late Twentieth Century.* Cambridge: Cambridge University Press.

———. 1992b. *Reproducing the Future: Anthropology, Kinship and the New Reproductive Technologies.* New York: Routledge.

Strehlow, T. G. H. 1947. *Aranda Traditions.* Victoria: Melbourne University Press.

———. 1965. Culture, Social Structure and Environment in Aboriginal Central Australia. In *Aboriginal Man in Australia,* ed. R. M. Berndt, 121–145. Nedlands: University of Western Australia.

———. 1970. Geography and the Totemic Landscape in Central Australia: A Functional Study. In *Australian Aboriginal Anthropology,* ed. R. M. Berndt. Nedlands: University of Western Australia.

———. 1971. *Songs of Central Australia.* Sydney: Angus and Robertson.

Stretton, H. 1975. *Ideas for Australian Cities.* Melbourne: Georgian House.

Sutton, P. 1978. Wik: Aboriginal Society and Territory, and Language at Cape Keerweer, Cape York Peninsula, Australia. Ph.D. Thesis. University of Queensland.

———. 1991. Language in Aboriginal Australia: Social Dialects in a Geographic Idiom. In *Language in Australia,* ed. S. Romaine, 49–66. Cambridge: Cambridge University Press.

Sutton, P., and A. Palmer. 1981. *Malak Malak (Daly River) Land Claim.* Darwin: Northern Land Council.

Swain, T. 1991. The Earth Mother Conspiracy: An Australian Episode. *Numen* 38(1):3–26.

———. 1993. *A Place for Strangers: Towards a History of Australian Aboriginal Being.* Melbourne: Cambridge University Press.

Tamisari, F. 1995. Body, Names and Movement: Images of Identity among the Yolngu of North-east Arnhem Land. Ph.D. Thesis. London School of Economics.

Taussig, M. 1993. *Mimesis and Alterity: A Particular History of the Senses.* New York and London: Routledge.

Tawney, R. H. 1938. *Equality.* 3d ed. London: George Allen and Unwin.

Thomson, D. 1939. The Seasonal Factor in Human Culture. *Proceedings of the Prehistoric Society* 5:209–221.

Tindale, N. B. 1925. Natives of Groote Eylandt and of the West Coast of the Gulf of Carpentaria, part 1. *Records of the South Australian Museum* 2:61–102.

———. 1974. *Aboriginal Tribes of Australia.* Berkeley: University of California Press.

———. 1976. Some Ecological Bases for Australian Tribal Boundaries. In *Tribes and Boundaries in Australia,* ed. N. Peterson, 12–29. Canberra: Australian Institute of Aboriginal Studies.

Tonkinson, M. 1990. Is It in the Blood? Australian Aboriginal Identity. In *Cultural Identity and Ethnicity in the Pacific,* ed J. Linnekin and L. Poyer, 191–218. Honolulu: University of Hawai'i Press.

Tonkinson, R. 1974. *The Jigalong Mob: Aboriginal Victors of the Desert Crusade.* Menlo Park, Calif.: Cummings.

———. 1991. *The Mardu Aborigines: Living the Dream in Australia's Desert.* 2d ed. Fort Worth, Tex.: Holt, Rinehart and Winston.

Trigger, D. S. 1987. Languages, Linguistic Groups and Status Relations at an Aboriginal Settlement in North-western Queensland, Australia. *Oceania* 57(3): 217–238.

———. 1989. Racial Ideologies in Australia's Gulf Country. *Ethnic and Racial Studies* 12(2):209–232.

———. 1992. *Whitefella Comin'.* Cambridge: Cambridge University Press.

Vincent, P. 1983. Noonkanbah. In *Aborigines, Land and Land Rights,* ed. N. Peterson and M. Langton, 327–338. Canberra: Australian Institute of Aboriginal Studies.

von Sturmer, J. 1978. Wik Region: Economy, Territoriality and Totemism in western Cape York Peninsula, North Queensland. Ph.D. Thesis. University of Queensland.

Ward, R. 1977. *A Nation for a Continent: The History of Australia, 1901–1975.* Richmond, Vic.: Heinemann Educational Australia.

Warner, W. L. 1931. Morphology and Functions of the Australian Murngin Type of Kinship, pt. 2. *American Anthropologist* 33:72–98.

———. 1937. *A Black Civilization.* New York: Harper.

White, R. 1981. *Inventing Australia: Images and Identity, 1688–1980.* Sydney: Allen and Unwin.

Whitlam, E. G. 1985. *The Whitlam Government, 1972–5*. Ringwood, Victoria: Viking Penguin.

Williams, N. 1986. *The Yolngu and Their Land*. Stanford, Calif.: Stanford University Press.

Wilson, P. 1982. *Black Death, White Hands*. Sydney: Allen and Unwin.

Wilton, J., and R. Bosworth. 1984. *Old Worlds and New Australia: The Post-War Migration Experience*. North Ryde, Sydney: Penguin.

Woldendorp, R. 1994. *Australia's Flying Doctors: The Royal Flying Doctor Service*. Sydney: Pan Macmillan.

Wolfe, P. 1994. Nation and MiscengeNation: Discursive Continuity in the Post-Mabo Era. *Social Analysis* 36:93–151.

Woodward, J. 1974. *Aboriginal Land Rights Commission: Second Report*. Canberra: Australian Government Publishing Service.

Wootten, H. 1992. Significant Aboriginal Sites in the Area of Proposed Junction Waterhole Dam, Alice Springs. Report to the Minister for Aboriginal Affairs under Section 10(4). Canberra: Australian Government Printing Service.

INDEX

Lightning Source UK Ltd.
Milton Keynes UK
UKHW010446080921
390191UK00001B/63